taste of home
appetizers
& SMALL PLATES

BOOKS

REIMAN MEDIA GROUP, INC. ● GREENDALE, WISCONSIN

taste of home   Reader's Digest

A TASTE OF HOME/READER'S DIGEST BOOK

© 2012 Reiman Media Group, LLC
5400 S. 60th St., Greendale WI 53129
All rights reserved.

Taste of Home and Reader's Digest are registered trademarks of The Reader's Digest Association, Inc.

EDITORIAL
Editor-in-Chief Catherine Cassidy

Executive Editor, Print and Digital Books Stephen C. George
Creative Director Howard Greenberg
Editorial Services Manager Kerri Balliet

Editor Janet Briggs
Associate Creative Director Edwin Robles Jr.
Content Production Manager Julie Wagner
Layout Designer Catherine Fletcher
Copy Chief Deb Warlaumont Mulvey
Project Proofreader Julie Schnittka
Recipe Asset System Business Analyst Colleen King
Recipe Testing & Editing Taste of Home Test Kitchen
Food Photography Taste of Home Photo Studio
Executive Assistant Marie Brannon
Editorial Assistant Marilyn Iczkowski

BUSINESS
Vice President, Publisher Jan Studin, jan_studin@rd.com
Regional Account Director Donna Lindskog, donna_lindskog@rd.com
Eastern Account Director Jennifer Dietz
Midwest & Western Account Director Jackie Fallon
Midwest Account Manager Lorna Phillips
Western Account Manager Joel Millikin
Michigan Sales Representative Linda C. Donaldson

Corporate Integrated Sales Director Steve Sottile
Vice President, Digital Sales and Development Dan Meehan
Digital Sales Planner Tim Baarda

General Manager, Taste of Home Cooking Schools Erin Puariea

Direct Response Katherine Zito, David Geller Associates

Executive Director, Brand Marketing Leah West
Associate Marketing Managers Betsy Connors, Emily Moore
Vice President, Creative Director Paul Livornese
Public Relations Manager Heidi Frank

Vice President, Magazine Marketing Dave Fiegel

READER'S DIGEST NORTH AMERICA
President Dan Lagani

President, Canada Tony Cioffi
President, Books and Home Entertaining Harold Clarke
Chief Financial Officer Howard Halligan
Vice President, General Manager, Reader's Digest Media Marilynn Jacobs
Chief Marketing Officer Renee Jordan
Vice President, Chief Sales Officer Mark Josephson
Vice President, General Manager, RD Milwaukee Lisa Karpinski
Vice President, Chief Strategy Officer Jacqueline Majers Lachman
Vice President, Marketing and Creative Services Elizabeth Tighe
Vice President, Chief Content Officer Liz Vaccariello

The Reader's Digest Association, Inc.
President and Chief Executive Officer: Robert E. Guth

For other Taste of Home books and products, visit us at **tasteofhome.com**.

For more Reader's Digest products and information, visit
rd.com (in the United States)
or see **rd.ca (in Canada).**

International Standard Book Number (10): 1-61765-116-8
International Standard Book Number (13): 978-1-61765-116-8
Library of Congress Control Number: 2010922368

Cover Photography
Art Directors Edwin Robles Jr., Gretchen Trautman
Photographers Rob Hagen, Lori Foy
Food Stylists Sarah Thompson, Alynna Malson
Set Stylist Dee Dee Jacq

Pictured on front cover:
Pepper-Crusted Tenderloin Crostini (p. 178); Stuffed Butterflied Shrimp (p. 194); Antipasto Kabobs (p. 73); Espresso Panna Cotta (p. 264); Wonton Kisses (p. 277); Zippy Cranberry Appetizer (p. 362); Brie with Apricot Topping (p. 122); and Veggie Wonton Quiches (p. 99).

Pictured on back cover:
Stuffed Chocolate Cherries (p. 290); Sangria (p. 324); and Chicken Bacon Bites (p. 206).

Printed in China.
3 5 7 9 10 8 6 4 2

table of contents

TASTE OF HOME APPETIZERS

taste of home appetizers & SMALL PLATES

With the 350 satisfying dips, spreads, wraps, rolls, beverages, nibblers, munchies, sweets and more in this fabulous collection of bite-size goodies, you'll be the hostess that serves the most sensational assortment of appetizers in town!

EVERYONE LOVES THE OPPORTUNITY TO SAMPLE DIFFERENT AND DELICIOUS foods at parties and gatherings. And appetizers are the tastiest way to tempt your guests and introduce them to fun, new flavors. Now you can serve up 350 of the most delectable dips and spreads, juicy chicken wings, dainty canapes, unique beverages, mouthwatering finger foods and scrumptious mini desserts—all easy to make and a delight to serve!

The recipes in this collection come from family cooks like you and have been tested by the experienced home economists in the Taste of Home Test Kitchen. So you can rest assured that these tasty tidbits will be a savory success.

In this book, you'll also discover make-ahead preparation tips, practical pointers for keeping party foods hot or cold, helpful hints for serving appetizers, time-saving tips and much more.

So turn to **Taste of Home Appetizers & Small Plates** for an abundance of appealing hors d'oeuvres…and make your next party a celebration of flavor!

Serving Up Appetizers

Whenever you offer friends and family appetizers or snacks, you invite them to get comfortable and share time with you and other guests.

Appetizers can be as simple as dip with chips for a casual night of TV watching, include heartier fare like sandwiches and pizza for Sunday football, serve as a first course to a festive meal, entertain a large group at an open house or even be the main meal for a special occasion.

Party Planning

Whether simple or fancy, savory or sweet, hot or cold, appetizers offer versatility and variety when entertaining. And as an added benefit, many appetizers can be made ahead of time—some even weeks in advance and then frozen—so you can be ready for guests at a moment's notice or relaxed when party time arrives.

When planning what appetizers to serve, don't overdo it. It's better to prepare a few good choices than to stress over making a lot of items. Start with one spectacular appetizer and then complete your menu with additional easy but delicious foods and beverages.

Choose from an assortment of hot, cold and room temperature foods. Select recipes that offer a variety of colors, textures (soft and crunchy) and flavors (sour, salty, savory, sweet, spicy or subtle). Mix in one or two lighter options to cater to guests concerned about calories or fat. And, look for appetizers that make a nice presentation and require no last-minute fussing.

How Much To Serve

The number of appetizers per person varies on the length of the party, the number of guests and the other items on your menu.

For a social hour before dinner, plan on serving three or four different appetizers and allow four to five pieces per person.

For an open-house affair, plan on serving four to five different appetizers and allow four to six pieces per person per hour.

For an appetizer buffet that is offered in place of a meal, plan on serving six to eight different appetizers and allow 10 to 14 pieces per person.

For larger groups, offer more types of appetizers. For eight guests, three types may be sufficient, 16 guests about four to five types and for 25 guests, serve six to eight types. The more variety you serve, the fewer servings of each type you'll need.

Food Quantities For Appetizers

When serving appetizers, no one wants to run out of food. But the challenge is to know how much will be enough.

Here are some guidelines to estimate how much you'll need per person. The larger the variety of appetizers you serve, the less of each type you will need.

appetizers	beverages (per hour)	miscellaneous
3 tablespoons dips	In warm weather, you may wish to have additional chilled beverages.	1 to 2 ounces chips
2 ounces cheese		4 crackers
3 to 4 cocktail wieners		4 fruit or vegetable dippers
1 to 2 ounces deli meat	1 to 2 cups soda, water or iced tea	1/2 ounce mixed nuts
3 tablespoons spreads	6 ounces juice	3 to 4 pickle slices or 1 pickle spear
2 to 4 small egg rolls	1 to 2 bottles beer	
3 to 4 meatballs	1/2 (750-ml) bottle wine	3 to 4 olives
1 to 2 slices pizza	3/4 cup hot coffee or tea	1 to 2 small rolls
2 to 4 miniature quiches	1/2 cup punch	3 to 4 ounces ice for beverages

Points About Food Safety

The general guideline when serving food is that cooked foods and uncooked foods that require refrigeration should not sit out at room temperature for more than 2 hours or 1 hour on hot days (90° or above). Hot foods should be kept hot (140°) and cold foods should be kept cold (40°). Here are some pointers for safely serving food:

- Divide the food among several serving dishes. Serve one dish, while the others are being chilled or kept warm. Replace the original serving dish as needed or every 2 hours (whichever comes first).

- To keep foods hot when serving, use insulated containers, warming trays, slow cookers or chafing dishes.

- To keep the back-up food hot, arrange on baking sheets and place in a 200° oven.

- To keep food cold, place on ice. You can easily improvise an ice bowl by placing dips, shrimp, cut-up fruits and salads in a bowl. Then set the bowl in a larger one filled with ice cubes or crushed ice. Replenish the ice as it melts throughout the party.

Hosting an Appetizer Party

Although hosting an appetizer party will require some planning, it's a fun way to entertain a group of people for any occasion.

To make it easy on you, include several make-ahead recipes on the menu.

A few weeks before the party:
Cook and freeze meatballs, savory cheesecakes and puffs or mini quiches, such as Crabmeat Appetizer Cheesecake (p. 140) or Mini Bacon Quiches (p. 119). For meatballs, just thaw and reheat in the sauce on your party day. For savory cheesecakes, thaw in the refrigerator 2 to 3 days before the party and bring to room temperature about 20 minutes before serving. Puffs and quiches can be reheated just before in a 300° oven until warm.

A few days before the party:
Make cheese balls and logs, flavored nut mixes and snack mixes. Store the mixes in airtight containers.

A day before the party:
Make tortilla-type roll-up sandwiches, dips and salsas. Cut up any fruit and vegetables that will be used for dippers. Prep any fillings for hot appetizers or any other food that can be made ahead.

The morning of your party:
Make hero-type sandwiches and assemble canapes. If possible, assemble and arrange any warm appetizers on baking sheets.

Before your guests arrive:
Place any long-cooking items, such as a baked dip in a bread shell, in the oven so that it will be ready to serve within half an hour after the party starts.

As the guests arrive:
Place some of the quickly baked items in the oven.

Arranging The Food

The way you arrange your food will encourage people to mingle with each other and move around your home. Food can be set up as a buffet, served from trays by waitstaff or family or casually placed throughout the house on tables. To keep people moving, set up the food and beverages in separate locations—even in separate rooms.

Buffets

For added visual interest to a buffet service, arrange various items such as phone books, sturdy boxes, inverted metal buckets, cake pans and cans as risers on your table (see figure 1). Drape them with a tablecloth and gently form it around the risers so that the cloth won't pull when platters of food are set on top (see figure 2).

When arranging the buffet, allow room on one end for the plates, and set the napkins and any utensils on the other end. This way your guests won't need to juggle the napkin and utensils while they serve themselves. Set the food back from the edge of the table to allow room for guests to set their plates down to serve themselves. For foods that need to be skewered, have a container of skewers or toothpicks alongside the serving dish.

If using candles, set them on the table so no one will need to reach over the flames to get the food. Small arrangements of flowers can be placed between serving dishes (see figure 3). Large arrangements should be placed out of reach, either in the middle of the buffet if service wraps around the table, or in the back if your table is against a wall.

If you're using a table for the buffet, remove the chairs from the table and arrange them in other areas in sitting groups. By removing the chairs, you make it easier for guests to move around the table and reach the food.

Trays

Trays can be used to circulate the food among the guests. This can be especially nice for hot finger foods, such as stuffed mushrooms or canapes. Offering food directly to people encourages them to sample the food. The trays will be emptied in a short period of time, eliminating concerns about food standing at room

Figure 1

Figure 2

Figure 3

temperature too long. Plus, the trays can easily be replenished with fresh tidbits.

For the best visual presentation, only place one or two types of food on a tray. Leave space around the food to prevent other pieces on the tray from being touched when one piece is picked up. Small tongs can aid in serving the appetizers from the tray. Or, if appropriate, use individual party picks with foods such as cubed cheese. Since the trays are being carried around, avoid making them too heavy. If you don't have enough trays for the occasion, consider renting them.

Placing Food Around the House

Placing appetizers in various locations throughout the party area invites people to walk around to see what other tasty bites are being served and, most importantly, to meet other guests. Scattered placement around the party area can work well with room temperature foods, chilled items and platters of hot appetizers. For items that need a slow cooker or chafing dish, a central location may be more convenient.

Tips to Make Your Guests Comfortable

Simple touches can enhance the comfort of your guests. Here are a few ideas to make your party even more enjoyable:

- Have music in the background to set the mood and still allow conversations to take place at a normal tone.

- Have chairs for people to sit (not everyone can stand for hours).

- Place the chairs in seating arrangements to encourage conversation.

- If you want your guests to use coasters, have plenty of them available and place them in noticeable locations.

- Have small tables and open surfaces on other furniture, where a guest may set down their glass or plate.

- Have an open floor plan so guests can easily walk from one room to the next. Consider stowing away pieces of furniture that are in the way.

- Have trash containers strategically placed around the area to prevent clutter from building up.

toasty treats

22

14

No matter what the occasion, oven-fresh appetizers will disappear quickly when passed around. With variety to choose from, like Feta Artichoke Bites (p. 39), Bacon-Pecan Stuffed Mushrooms (p. 17), Spinach Squares (p. 22) or Cheese Boereg (p. 14), you're certain to find something that will appeal to your friends.

Just because these oven-fresh favorites take time to heat, don't hesitate to add them to your menu mix. Simply keep a tray warm in the oven or cook them in batches while you enjoy time with guests.

spinach-cheese mushroom caps

24 large fresh mushrooms

¼ cup chopped onion

2 garlic cloves, minced

1 tablespoon olive oil

1 package (8 ounces) cream cheese, softened

1 package (10 ounces) frozen chopped spinach, thawed and squeezed dry

½ cup plus 2 tablespoons shredded Parmesan cheese, *divided*

½ cup crumbled feta cheese

1 bacon strip, cooked and crumbled

½ teaspoon salt

1 Remove stems from mushrooms; set caps aside. Finely chop the stems. In a skillet, saute the chopped mushrooms, onion and garlic in oil until tender.

2 In a mixing bowl, beat cream cheese until smooth. Add the spinach, ½ cup Parmesan cheese, feta cheese, bacon, salt and mushroom mixture. Spoon into mushroom caps. Sprinkle with the remaining Parmesan cheese.

3 Place on a baking sheet. Bake at 400° for 15 minutes or until golden brown.

YIELD: 2 DOZEN.

Sandy Herman, Marietta, Georgia

Dainty finger foods like these mushrooms are a wonderful way to welcome guests into your home. A hearty spinach filling will tide folks over until the meal is served.

seasoned potato wedges

1/3 cup all-purpose flour

1/3 cup grated Parmesan cheese

1 teaspoon paprika

3 large baking potatoes (about 2 3/4 pounds)

1/3 cup milk

1/4 cup butter, *divided*

SOUR CREAM DIP:

2 cups (16 ounces) sour cream

8 bacon strips, cooked and crumbled

2 tablespoons minced chives

1/2 teaspoon garlic powder

1 In a large resealable plastic bag, combine the flour, Parmesan cheese and paprika. Cut each potato into eight wedges; dip in milk. Place in the bag, a few at a time, and shake to coat.

2 Place potatoes in a greased 15-in. x 10-in. x 1-in. baking pan. Drizzle with 2 tablespoons butter. Bake, uncovered, at 400° for 20 minutes.

3 Turn wedges; drizzle with remaining butter. Bake 20-25 minutes longer or until potatoes are tender and golden brown.

4 In a large bowl, combine the dip ingredients. Serve with the warm potato wedges.

YIELD: 6-8 SERVINGS.

Karen Trewin, Decorah, Iowa

These baked wedges, seasoned with Parmesan cheese and served with a sour cream dip, make a nice alternative to french fries or baked potatoes. They go great with grilled steak, but my family enjoys them as snacks, too.

cheese boereg

Jean Ecos, Hartland, Wisconsin

This Armenian appetizer has a rich-tasting cheese filling, which is baked between buttery layers of phyllo dough.

1 egg, lightly beaten

1 egg white, lightly beaten

1 cup ricotta cheese

¼ cup minced fresh parsley

4 cups (16 ounces) shredded part-skim mozzarella *or* Muenster cheese

10 sheets phyllo dough (18 inches x 14 inches)

½ cup butter, melted

1 In a bowl, combine the egg, egg white, ricotta and parsley. Stir in mozzarella; set aside.

2 Unroll phyllo dough; cut stack of sheets in half widthwise. Place one sheet of phyllo dough in a greased 13-in. x 9-in. baking pan; brush with butter. Repeat nine times. Keep remaining dough covered with plastic wrap and a damp towel to prevent it from drying out.

3 Spread the cheese mixture evenly over the top. Layer with the remaining dough, brushing the butter on every other sheet.

4 Bake at 350° for 25-30 minutes or until golden brown. Cut into triangles or squares.

YIELD: 16-20 APPETIZERS.

pizza poppers

4 to 4½ cups all-purpose flour

⅓ cup sugar

1 package (¼ ounce) active dry yeast

1 teaspoon dried oregano

½ teaspoon salt

1 cup water

1 tablespoon shortening

1 egg

3 cups (12 ounces) shredded part-skim mozzarella cheese

1⅓ cups minced pepperoni (about 5 ounces)

2 cups pizza sauce, warmed

1 In a large mixing bowl, combine 2 cups flour, sugar, yeast, oregano and salt. In a saucepan, heat water and shortening to 120°-130°. Add to dry ingredients; beat until moistened. Add egg; beat on medium speed for 1 minute. Stir in cheese and pepperoni; mix well. Stir in enough remaining flour to form a soft dough.

2 Turn onto a floured surface; knead until smooth and elastic, about 6-8 minutes. Place in a greased bowl, turning once to grease top. Cover and let rise in a warm place until doubled, about 1 hour.

3 Punch dough down. Turn onto a lightly floured surface; divide into four pieces. Divide each piece into eight balls. Roll each ball into a 12-in. rope. Tie into a loose knot, leaving two long ends. Fold top end under roll; bring bottom end up and press into center of roll. Place on greased baking sheets. Cover and let rise until doubled, about 30 minutes.

4 Bake at 375° for 10-12 minutes or until golden brown. Serve warm with pizza sauce.

YIELD: 32 APPETIZERS.

Denise Sargent, Pittsfield, New Hampshire
Both my husband and I are big pizza fans, so we created these pizza rolls. They'll go fast at any gathering.

bacon-pecan stuffed mushrooms

1 pound large fresh mushrooms

4 tablespoons butter, *divided*

2 tablespoons vegetable oil

¼ teaspoon salt

2 tablespoons finely chopped onion

1 cup soft bread crumbs

6 bacon strips, cooked and crumbled

2 tablespoons chopped pecans

2 tablespoons sherry *or* beef broth

2 tablespoons sour cream

2 tablespoons minced chives

1 Remove mushroom stems (discard or save for another use). In a large skillet, heat 2 tablespoons butter and oil over medium-high heat. Saute mushroom caps for 2 minutes on each side; sprinkle with salt. Remove with a slotted spoon to paper towels.

2 In the same skillet, saute the onion in remaining butter until tender. Remove skillet from the heat; stir in the remaining ingredients.

3 Spoon into mushroom caps. Place on a broiler pan; broil 5 in. from the heat for 2-3 minutes or until filling is browned. Serve warm.

YIELD: 12-14 APPETIZERS.

Beverly Pierce, Indianola, Mississippi
When I had some kitchen remodeling done a few years ago, this recipe disappeared. But I'd shared it so often that I had no trouble getting a copy.

cheddar artichoke quiche cups

2 jars (7½ ounces *each*) marinated artichoke hearts

1 small onion, finely chopped

1 garlic clove, minced

4 eggs, beaten

¼ cup dry bread crumbs

¼ teaspoon ground mustard

⅛ teaspoon dried oregano

⅛ teaspoon pepper

⅛ teaspoon hot pepper sauce

2 cups (8 ounces) shredded cheddar cheese

2 tablespoons minced fresh parsley

1 Drain artichokes, reserving half of the marinade. Chop artichokes; set aside. In a skillet, saute onion and garlic in reserved marinade until tender; set aside.

2 In a large bowl, combine the eggs, bread crumbs, mustard, oregano, pepper and hot pepper sauce. Stir in the cheese, parsley, reserved artichokes and onion mixture.

3 Fill miniature muffin cups three-fourths full. Bake at 325° for 15-17 minutes or until set. Cool for 5 minutes before removing from pan to wire racks. Serve warm. Refrigerate leftovers.

YIELD: 4 DOZEN.

Fran Dell, Las Vegas, Nevada

No one can resist sampling these savory bites chock-full of artichokes, onions and cheese. They're at the top of my family's list for every holiday gathering. There are never any left!

onion blossoms

2 large sweet onions, unpeeled
1/2 cup mayonnaise
1/2 cup sour cream
1 tablespoon chili powder
2 1/2 teaspoons Cajun seasoning, *divided*
1 1/4 cups all-purpose flour
1 cup milk
Oil for deep-fat frying

1 Leaving the root end intact, peel the outer skin of the onion. Cut a small slice off the top. Starting at the top of the onion and on one side, make a cut downward toward the root end, stopping 1/2 in. from the bottom. Make additional cuts 1/8 in. from the first until there are cuts completely across top of onion.

2 Turn the onion a quarter turn so the slices are horizontal to you. Repeat the cuts 1/8 in. apart from each other until there is a checkerboard pattern across entire top of onion.

3 For dip, in a small bowl, combine the mayonnaise, sour cream, chili powder and 1 1/2 teaspoons Cajun seasoning. Mix well and set aside.

4 In a 1-gallon plastic bag, combine the flour and the remaining Cajun seasoning. Place milk in a small deep bowl. Coat the cut onion in flour, then dip into milk and back into the flour mixture.

5 Fry in enough oil to cover onion at 350° for 5 minutes or until golden, turning once. Remove from oil; place on serving plate. Discard the very center of the fried onion blossom. Place a few spoonfuls of dip in the center of blossom and serve immediately.

YIELD: 4 SERVINGS.

Jeanne Bennett, Minden, Louisiana

Onion blossoms are a popular appetizer served at many restaurants. Now you can easily make them at home with this delicious recipe.

---

sausage cheese squares

1 tube (8 ounces) refrigerated crescent rolls

1 package (8 ounces) brown-and-serve sausage links, thawed and sliced ½ inch thick

2 cups (8 ounces) shredded Monterey Jack cheese

4 eggs

¾ cup milk

2 tablespoons chopped green pepper

½ teaspoon salt

¼ teaspoon pepper

1 Unroll dough; place in an ungreased 13-in. x 9-in. baking dish. Press onto bottom and ½ in. up sides to form a crust. Top with sausage and cheese. Beat eggs in a bowl; add remaining ingredients. Carefully pour over cheese.

2 Bake, uncovered, at 425° for 20-25 minutes or until a knife inserted near the center comes out clean. Cut into small squares.

YIELD: 12-16 SERVINGS.

Helen McFadden, Sierra Vista, Arizona

My grandsons tried these savory morsels for the first time as youngsters and loved them. Though they're all grown up now, the boys still request the squares—and I'm happy to oblige!

deep-fried potato skins

4 large baking potatoes

2 cups (16 ounces) sour cream

1 envelope onion soup mix

1 tablespoon finely chopped onion

5 garlic cloves, minced

Dash hot pepper sauce

Oil for deep-fat frying

½ cup shredded cheddar cheese

½ cup shredded Swiss cheese

6 to 8 bacon strips, cooked and crumbled

4 teaspoons minced chives *or* green onion

1 Bake potatoes at 400° for 1 hour or until tender.

2 Meanwhile, for dip, combine sour cream, soup mix, onion, garlic and hot pepper sauce in a bowl. Cover; chill until serving.

3 When potatoes are cool enough to handle, cut in half lengthwise. Scoop out pulp, leaving a ¼-in. shell (save pulp for another use). With a scissors, cut each potato half into three lengthwise strips.

4 In an electric skillet or deep-fat fryer, heat oil to 375°. Fry skins in oil for 2-3 minutes or until golden brown and crisp.

5 Place potato skins in a 15-in. x 10-in. x 1-in. baking pan. Combine the cheeses and bacon; sprinkle over potatoes. Broil 4 in. from the heat for 1-2 minutes or until cheese is melted. Sprinkle with chives. Serve with the dip.

YIELD: 2 DOZEN.

Leslie Cunnian, Peterborough, Ontario

The combination of potatoes, cheese, bacon and garlic dip in this recipe is fantastic. The skins can be served as an appetizer or as a side dish with roast prime rib or any other entree you choose.

spinach squares

Patricia Kile, Greentown, Pennsylvania

Even people who don't care for spinach can't pass up these satisfying squares when they're set out.

2 tablespoons butter, *divided*

1 cup milk

3 eggs

1 cup all-purpose flour

1 teaspoon baking powder

¾ teaspoon salt

½ teaspoon dried oregano

¼ teaspoon pepper

¼ teaspoon dried basil

¼ teaspoon dried thyme

2 packages (10 ounces *each*) frozen chopped spinach, thawed and squeezed dry

2 cups (8 ounces) shredded cheddar cheese

2 cups (8 ounces) shredded Monterey Jack cheese

1 cup chopped onion

Sliced pimientos, optional

1 Brush the bottom and sides of a 13-in. x 9-in. baking dish with 1 tablespoon butter; set aside. In a large mixing bowl, combine remaining butter and next nine ingredients. Stir in spinach, cheeses and onion.

2 Spread in pan. Bake, uncovered, at 350° for 30-35 minutes or until a toothpick inserted near the center comes out clean and edges are lightly browned. Cut into squares. Garnish with pimientos if desired.

YIELD: 4 DOZEN.

prosciutto puffs

1 cup water

6 tablespoons butter

1/8 teaspoon pepper

1 cup all-purpose flour

5 eggs

3/4 cup finely chopped prosciutto
  or fully cooked ham

1/4 cup minced chives

1 In a large saucepan, bring the water, butter and pepper to a boil. Add flour all at once and stir until a smooth ball forms. Remove from the heat; let stand for 5 minutes.

2 Add the eggs, one at a time, beating well after each addition. Continue beating until the mixture is smooth and shiny. Stir in the prosciutto and chives.

3 Drop by heaping teaspoonfuls onto greased baking sheets. Bake at 425° for 18-22 minutes or until golden brown. Remove to wire racks. Serve warm. Refrigerate leftovers.

YIELD: 4 1/2 DOZEN.

Nella Parker, Hersey, Michigan

Your guests will come back for seconds and even thirds of these light and tasty puffs. They're so delicious that they practically melt in your mouth.

tater-dipped veggies

1 cup instant potato flakes

1/3 cup grated Parmesan cheese

1/2 teaspoon celery salt

1/4 teaspoon garlic powder

1/4 cup butter, melted and cooled

2 eggs

4 to 5 cups raw bite-size vegetables (mushrooms, peppers, broccoli, cauliflower, zucchini *and/or* parboiled carrots)

Prepared ranch salad dressing *or* dip, optional

1 In a small bowl, combine the potato flakes, Parmesan cheese, celery salt, garlic powder and butter. In another bowl, beat eggs. Dip vegetables, one at a time, into egg, then into potato mixture; coat well.

2 Place on an ungreased baking sheet. Bake at 400° for 20-25 minutes. Serve with dressing or dip if desired.

YIELD: 6-8 SERVINGS.

Earleen Lillegard, Prescott, Arizona

Deep-fried vegetables are terrific, but it's not always convenient to prepare them for company. Here's a recipe that produces the same deliciously crisp results in the oven. Serve with your favorite ranch-style dressing as a dip.

fried corn balls

1 egg, lightly beaten

1 can (8¼ ounces) cream-style corn

¾ cup crushed saltines (about 22 crackers)

½ teaspoon sugar

½ teaspoon baking powder

Oil for deep-fat frying

1 In a bowl, combine the first five ingredients to form a soft batter.

2 In an electric skillet or deep-fat fryer, heat oil to 375°. Drop batter by rounded teaspoonfuls; fry until golden brown, about 1 minute on each side. Drain on paper towels. Serve warm.

YIELD: ABOUT 2 DOZEN.

Ronnie-Ellen Timoner, Middletown, New York

These bite-size treats are so easy to make. Serve them as an appetizer or as a side to a beef or chicken entree.

bacon water chestnut wraps

1 pound sliced bacon

2 cans (8 ounces *each*) whole water chestnuts, drained

1/2 cup packed brown sugar

1/2 cup mayonnaise

1/4 cup chili sauce

1 Cut bacon strips in half crosswise. In a skillet over medium heat, cook bacon until almost crisp; drain. Wrap each bacon piece around a water chestnut and secure with a toothpick. Place in an ungreased 13-in. x 9-in. baking dish.

2 Combine the brown sugar, mayonnaise and chili sauce; pour over water chestnuts. Bake, uncovered, at 350° for 30 minutes or until hot and bubbly.

YIELD: ABOUT 2½ DOZEN.

Laura Mahaffey, Annapolis, Maryland

The holidays around our house just wouldn't be the same without these classic wraps. Through the years, Christmas Eve guests have proved it's impossible to eat just one.

tomato leek tarts

1 package (15 ounces) refrigerated pie pastry

4 ounces provolone cheese, shredded

1 pound leeks (white portion only), sliced

6 medium plum tomatoes, thinly sliced

¼ cup grated Parmesan cheese

1½ teaspoons garlic powder

⅛ teaspoon pepper

1 cup (8 ounces) shredded part-skim mozzarella cheese

1 Place both pastry sheets on greased baking sheets. Sprinkle each with provolone cheese, leaving 1 in. around edges. Arrange leeks and tomato slices over provolone cheese. Sprinkle with Parmesan cheese, garlic powder and pepper. Top with mozzarella cheese. Fold edges over filling.

2 Bake at 425° for 18-22 minutes or until crusts are lightly browned. Cut into wedges. Serve warm.

YIELD: 2 TARTS.

Kathleen Tribble, Santa Ynez, California

You'll get two attractive, rustic-looking tarts from this delicious recipe. The crisp pastry crust cuts easily into wedges.

spinach spirals with mushroom sauce

¾ pound fresh mushrooms, sliced

¼ cup butter

3 tablespoons all-purpose flour

1 cup chicken broth

1 cup half-and-half cream

2 tablespoons sherry *or* additional chicken broth

1 teaspoon Dijon mustard

½ teaspoon lemon juice

SPINACH ROLL:

½ cup dry bread crumbs

3 packages (10 ounces *each*) frozen chopped spinach, thawed and squeezed dry

6 tablespoons butter, melted

¼ teaspoon salt

⅛ teaspoon pepper

⅛ teaspoon ground nutmeg

4 eggs, *separated*

¼ cup grated Parmesan cheese

1 In a large skillet, saute mushrooms in butter for 2-3 minutes. Stir in flour until blended; cook 2-3 minutes longer or until liquid is absorbed. Gradually stir in broth and cream. Bring to a boil. Remove from the heat; stir in the sherry or additional broth, mustard and lemon juice. Cool for 15 minutes.

2 Line a greased 15-in. x 10-in. x 1-in. baking pan with parchment paper; grease the paper. Sprinkle with bread crumbs; set aside. In a large bowl, combine the spinach, butter, salt, pepper, nutmeg and egg yolks. In a small mixing bowl, beat egg whites on high speed until stiff peaks form. Gradually fold into spinach mixture. Gently spoon over bread crumbs; press down lightly using a rubber spatula. Sprinkle with Parmesan cheese.

3 Bake at 350° for 12-15 minutes or until center springs back when lightly touched. Cover with a piece of greased foil; immediately invert pan onto foil. Gently peel away parchment paper.

4 Spread 1 cup mushroom sauce over the spinach mixture to within 1 in. of edges. Roll up jelly-roll style, starting with a short side and peeling foil away while rolling. Cut into slices. Reheat remaining mushroom sauce; serve with spinach spirals.

YIELD: 12 SERVINGS.

Mrs. Archie Potts, San Antonio, Texas

I never thought I liked spinach until I tried these pretty spirals topped with a creamy mushroom sauce! It is a delicious dish to serve at a festive gathering.

fried cheese nuggets

½ cup dry bread crumbs

1 tablespoon sesame seeds

2 eggs, lightly beaten

1 package (10 ounces) extra-sharp cheddar cheese

Oil for deep-fat frying

1 In a shallow bowl, combine bread crumbs and sesame seeds. Place eggs in another shallow bowl. Cut cheese into ¾-in. cubes; dip in eggs, then coat with crumb mixture. Refrigerate for 15 minutes or until coating is set.

2 In an electric skillet or deep-fat fryer, heat 1 in. oil to 375°. Fry cheese cubes for 1-2 minutes or until browned. Drain on paper towels. Serve warm.

YIELD: 2 DOZEN.

Pat Waymire, Yellow Springs, Ohio

There's just something about cheese that folks can't resist, and these cheese nuggets are no exception. I barely finish making a batch before they disappear!

bacon-wrapped scallops

20 fresh baby spinach leaves

10 uncooked sea scallops, halved

10 bacon strips, halved widthwise

Lemon wedges

1 Fold a spinach leaf around each scallop half. Wrap bacon over spinach and secure with a toothpick. Place on baking sheet or broiler pan.

2 Broil 3-4 in. from the heat for 6 minutes on each side or until the bacon is crisp and the scallops are opaque. Squeeze lemon over each. Serve immediately.

YIELD: 20 APPETIZERS.

Pamela MacCumbee, Berkeley Springs, West Virginia

When I'm looking for a more elegant appetizer, this is the recipe I reach for. I've also served these savory scallops for dinner.

italian garlic breadsticks

Taste of Home Test Kitchen

A seasoned Parmesan cheese coating gives refrigerated breadsticks a terrific taste twist. The wonderful aroma of these breadsticks baking is so irresistible, you may need to make another batch!

½ cup grated Parmesan cheese

2 teaspoons Italian seasoning

1 teaspoon garlic powder

¼ cup butter, melted

1 tube (11 ounces) refrigerated breadsticks

1 In a shallow bowl, combine the cheese, Italian seasoning and garlic powder. Place butter in another shallow bowl. Separate dough into individual breadsticks. Dip in butter, then in cheese mixture. Twist 2-3 times and place on an ungreased baking sheet.

2 Bake at 375° for 12-14 minutes or until golden brown. Serve immediately.

YIELD: 1 DOZEN.

mini phyllo tacos

1 pound lean ground beef (90% lean)

½ cup finely chopped onion

1 envelope taco seasoning

¾ cup water

1¼ cups shredded Mexican cheese blend, *divided*

2 packages (1.9 ounces *each*) frozen miniature phyllo tart shells

1 In a small skillet, cook beef and onion over medium heat until meat is no longer pink; drain. Stir in taco seasoning and water. Bring to a boil. Reduce heat; simmer, uncovered for 5 minutes. Remove from the heat; stir in ½ cup cheese blend.

2 Place tart shells in an ungreased 15-in. x 10-in. x 1-in. baking pan. Fill with taco mixture.

3 Bake at 350° for 6 minutes. Sprinkle with remaining cheese blend; bake 2-3 minutes longer or until cheese is melted.

YIELD: 2½ DOZEN.

Roseann Weston, Philipsburg, Pennsylvania

For a winning appetizer, serve crispy phyllo cups filled with taco-seasoned ground beef and zesty shredded cheese.

blue cheese crostini

4 ounces cream cheese, softened

3 tablespoons butter, softened

1 cup (4 ounces) crumbled blue cheese

¼ cup finely chopped walnuts, toasted

15 slices French bread (½ inch thick), lightly toasted

1 medium ripe pear

1 In a small mixing bowl, beat the cream cheese and butter until smooth. Stir in the blue cheese and walnuts. Spread evenly over the toasted bread.

2 Place on a baking sheet. Broil 3-4 in. from the heat for 3-4 minutes or until cheese is bubbly. Core pear and cut into 30 thin slices. Place two pear slices on each crostini. Serve warm.

YIELD: 15 APPETIZERS.

Kate Hilts, Grand Rapids, Michigan

My sister-in-law gave me this great recipe, which includes two of my favorite ingredients—blue cheese and pears. Yum!

bacon nachos

½ pound ground beef

4 cups tortilla chips

¼ cup real bacon bits

2 cups (8 ounces) shredded cheddar cheese

½ cup guacamole dip

½ cup sour cream

Chopped tomatoes and green onions, optional

1 In a small skillet, cook beef over medium heat until no longer pink; drain. Place the tortilla chips on a microwave-safe serving plate. Layer with the beef, bacon and cheese.

2 Microwave, uncovered, on high for 1-2 minutes or until cheese is melted. Top with guacamole and sour cream. Sprinkle with the tomatoes and onions if desired.

YIELD: 4-6 SERVINGS.

EDITOR'S NOTE: This recipe was tested in a 1,100-watt microwave.

Ruth Ann Bott, Lake Wales, Florida

These crispy nachos have always been a big hit in our house. Topped with kid-friendly ingredients, they're sure to be requested by your children.

crunchy onion sticks

2 eggs, lightly beaten

2 tablespoons butter, melted

1 teaspoon all-purpose flour

½ teaspoon garlic salt

½ teaspoon dried parsley flakes

¼ teaspoon onion salt

2 cans (2.8 ounces *each*) french-fried onions, crushed

1 tube (8 ounces) refrigerated crescent rolls

1 In a shallow bowl, combine the first six ingredients. Place the onions in another shallow bowl. Separate crescent dough into four rectangles; seal perforations. Cut each rectangle into eight strips. Dip each strip in egg mixture, then roll in onions.

2 Place 2 in. apart on ungreased baking sheets. Bake at 375° for 10-12 minutes or until golden brown. Immediately remove from baking sheets. Serve warm.

YIELD: 32 APPETIZERS.

Leora Muellerleile, Turtle Lake, Wisconsin

Although I've been collecting recipes for more than 50 years, I never tire of tried-and-true ones like this.

crab puffs

1 cup plus 1 tablespoon water

½ cup butter

1 tablespoon ground mustard

1 teaspoon salt

1 teaspoon ground cumin

⅛ teaspoon hot pepper sauce

1 cup all-purpose flour

4 eggs

2 cups (8 ounces) shredded Swiss cheese

1 can (6 ounces) crabmeat, drained, flaked and cartilage removed

1 In a large saucepan, bring the water, butter, mustard, salt, cumin and hot pepper sauce to a boil. Add flour all at once and stir until a smooth ball forms. Remove from the heat; let stand for 5 minutes.

2 Add eggs, one at a time, beating well after each addition. Continue beating until smooth and shiny. Stir in the cheese and crab.

3 Drop by rounded teaspoonfuls 2 in. apart onto greased baking sheets. Bake at 400° for 23-26 minutes or until golden brown. Remove to wire racks. Serve warm.

YIELD: ABOUT 4 DOZEN.

Nadia Miheyev, Richmond Hill, New York

If you're looking for a scrumptious way to get a party started, bring out a tray of these cheesy crab puffs. They bake up golden brown and taste wonderful right out of the oven. Try serving them with soup.

fried onion rings

1 large Vidalia *or* sweet onion

¾ cup all-purpose flour

¼ cup cornmeal

½ teaspoon baking powder

½ teaspoon salt

¼ teaspoon baking soda

¼ teaspoon cayenne pepper

1 egg

1 cup buttermilk

Oil for deep-fat frying

LIME DIPPING SAUCE:

⅔ cup mayonnaise

3 tablespoons honey

2 tablespoons lime juice

2 tablespoons spicy brown *or* horseradish mustard

1 teaspoon prepared horseradish

1 Cut onion into ½-in. slices; separate into rings. In a bowl, combine the flour, cornmeal, baking powder, salt, baking soda and cayenne. Combine the egg and buttermilk; stir into dry ingredients just until moistened.

2 In an electric skillet or deep-fat fryer, heat 1 in. of oil to 375°. Dip onion rings into batter. Fry a few at a time for 1 to 1½ minutes on each side or until golden brown. Drain on paper towels (keep warm in a 300° oven).

3 In a small bowl, combine sauce ingredients. Serve with onion rings.

YIELD: 4 SERVINGS.

Christine Wilson, Sellersville, Pennsylvania

Sweet Vidalia onion rings are deep-fried to a crispy golden brown, then served with a cool and zesty lime dipping sauce.

jalapeno poppers

2 jars (11½ ounces *each*) jalapeno peppers

1 package (8 ounces) cream cheese, softened

1 cup (4 ounces) shredded cheddar cheese

¼ cup grated Parmesan cheese

1 tablespoon dried parsley flakes

2 teaspoons garlic salt

2 teaspoons paprika

¼ cup all-purpose flour

3 eggs

1 cup crushed cornflakes

½ cup dry bread crumbs

Oil for frying

SAUCE:

¼ cup mayonnaise

¼ cup prepared Russian salad dressing

1 teaspoon prepared horseradish

1 teaspoon dried parsley flakes

½ teaspoon pepper

¼ teaspoon salt

Dash Louisiana-style hot sauce

1 Select 12-16 large jalapenos from jars; pat dry with paper towels (refrigerate any remaining jalapenos for another use). Remove stems from jalapenos; cut a lengthwise slit on one side. Discard seeds. In a small mixing bowl, combine the cheeses, parsley, garlic salt and paprika. Pipe or stuff into each pepper.

2 Place flour in a shallow bowl. In another shallow bowl, lightly beat the eggs. In a separate bowl, combine cornflakes and bread crumbs. Roll jalapenos in flour, dip in eggs, then roll in crumbs. Dip again in eggs, then roll in crumbs to completely coat.

3 In an electric skillet, heat ¼ in. of oil to 375°. Fry peppers, a few at a time, for 30-60 seconds or until lightly browned. Drain on paper towels. In a small bowl, combine sauce ingredients. Serve with warm peppers.

YIELD: 12-16 APPETIZERS.

EDITOR'S NOTE: When cutting or seeding hot peppers, use rubber or plastic gloves to protect your hands. Avoid touching your face.

James Brophy, Feasterville Trevose, Pennsylvania

After sampling similar poppers at a wedding reception, I wanted to create my own recipe. The creamy filling pairs well with the spicy peppers.

potato nachos

8 medium red potatoes

1 envelope ranch salad dressing mix

1 jar (12 ounces) pickled jalapeno pepper slices, drained

2 cups (8 ounces) shredded cheddar cheese

2 cups (8 ounces) shredded Monterey Jack cheese

2 cups (16 ounces) sour cream

6 to 8 green onions, chopped

1 Place potatoes in a saucepan and cover with water. Bring to a boil. Reduce heat; cover and cook for 15-20 minutes or just until tender. Drain; cool slightly.

2 Cut the potatoes into $\frac{1}{4}$-in.-thick slices. Place in a single layer in three greased 15-in. x 10-in. x 1-in. baking pans. Top each with the salad dressing mix, a jalapeno slice, cheddar cheese and Monterey Jack cheese.

3 Bake, uncovered, at 350° for 10-12 minutes or until cheese is melted. Top with sour cream and green onions.

YIELD: 12 SERVINGS.

Tony Horton, Van Buren, Arkansas

Cheese, jalapeno pepper, sour cream and green onions top these pretty potato slices, seasoned with dry ranch dressing mix. I love to serve them to guests, and they love to eat them. You can use them as an appetizer or even as a side dish.

feta artichoke bites

1 jar (7½ ounces) marinated artichoke hearts

1 cup diced seeded tomatoes

1 cup (4 ounces) crumbled feta cheese

⅓ cup grated Parmesan cheese

2 green onions, thinly sliced

1 loaf sourdough baguette (about 20 inches long)

1 Drain artichokes, reserving 2 tablespoons marinade. Chop artichokes; place in a large bowl. Stir in tomatoes, cheeses, onions and reserved marinade. Cover and refrigerate for 1 hour.

2 Cut baguette into ½-in. slices. Spread with artichoke mixture. Place on an ungreased baking sheet. Broil 4-6 in. from the heat for 4-5 minutes or until edges of bread are browned. Serve immediately.

YIELD: ABOUT 12 SERVINGS.

Louise Leach, Chino, California

You can prepare the flavorful topping for this appetizer ahead of time. Then, when it's time to serve them, spread the topping onto slices of bread and broil for a fast, festive snack.

eggplant snack sticks

1 medium eggplant (1¼ pounds)

½ cup toasted wheat germ

½ cup grated Parmesan cheese

1 teaspoon Italian seasoning

¾ teaspoon garlic salt

½ cup egg substitute

1 cup meatless spaghetti sauce, warmed

1 Cut eggplant lengthwise into ½-in.-thick slices, then cut each slice lengthwise into ½-in. strips. In a shallow dish, combine the wheat germ, cheese, Italian seasoning and garlic salt. Dip eggplant sticks in egg substitute, then coat with wheat germ mixture. Arrange in a single layer on a baking sheet coated with cooking spray.

2 Spritz eggplant with cooking spray. Broil 4 in. from the heat for 3 minutes. Remove from the oven. Turn sticks and spritz with cooking spray. Broil 2 minutes longer or until golden brown. Serve immediately with spaghetti sauce.

YIELD: 8 SERVINGS.

Mary Murphy, Atwater, California

Coated with Italian seasoning, Parmesan cheese and garlic salt, my veggie sticks are broiled so there's no guilt when guests crunch into them.

fruit 'n' almond-stuffed brie

2/3 cup sliced almonds

1/3 cup chopped dried apricots

1/4 cup brandy

1 sheet frozen puff pastry, thawed

1 round (8 ounces) Brie cheese, rind removed

1 egg, lightly beaten

RASPBERRY SAUCE:

1/2 cup sugar

1 tablespoon cornstarch

1/2 cup cold water

2 cups fresh *or* frozen raspberries

Assorted crackers

1 In a small saucepan with high sides, combine the almonds, apricots and brandy. Cook and stir over medium-low heat until liquid is almost evaporated. Remove from the heat; set aside.

2 On a lightly floured surface, roll puff pastry into an 11-in. x 9-in. rectangle. Cut cheese in half horizontally; place bottom half in the center of pastry. Spread with half of the almond mixture. Top with remaining cheese and almond mixture.

3 Fold pastry around cheese; trim excess dough. Pinch edges to seal. Place seam side down on ungreased baking sheet. Brush with egg.

4 Bake at 375° for 30-35 minutes or until puffed and golden brown.

5 In a small saucepan, combine the sugar, cornstarch and water until smooth; add raspberries. Bring to a boil over medium heat, stirring constantly. Cook and stir for 1 minute or until slightly thickened. Strain and discard seeds. Transfer sauce to a small pitcher or bowl; serve with stuffed Brie and crackers.

YIELD: 8 SERVINGS.

Douglas Wasdyke, Effort, Pennsylvania
Our friends enjoy this special appetizer as part of all our celebrations. An apricot filling and a raspberry topping make every bite cheesy and fruity.

shrimp puffs

2 eggs, *separated*

¾ cup milk

1 tablespoon vegetable oil

1 cup all-purpose flour

1½ teaspoons baking powder

1½ teaspoons onion powder

1 teaspoon salt

½ teaspoon pepper

3 cups cooked rice

1 pound uncooked shrimp, peeled, deveined and chopped *or* 2 cans (4½ ounces *each*) small shrimp, drained

¼ cup minced fresh parsley

½ teaspoon hot pepper sauce

Oil for deep-fat frying

1 In a large bowl, beat the egg yolks, milk and oil. Combine the flour, baking powder, onion powder, salt and pepper; add to yolk mixture and mix well. Stir in the rice, shrimp, parsley and hot pepper sauce.

2 In a mixing bowl, beat the egg whites until soft peaks form; fold into shrimp mixture.

3 In an electric skillet or deep-fat fryer, heat oil to 350°. Drop batter by tablespoons into hot oil. Fry the puffs, a few at a time, for 1½ minutes on each side or until browned and puffy. Drain on paper towels. Serve warm.

YIELD: ABOUT 4 DOZEN.

Maudry Ramsey, Sulphur, Louisiana

Shrimp and rice are two foods that are abundant in our area. These shrimp puffs are my family's favorite.

calico clams casino

3 cans (6½ ounces *each*) minced clams

1 cup (4 ounces) shredded part-skim mozzarella cheese

1 cup (4 ounces) shredded cheddar cheese

4 bacon strips, cooked and crumbled

3 tablespoons seasoned bread crumbs

3 tablespoons butter, melted

2 tablespoons *each* finely chopped onion, celery and sweet red, yellow and green peppers

1 garlic clove, minced

Dash dried parsley flakes

1 Drain clams, reserving 2 tablespoons clam juice. In a large bowl, combine the clams and all the remaining ingredients; stir in the reserved clam juice. Spoon into greased 6-oz. custard cups or clamshell dishes; place on baking sheets.

2 Bake at 350° for 10-15 minutes or until heated through and lightly browned.

YIELD: 8 SERVINGS.

Paula Sullivan, Barker, New York

A few years ago, I came across this recipe in the back of my files when I was looking for a special appetizer. Everyone raved about it. Now it's an often-requested dish.

creamy herb slices

1 package (8 ounces) cream cheese, softened

1 tablespoon minced fresh parsley

1 tablespoon minced chives

2 teaspoons chopped green onions

2 garlic cloves, minced

1 teaspoon dill weed

½ teaspoon pepper

1 loaf (½ pound) French bread

In a small bowl, combine the first seven ingredients. Cut bread into ½-in. slices; spread each slice with 1 tablespoon cream cheese mixture. Place on ungreased baking sheets. Bake at 400° for 7 minutes or broil for 2 minutes until golden brown.

YIELD: ABOUT 22 APPETIZERS.

Kelly Schulz, Oak Lawn, Illinois

These dressed-up slices of French bread make a satisfying snack…plus, they go well with soup or salad. I have to move fast after putting them out—or there are none left for me!

onion tart

1 unbaked pastry shell (9 inches)

2 medium sweet onions, thinly sliced

2 tablespoons olive oil

3 eggs

1/2 cup crumbled feta cheese

1/2 teaspoon salt

1/4 teaspoon coarsely ground pepper

1/8 teaspoon ground nutmeg

1/8 teaspoon hot pepper sauce

3/4 cup half-and-half cream

1/2 cup milk

1 tablespoon Dijon mustard

6 green onions, thinly sliced

2 tablespoons minced chives

1/3 cup grated Parmesan cheese

1 Line unpricked pastry shell with a double thickness of heavy-duty foil. Bake at 450° for 8 minutes. Remove foil; bake 5 minutes longer. Cool on a wire rack.

2 In a small skillet, saute the onions in oil until tender; cool. In a food processor, combine the eggs, feta cheese, salt, pepper, nutmeg and hot pepper sauce; cover and process until smooth. Gradually add cream and milk; process until blended.

3 Brush the inside of crust with mustard. Sprinkle the green onions, chives and sauteed onions over crust. Carefully pour egg mixture over onions. Sprinkle with Parmesan cheese.

4 Bake at 375° for 30-40 minutes or until a knife inserted near the center comes out clean. Let stand for 10 minutes before cutting. Serve warm.

YIELD: 12 SERVINGS.

Christine Andreas, Huntingdon, Pennsylvania
Onion lovers are sure to be asking for second helpings of this appetizing tart—it uses two kinds of onions! Parmesan and feta cheese, nutmeg and hot pepper sauce enhance the flavor nicely. With its quiche-like filling, the dish is ideal for a brunch or buffet.

chicken nut puffs

1½ cups finely chopped cooked
  chicken

⅓ cup chopped almonds, toasted

1 cup chicken broth

½ cup vegetable oil

2 teaspoons Worcestershire sauce

1 tablespoon dried parsley flakes

1 teaspoon seasoned salt

½ to 1 teaspoon celery seed

⅛ teaspoon cayenne pepper

1 cup all-purpose flour

4 eggs

1 Combine the chicken and almonds; set aside. In a saucepan, combine the next seven ingredients; bring to a boil. Add flour all at once; stir until a smooth ball forms. Remove from the heat; let stand for 5 minutes.

2 Add eggs, one at a time, beating well after each. Beat until smooth. Stir in chicken and almonds.

3 Drop by heaping teaspoonfuls onto greased baking sheets. Bake at 450° for 12-14 minutes or until golden brown. Serve warm.

YIELD: ABOUT 6 DOZEN.

Jo Groth, Plainfield, Iowa

Of the 15 to 20 items I set out when hosting holiday parties, these savory puffs are the first to get snapped up. People enjoy the zippy flavor. They're a nice finger food to eat since they're not sticky or drippy.

cajun canapes

Jerri Peachee, Gentry, Arkansas

I came across these filled biscuits at a party—and now they're a family-favorite snack.

2 tubes (12 ounces *each*) refrigerated buttermilk biscuits

½ pound bulk pork sausage, cooked and drained

1½ cups (6 ounces) shredded cheddar cheese

¼ cup chopped green pepper

¼ cup mayonnaise

2 green onions, chopped

2 teaspoons lemon juice

½ teaspoon salt

½ teaspoon paprika

¼ teaspoon garlic powder

¼ teaspoon dried thyme

⅛ to ¼ teaspoon cayenne pepper

1 Bake biscuits according to package directions, except turn biscuits over halfway through baking. Remove from pans to wire racks to cool completely.

2 Using a melon baller, scoop out the center of each biscuit, leaving a ⅜-in. shell (discard biscuit center). In a bowl, combine the remaining ingredients. Spoon about 1 tablespoonful into the center of each biscuit.

3 Place on an ungreased baking sheet. Bake at 400° for 8-10 minutes or until heated through. Serve warm.

YIELD: 20 APPETIZERS.

cool nibbles

76

51

Chill out with easy appetizers you can plate before your party starts. Count on time-savers like Zesty Marinated Shrimp (p. 57), Savory Cheese Cutouts (p. 76) and Potato Salad Bites (p. 51).

For food-safe service, arrange appetizers on multiple plates. Then serve one plate while you keep the others refrigerated. Just refill as needed. Place a serving dish of items like shrimp or deviled eggs on a bed of ice for a presentation that's both practical and pretty. Avoid setting warm and cold appetizers on a platter together.

ham 'n' cheese pinwheels

1 carton (8 ounces) whipped cream cheese

½ cup finely chopped walnuts

1 tablespoon ranch salad dressing mix

1 garlic clove, minced

9 thin slices deli ham

In a bowl, combine the cream cheese, walnuts, salad dressing mix and garlic. Spread about 2 tablespoons over each ham slice; roll up tightly and wrap in plastic wrap. Refrigerate for at least 2 hours. Unwrap; cut into 1-in. slices.

YIELD: ABOUT 4 DOZEN.

Andrea Bolden, Unionville, Tennessee

This recipe is a convenient make-ahead treat. I love the garlic flavor in these roll-ups. Every time I serve them, they're a hit.

potato salad bites

10 small red potatoes

¼ cup chopped pimiento-stuffed olives

2 teaspoons minced fresh parsley

1 teaspoon finely chopped onion

½ cup mayonnaise

1¾ teaspoons Dijon mustard

⅛ teaspoon pepper

¼ teaspoon salt

Paprika

Parsley sprigs, optional

1 Place the potatoes in a saucepan and cover with water. Bring to a boil. Reduce heat; cover and cook for 12-15 minutes or until tender. Drain and place potatoes in ice water; drain and pat dry.

2 Peel two potatoes; finely dice and place in a small bowl. Cut the remaining potatoes in half. With a melon baller, scoop out pulp, leaving a ⅜-in. shell; set shells aside. Dice pulp and add to bowl. Stir in olives, parsley and onion. Combine the mayonnaise, mustard and pepper; gently stir into potato mixture.

3 Sprinkle potato shells with salt; stuff with potato salad. Sprinkle with paprika. Refrigerate for at least 1 hour before serving. Garnish with parsley if desired.

YIELD: 16 APPETIZERS.

Stephanie Sheridan, Plainfield, Vermont
Potatoes make the perfect platform for this colorful potato salad. They take just two or three bites, so you don't need a fork.

beef canapes with cucumber sauce

Taste of Home Test Kitchen

A homemade cucumber-yogurt sauce complements tender slices of beef in this recipe. Since both the meat and sauce are prepared in advance, this recipe requires very little last-minute preparation.

4 cups (32 ounces) plain yogurt

1 whole beef tenderloin (1½ pounds)

2 tablespoons olive oil, *divided*

1 teaspoon salt, *divided*

¼ teaspoon plus ⅛ teaspoon white pepper, *divided*

1 medium cucumber, peeled, seeded and diced

1 tablespoon finely chopped onion

1 garlic clove, minced

1 tablespoon white vinegar

1 (1 pound) French bread baguette, cut into 36 thin slices

1 cup fresh arugula

1 Line a fine mesh strainer with two layers of cheesecloth; place over a bowl. Place yogurt in strainer. Cover and refrigerate for at least 4 hours or overnight.

2 Rub tenderloin with 1 tablespoon oil. Sprinkle with ½ teaspoon salt and ¼ teaspoon white pepper. In a large skillet, cook the beef tenderloin over medium-high heat until browned on all sides. Transfer meat to a shallow roasting pan. Bake at 400° for 25-30 minutes or until a meat thermometer reads 145°. Cool on a wire rack for 1 hour. Cover and refrigerate.

3 Transfer yogurt from strainer to another bowl (discard yogurt liquid). Add the cucumber, onion, garlic and remaining salt and white pepper. In a small bowl, whisk the vinegar and remaining oil; stir into yogurt mixture.

4 Thinly slice tenderloin. Spread yogurt mixture over bread slices; top with beef and arugula. Serve immediately or cover and refrigerate until serving.

YIELD: 3 DOZEN.

artichoke crostini

1 sourdough baguette (1 pound)

2 cups chopped seeded tomatoes

1 can (14 ounces) water-packed artichoke hearts, rinsed, drained and chopped

2 tablespoons minced fresh basil

2 tablespoons olive oil

½ teaspoon seasoned salt

⅛ teaspoon pepper

1 Cut the baguette into 32 slices. Place on an ungreased baking sheet; spritz bread with cooking spray. Bake at 325° for 7-10 minutes or until crisp. Cool on a wire rack.

2 In a bowl, combine the tomatoes, artichokes, basil, oil, seasoned salt and pepper. Spoon onto bread slices.

YIELD: 32 APPETIZERS.

Janne Rowe, Wichita, Kansas

This appetizer is wonderful when vine-ripened tomatoes are at their best. I often rely on these fresh-tasting slices for parties and other events.

party puffs

1 cup water

½ cup butter

1 cup all-purpose flour

4 eggs

EGG SALAD FILLING:

6 hard-cooked eggs, chopped

⅓ cup mayonnaise

3 tablespoons chutney, finely chopped

2 green onions, finely chopped

1 teaspoon salt

½ teaspoon curry powder

HAM SALAD FILLING:

1 can (4¼ ounces) deviled ham

1 package (3 ounces) cream cheese, softened

2 tablespoons finely chopped green pepper

1½ teaspoons prepared horseradish

1 teaspoon lemon juice

1 In a saucepan over medium heat, bring water and butter to a boil. Add flour all at once and stir until a smooth ball forms. Remove from the heat; let stand for 5 minutes.

2 Add eggs, one at a time, beating well after each addition. Continue beating until mixture is smooth and shiny. Drop by teaspoonfuls 2 in. apart onto greased baking sheets.

3 Bake at 400° for 20-25 minutes or until lightly browned. Remove to wire racks. Immediately cut a slit in each puff to allow steam to escape; cool completely.

4 In separate bowls, combine the ingredients for egg salad filling and ham salad filling. Split puffs and remove soft dough from inside. Just before serving, spoon filling into puffs; replace tops. Refrigerate the leftovers.

YIELD: 7½ DOZEN.

Karen Owen, Rising Sun, Indiana

For a substantial party starter, you can't go wrong with mini sandwiches. Instead of serving egg or ham salad on ordinary bread, I like to present them in homemade puff pastry.

red pepper green bean roll-ups

1/2 pound fresh green beans, trimmed

1/2 cup Italian salad dressing

15 slices white bread

1/4 cup mayonnaise

2 tablespoons spicy brown mustard

1 jar (7 1/4 ounces) roasted sweet red peppers, well drained

1/3 cup butter, melted

1/2 cup packed minced fresh parsley

1 Place green beans in a large saucepan and cover with water. Bring to a boil; cook, uncovered, for 6-8 minutes or until crisp-tender. Drain and rinse in cold water. Pat dry with paper towels. Place the beans in a large resealable plastic bag; add salad dressing. Seal bag and toss to coat; refrigerate overnight.

2 Trim crusts from bread. With a rolling pin, flatten each slice slightly. Combine mayonnaise and mustard; spread about 1 teaspoon on each slice of bread.

3 Cut roasted peppers into 1/2-in. slices. Drain and discard marinade. Place three green beans and two pepper slices on each slice of bread. Roll up from a long side and secure with a toothpick. Brush with butter; roll in parsley. Cover and refrigerate until serving. Just before serving, discard toothpicks and cut each roll into three pieces.

YIELD: 45 APPETIZERS.

Marie Rizzio, Interlochen, Michigan

Delicious and healthy, this appetizer is a yummy way to eat green beans. The roll-ups can be prepared early in the day, and guests always comment on how unique they are.

zesty marinated shrimp

½ cup vegetable oil

½ cup lime juice

½ cup thinly sliced red onion

12 lemon slices

1 tablespoon minced fresh parsley

½ teaspoon salt

½ teaspoon dill weed

⅛ teaspoon hot pepper sauce

2 pounds medium shrimp, cooked, peeled and deveined

In a large bowl, combine the first eight ingredients. Stir in shrimp. Cover and refrigerate for 4 hours, stirring occasionally. Drain before serving.

YIELD: 12 SERVINGS.

Mary Jane Guest, Alamosa, Colorado

These easy shrimp look impressive on a buffet table and taste even better! The zesty sauce has a wonderful, spicy citrus flavor. I especially like this recipe because I can always prepare it well ahead of time.

marinated mushrooms

1 pound small fresh mushrooms

1 small onion, thinly sliced

1/3 cup white wine vinegar

1/3 cup vegetable oil

1 teaspoon salt

1 teaspoon ground mustard

In a large saucepan, combine all the ingredients. Bring to a boil over medium-high heat. Cook, uncovered, for 6 minutes, stirring once. Cool to room temperature. Transfer to a bowl; cover and refrigerate overnight.

YIELD: 3 CUPS.

Mark Curry, Buena Vista, Colorado
Add these flavorful mushrooms to an antipasto platter,
toss in a salad or just serve by themselves.

shrimp 'n' snow pea wrap-ups

1 cup oil and vinegar salad dressing

1 teaspoon minced fresh gingerroot

1 garlic clove, minced

1 pound cooked medium shrimp, peeled and deveined (about 36)

2 cups water

4 ounces fresh snow peas (about 36)

1 In a large bowl, combine the salad dressing, ginger and garlic. Stir in shrimp; cover and refrigerate for 2 hours.

2 Meanwhile, in a small saucepan, bring water to a boil. Add snow peas; cover and boil for 1 minute. Drain and immediately place peas in ice water; drain and pat dry.

3 Drain and discard marinade from shrimp. Wrap a snow pea around each shrimp; secure with a toothpick. Chill until serving.

YIELD: ABOUT 3 DOZEN.

Earnestine Jackson, Beaumont, Texas

This variation on marinated shrimp gets a splash of color from snow peas.

---

herbed deviled eggs

6 hard-cooked eggs

2 tablespoons minced chives

2 tablespoons plain yogurt

2 tablespoons mayonnaise

1 tablespoon chopped fresh tarragon

1 tablespoon minced fresh parsley

2½ teaspoons prepared mustard

1 teaspoon snipped fresh dill

Salt and pepper to taste

Cut eggs in half lengthwise; remove yolks and set whites aside. In a small bowl, mash yolks with a fork. Stir in the remaining ingredients. Pipe or stuff into egg whites. Refrigerate until serving.

YIELD: 1 DOZEN.

Sue Seymour, Valatie, New York

Wondering what to do with hard-cooked eggs when Easter is past? This version of deviled eggs offers a mix of herbs in the filling.

---

salmon canapes

1 package (8 ounces) cream cheese

1 teaspoon snipped fresh dill *or*
   ¼ teaspoon dill weed

36 slices cocktail rye bread

12 ounces sliced smoked salmon

1 medium red onion, thinly sliced
   and separated into rings

Fresh dill sprigs, optional

In a small mixing bowl, combine cream cheese and dill. Spread on rye bread. Top with salmon and red onion. Garnish with dill sprigs if desired.

YIELD: 12 SERVINGS.

Tristin Crenshaw, Tucson, Arizona

My boyfriend's mother gave me the idea for this classy appetizer that I serve for Sunday brunch and special occasions like New Year's Eve. The textures and flavors of the dill, cream cheese and smoked salmon are scrumptious together. Spread on cocktail rye bread, it's sure to be the toast of your buffet!

oriental pork tenderloin

1 cup soy sauce

½ cup packed brown sugar

2 tablespoons red wine vinegar

2 teaspoons red food coloring, optional

1 garlic clove, minced

1 teaspoon ground ginger

1 teaspoon salt

½ teaspoon pepper

3 pork tenderloins (about 1 pound *each*)

Sesame seeds, toasted

1 In a bowl, combine the first eight ingredients; mix well. Remove ½ cup for basting; cover and refrigerate. Pour the remaining marinade into a large resealable plastic bag; add tenderloins. Seal bag and turn to coat; refrigerate overnight.

2 Drain and discard marinade from pork. Place pork on a rack in a shallow roasting pan. Bake, uncovered, at 350° for 55-60 minutes or until a meat thermometer reads 160°, brushing with the reserved marinade every 15 minutes.

3 Sprinkle with sesame seeds. Cool for 30 minutes. Refrigerate for 2 hours or overnight. Cut into thin slices.

YIELD: 8-10 SERVINGS.

Diana Beyer, Graham, Washington

I first made this appetizer on Christmas Eve a few years ago, and it has since become a tradition.

nutty apple wedges

1 medium unpeeled tart apple, cored

½ cup peanut butter

1 cup crushed cornflakes

Cut apple into 12 thin wedges. Spread peanut butter on cut sides; roll in the cornflakes.

YIELD: 4-6 SERVINGS.

Beatrice Richard, Posen, Michigan

A crunchy coating turns apples and peanut butter into a finger-licking, after-school surprise. Even young kids will have a blast spreading peanut butter on the apple wedges and rolling them in cornflake crumbs.

tortellini appetizers

4 garlic cloves, peeled

2 tablespoons olive oil, *divided*

1 package (10 ounces) refrigerated spinach tortellini

1 cup mayonnaise

¼ cup grated Parmesan cheese

¼ cup milk

¼ cup prepared pesto

⅛ teaspoon pepper

1 pint grape tomatoes

26 frilled toothpicks

1 Place garlic cloves on a double thickness of heavy-duty foil; drizzle with 1 tablespoon oil. Wrap foil around garlic. Bake at 425° for 20-25 minutes or until tender. Cool for 10-15 minutes.

2 Meanwhile, cook tortellini according to package directions; drain and rinse in cold water. Toss with remaining oil; set aside. In a small bowl, combine the mayonnaise, Parmesan cheese, milk, pesto and pepper. Mash garlic into pesto mixture; stir until combined.

3 Alternately thread tortellini and tomatoes onto toothpicks. Serve with pesto dip. Refrigerate leftovers.

YIELD: ABOUT 2 DOZEN (1½ CUPS DIP).

Cheryl Lama, Royal Oak, Michigan

The festive green and red of this appetizer will make it a welcomed addition to your holiday buffet table. Store-bought pesto keeps the preparation fast. Sometimes I like to heat the garlic in a skillet and use skewers for a different look.

red pepper bruschetta

1 whole garlic bulb

1 teaspoon plus 2 tablespoons olive oil, *divided*

2 medium sweet red peppers, halved and seeded

3 tablespoons minced fresh parsley

2 tablespoons minced fresh basil *or 2 teaspoons dried basil*

1 tablespoon lemon juice

½ teaspoon salt

¼ teaspoon pepper

1 French bread baguette (about 12 ounces)

1 Remove papery outer skin from garlic bulb (do not peel or separate cloves). Brush with 1 teaspoon oil. Wrap in heavy-duty foil. Bake at 425° for 30-35 minutes or until softened. Cool.

2 Broil red peppers 4 in. from the heat until skins blister, about 10 minutes. Immediately place peppers in a bowl; cover with plastic wrap and let stand for 15-20 minutes.

3 Peel off and discard charred skin from peppers and coarsely chop. Cut top off garlic head, leaving root end intact. Squeeze softened garlic from bulb and finely chop.

4 In a bowl, combine the parsley, basil, lemon juice, salt, pepper and remaining oil. Add peppers and garlic; mix well. Cut bread into 16 slices, ½ in. thick; broil until lightly toasted. Top with pepper mixture. Serve immediately.

YIELD: 8 SERVINGS.

Taste of Home Test Kitchen

Roasted red peppers take the place of tomatoes in this twist on traditional bruschetta. If your bakery doesn't offer baguettes, buy regular French bread instead then cut the slices in half to create the crunchy snacks.

asian spring rolls

3 tablespoons lime juice

1 tablespoon hoisin sauce

1 teaspoon sugar

1 teaspoon salt

3 ounces uncooked Asian rice noodles

1 large carrot, grated

1 medium cucumber, peeled, seeded and julienned

1 medium jalapeno pepper, seeded and chopped

1/3 cup chopped dry roasted peanuts

8 spring roll wrappers *or* rice papers (8 inches)

1/2 cup loosely packed fresh cilantro

PEANUT SAUCE:

2 garlic cloves, minced

1/2 to 1 teaspoon crushed red pepper flakes

2 teaspoons vegetable oil

1/4 cup hoisin sauce

1/4 cup creamy peanut butter

2 tablespoons tomato paste

1/2 cup hot water

1 In a small bowl, combine the lime juice, hoisin sauce and sugar; set aside. In a large saucepan, bring 2 qts. water and salt to a boil. Add noodles; cook for 2-3 minutes or until tender. Drain and rinse with cold water. Transfer to a bowl and toss with 2 tablespoons reserved lime juice mixture; set aside. In another bowl, combine carrot, cucumber, jalapeno and peanuts. Toss with remaining lime juice mixture; set aside.

2 Soak the spring roll wrappers in cool water for 5 minutes. Carefully separate and place on a flat surface. Top each with several cilantro leaves. Place 1/4 cup carrot mixture and 1/4 cup noodles down the center of each wrapper to within 1 1/2 in. of ends. Fold both ends over filling; fold one long side over the filling, then carefully roll up tightly. Place seam side down on serving plate. Cover with damp paper towels and refrigerate until serving.

3 In a small saucepan, cook garlic and pepper flakes in oil for 2 minutes. Add the remaining sauce ingredients; cook and stir until combined and thickened. Serve with spring rolls.

YIELD: 8 SPRING ROLLS (1 CUP SAUCE).

EDITOR'S NOTE: When cutting or seeding hot peppers, use rubber or plastic gloves to protect your hands. Avoid touching your face.

Nirvana Harris, Mundelein, Illinois

The peanut dipping sauce is slightly spicy but really complements these traditional vegetable-filled spring rolls.

stuffed banana peppers

2 packages (8 ounces *each*)
cream cheese, softened

1 envelope ranch salad
dressing mix

1 cup (4 ounces) finely shredded
cheddar cheese

5 bacon strips, cooked and
crumbled

8 mild banana peppers
(about 6 inches long), halved
lengthwise and seeded

In a small mixing bowl, combine the cream cheese, salad dressing mix, cheese and bacon until blended. Pipe or stuff into pepper halves. Cover and refrigerate until serving. Cut into 1¼-in. pieces.

YIELD: 8-10 SERVINGS.

EDITOR'S NOTE: When cutting or seeding banana peppers, use rubber or plastic gloves to protect your hands. Avoid touching your face.

Cathy Kidd, Medora, Indiana

I received this recipe from a customer while working at my sister's produce market. The peppers can be made a day in advance, making them great for get-togethers.

pickled eggs and beets

1 can (14½ ounces) sliced beets

½ cup sugar

¼ cup white vinegar

½ cinnamon stick

6 whole cloves, optional

8 hard-cooked eggs, shelled

1 Drain beets, reserving juice. Add enough water to juice to measure ¾ cup; place in saucepan. Add the sugar, vinegar, cinnamon stick and cloves if desired; bring to a boil. Remove from the heat.

2 Place eggs in a bowl; top with beets. Pour liquid over all. Cover and refrigerate for 4 hours or overnight. Remove the cinnamon stick and cloves before serving.

YIELD: 8 SERVINGS.

Ellen Benninger, Stoneboro, Pennsylvania

This is a regional specialty. I like this particular recipe because the eggs are not too puckery, and it's so easy to prepare.

chicken ham pinwheels

4 boneless skinless chicken breast halves

1/8 teaspoon plus 1/2 teaspoon dried basil, *divided*

1/8 teaspoon salt

1/8 teaspoon garlic salt

1/8 teaspoon pepper

4 thin slices deli ham

2 teaspoons lemon juice

Paprika

1/2 cup mayonnaise

1 teaspoon grated orange peel

1 teaspoon orange juice

1 Flatten chicken to 1/4-in. thickness. Combine 1/8 teaspoon basil, salt, garlic salt and pepper; sprinkle over the chicken. Top each with a ham slice.

2 Roll up jelly-roll style; place seam side down in a greased 11-in. x 7-in. baking dish. Drizzle with lemon juice and sprinkle with paprika. Bake, uncovered, at 350° for 30 minutes or until chicken juices run clear. Cover and refrigerate.

3 Meanwhile, in a bowl, combine the mayonnaise, orange peel, orange juice and remaining basil. Cover and refrigerate until serving. Cut chicken rolls into 1/2-in. slices. Serve with the orange spread.

YIELD: 24 SERVINGS.

Laura Mahaffey, Annapolis, Maryland

These pretty pinwheels have been a part of our annual Christmas Eve appetizer buffet for many years. I love them because they can be made a day in advance and taste great alone or served with crackers.

asparagus beef roll-ups

1½ cups water

36 fresh asparagus spears, trimmed

1 carton (8 ounces) spreadable chive and onion cream cheese

3 to 5 tablespoons prepared horseradish

2 packages (5 ounces *each*) thinly sliced roast beef

1 In a large skillet, bring water to a boil. Add asparagus; cover and boil for 2-3 minutes or until crisp-tender. Drain and immediately place asparagus in ice water. Drain and pat dry.

2 In a small mixing bowl, combine cream cheese and horseradish. Pat beef slices dry with paper towels. Spread each slice with a thin layer of cream cheese mixture; top with an asparagus spear. Roll up tightly. Refrigerate until serving.

YIELD: 3 DOZEN.

Kris Krueger, Plano, Texas

I created these easy and elegant appetizers with asparagus spears, roast beef slices and a cream cheese-horseradish spread. I make them for all of my parties and have received many recipe requests. They're a snap to assemble.

cream-filled strawberries

18 large fresh strawberries

1 cup cold fat-free milk

1 package (1 ounce) sugar-free instant vanilla pudding mix

2 cups reduced-fat whipped topping

¼ teaspoon almond extract

1 Remove stems from strawberries; cut a deep X in the top of each berry. Spread berries apart.

2 In a bowl, whisk milk and pudding mix for 2 minutes. Fold in whipped topping and almond extract. Pipe or spoon about 5 teaspoons into each berry. Chill until serving.

YIELD: 18 STRAWBERRIES.

Karin Poroslay, Wesley Chapel, Florida

These plump berries filled with a creamy pudding mixture are so elegant-looking and luscious-tasting that they're perfect for parties or holiday gatherings.

cucumber canapes

1 cup mayonnaise

1 package (3 ounces) cream cheese, softened

1 tablespoon grated onion

1 tablespoon minced chives

½ teaspoon cider vinegar

½ teaspoon Worcestershire sauce

1 garlic clove, minced

¼ teaspoon paprika

⅛ teaspoon curry powder

⅛ teaspoon *each* dried oregano, thyme, basil, parsley flakes and dill weed

1 loaf (1 pound) white *or* rye bread

2 medium cucumbers, scored and thinly sliced

Diced pimientos and additional dill weed

1 In a blender or food processor, combine the mayonnaise, cream cheese, onion, chives, vinegar, Worcestershire sauce and seasonings. Cover and process until blended. Cover and refrigerate for 24 hours.

2 Using a 2½-in. biscuit cutter, cut out circles from bread slices. Spread mayonnaise mixture over bread; top with cucumber slices. Garnish with pimientos and dill.

YIELD: 2 DOZEN.

Nadine Whittaker, South Plymouth, Massachusetts
I always get requests for the recipe whenever I serve these delicate finger sandwiches with a creamy herb spread and festive red and green garnishes.

shrimp salad on endive

1/3 cup mayonnaise

1/2 teaspoon lemon juice

1/4 teaspoon dill weed

1/4 teaspoon seafood seasoning

1/8 teaspoon salt

1/8 teaspoon pepper

1/2 pound cooked shrimp, chopped

1 green onion, sliced

2 tablespoons chopped celery

1 tablespoon diced pimientos

2 heads Belgian endive, separated into leaves

In a small bowl, combine the first six ingredients. Stir in the shrimp, onion, celery and pimientos. Spoon 1 tablespoonful onto each endive leaf; arrange on a platter. Refrigerate until serving.

YIELD: ABOUT 1 1/2 DOZEN.

Taste of Home Test Kitchen

This simple-to-prepare shrimp salad is served on endive leaves for a fresh-from-the-sea version of lettuce wraps.

cucumber ham roll-ups

1 medium cucumber

1 package (8 ounces) cream cheese, softened

2 tablespoons prepared mustard

1 teaspoon dill weed

8 thin rectangular slices deli ham

1 Peel cucumber; cut in half lengthwise. Scoop out seeds with a spoon. Cut each half lengthwise into four strips; set aside.

2 In a small mixing bowl, combine the cream cheese, mustard and dill. Spread about 2 tablespoons over each ham slice. Place a cucumber strip on the wide end; roll up tightly jelly-roll style. Cut off any of the cucumber that extends beyond ham slice. Wrap tightly in plastic wrap and refrigerate for at least 2 hours. Cut into ¾-in. slices.

YIELD: ABOUT 4 DOZEN.

Debbie Smith, Urbana, Ohio

I came across this recipe looking for a new dish to take to a card party. Everyone loves these refreshing roll-ups—even the kids!

guacamole-stuffed eggs

6 hard-cooked eggs

¼ cup guacamole dip

1 teaspoon lime juice

1 tablespoon minced fresh cilantro

¼ teaspoon salt, optional

Paprika, optional

Cut eggs in half lengthwise; remove yolks and set whites aside. In a small bowl, mash yolks with a fork. Stir in the guacamole, lime juice, cilantro and salt if desired. Pipe or stuff into egg whites. Refrigerate until serving. Sprinkle with paprika if desired. Refrigerate until serving.

YIELD: 1 DOZEN.

Phy Bresse, Lumberton, North Carolina

Want a quick and easy way to surprise guests? Try my south-of-the-border variation on deviled eggs. Friends say they're wonderful.

sweet-sour deviled eggs

12 hard-cooked eggs

⅓ cup plus 1 tablespoon mayonnaise

5 teaspoons sugar

5 teaspoons cider vinegar

1 teaspoon prepared mustard

½ teaspoon salt

¼ teaspoon pepper

Paprika and minced fresh parsley

Slice eggs in half lengthwise; remove yolks and set whites aside. In a small bowl, mash yolks with a fork. Add the mayonnaise, sugar, vinegar, mustard, salt and pepper. Pipe or stuff into egg whites. Garnish with paprika and parsley. Refrigerate until serving.

YIELD: 2 DOZEN.

Claudia Millhouse, Myersville, Maryland

Folks will be sweet on these appetizers when they try them! My family doesn't like traditional deviled eggs, but they gobble this sweet-sour version right up.

antipasto kabobs

1 package (9 ounces) refrigerated cheese tortellini

40 pimiento-stuffed olives

40 large pitted ripe olives

¾ cup Italian salad dressing

40 thin slices pepperoni

20 thin slices hard salami, halved

1 Cook tortellini according to package directions; drain and rinse in cold water.

2 In a resealable plastic bag, combine the tortellini, olives and salad dressing. Seal and refrigerate for 4 hours or overnight.

3 Drain and discard dressing. For each appetizer, thread a stuffed olive, folded pepperoni slice, tortellini, folded salami piece and ripe olive on a toothpick or short skewer.

YIELD: 40 APPETIZERS.

Denise Hazen, Cincinnati, Ohio

My husband and I met at a cooking class, and we have loved creating menus and entertaining ever since. These do-ahead mini skewers are always a hit.

pork pinwheels

GARLIC MAYONNAISE:
- 1 large whole garlic bulb
- 2 teaspoons olive oil
- 1/2 cup mayonnaise
- 1 to 3 teaspoons milk, optional

STUFFING:
- 3 medium leeks (white portion only), thinly sliced
- 4 tablespoons olive oil, *divided*
- 1 cup minced fresh parsley
- 1/4 cup grated Parmesan cheese
- 1 tablespoon minced fresh thyme *or* 1 teaspoon dried thyme
- 1/4 teaspoon salt
- 1/4 teaspoon pepper
- 1/4 cup chopped walnuts
- 2 pork tenderloins (3/4 pound *each*)

1 Remove the papery outer skin from garlic (do not peel or separate cloves). Cut top off garlic bulb. Brush with oil. Wrap bulb in heavy-duty foil. Bake at 425° for 30-35 minutes or until softened. Cool for 10-15 minutes. Squeeze softened garlic into a small bowl; mash until smooth. Stir in mayonnaise and milk if needed to achieve a creamy consistency. Cover and refrigerate for at least 3 hours.

2 In a large skillet, saute leeks in 1 tablespoon oil until tender; remove from the heat. In a blender or food processor, combine the parsley, Parmesan cheese, thyme, salt and pepper. While processing, gradually add the remaining oil until creamy. Add walnuts and leek mixture; coarsely chop. Set aside.

3 Make a lengthwise slit in each tenderloin to within 1/2 in. of the opposite side. Open tenderloins so they lie flat; cover with plastic wrap. Flatten to 3/4-in. thickness; remove plastic wrap. Spread leek mixture to within 1 in. of edges. Roll up from a long side; tie with kitchen string to secure. Place tenderloins seam down on a rack in a shallow roasting pan. Bake, uncovered, at 325° for 45-55 minutes or until a meat thermometer reads 160°. Let stand for 15 minutes. Cover and refrigerate. Discard string; cut pork into 1/2-in. slices. Serve with garlic mayonnaise.

YIELD: ABOUT 2 1/2 DOZEN.

Mary Lou Wayman, Salt Lake City, Utah

A flavorful filling peeks out from the swirled slices of pork.

This appetizer is enhanced with garlic mayonnaise.

crispy cheese twists

6 tablespoons butter, softened

1 garlic clove, minced

1/8 teaspoon pepper

1 cup (4 ounces) shredded cheddar cheese

2 tablespoons milk

1 tablespoon minced fresh parsley

1 tablespoon snipped fresh dill *or* 1 teaspoon dill weed

1 cup all-purpose flour

1 In a mixing bowl, combine the butter, garlic and pepper; beat until light and fluffy. Stir in cheese, milk, parsley and dill. Gradually add flour, mixing thoroughly.

2 Divide dough into 20 pieces. Roll each piece into a 10-in. log; cut each in half and twist together. Place 1 in. apart on an ungreased baking sheet. Bake at 375° for 10-12 minutes or until golden brown. Remove to wire racks to cool.

YIELD: 20 TWISTS.

Mary Maxeiner, Lakewood, Colorado

My grown son enjoys these cheese twists so much that I'll often prepare an extra batch just for him. They make a great anytime snack.

white bean bruschetta

1 cup canned great northern beans, rinsed and drained

3 plum tomatoes, seeded and chopped

1/4 cup chopped pitted Greek olives

6 tablespoons olive oil, *divided*

1/4 cup fresh basil leaves, cut into strips

1 tablespoon minced garlic

Salt and pepper to taste

1 French bread baguette, cut into 1/3-inch-thick slices

1 package (5.3 ounces) goat cheese

In a bowl, combine the beans, tomatoes, olives, 4 tablespoons oil, basil, garlic, salt and pepper. Place bread slices on an ungreased baking sheet. Brush with remaining oil. Broil 3-4 in. from the heat until golden, about 1 minute. Spread with cheese; top with bean mixture. Serve immediately.

YIELD: ABOUT 20 SERVINGS.

Kristin Arnett, Elkhorn, Wisconsin

This fabulous bruschetta has a Tuscan flavor. I've made it many times to serve when entertaining because it's quick and easy.

savory cheese cutouts

J.R. Smosna, Warren, Pennsylvania

This recipe is always a success because the dough is easy to work with and cuts well. The appetizer can be made year-round using cookie cutter shapes to suit the season.

2 cups all-purpose flour

1 cup (4 ounces) shredded Swiss cheese

1 teaspoon sugar

1 teaspoon salt

1/2 teaspoon ground mustard

1/8 to 1/4 teaspoon cayenne pepper

1/2 cup plus 2 tablespoons cold butter

9 tablespoons dry white wine *or* chicken broth

1 egg, lightly beaten

Sesame seeds *and/or* poppy seeds

1 In a bowl, combine the first six ingredients; cut in butter until the mixture resembles coarse crumbs. Gradually add wine or broth, tossing with a fork until dough forms a ball.

2 On a lightly floured surface, roll out dough to 1/8-in. thickness. Cut with floured 2-in. cookie cutters. Place 1 in. apart on ungreased baking sheets.

3 Brush tops with egg; sprinkle with sesame and/or poppy seeds. Bake at 400° for 10-12 minutes or until lightly browned. Remove to wire racks to cool.

YIELD: 6 DOZEN.

fruit 'n' cheese kabobs

1 block (1 pound) Colby-Monterey Jack cheese

1 block (1 pound) cheddar cheese

1 block (1 pound) baby Swiss cheese

1 fresh pineapple, peeled, cored and cut into 2-inch chunks

1 to 2 pounds seedless green *or* red grapes

3 pints strawberries

Cut cheese into chunks or slices. If desired, cut into shapes with small cutters. Alternately thread cheese and fruit onto wooden skewers. Serve immediately.

YIELD: ABOUT 3 DOZEN.

Taste of Home Test Kitchen

This simple, nutritious snack is a snap to put together, much to the delight of busy hostesses!

shrimp lover squares

1 tube (8 ounces) refrigerated crescent rolls

1 package (8 ounces) cream cheese, softened

¼ cup sour cream

½ teaspoon dill weed

⅛ teaspoon salt

½ cup seafood sauce

24 cooked medium shrimp, peeled and deveined

½ cup chopped green pepper

⅓ cup chopped onion

1 cup (4 ounces) shredded Monterey Jack cheese

1 In a greased 13-in. x 9-in. baking dish, unroll crescent dough into one long rectangle; seal seams and perforations. Bake at 375° for 10-12 minutes or until golden brown. Cool completely on a wire rack.

2 In a small mixing bowl, beat the cream cheese, sour cream, dill and salt until smooth. Spread over crust. Top with seafood sauce, shrimp, green pepper, onion and cheese. Cover and refrigerate for 1 hour. Cut into squares.

YIELD: 2 DOZEN.

Ardyce Piehl, Poynette, Wisconsin

These delicious shrimp squares are part of an appetizer buffet I prepare for family every year. We often enjoy having a variety of appetizers as a meal while playing board games or watching movies together.

marinated mushrooms and cheese

½ cup sun-dried tomatoes
   (not packed in oil), julienned

1 cup boiling water

½ cup olive oil

½ cup white wine vinegar

2 garlic cloves, minced

½ teaspoon salt

½ pound sliced fresh mushrooms

8 ounces Monterey Jack cheese,
   cubed

In a small bowl, combine the tomatoes and water. Let stand for 5 minutes; drain. In a large resealable plastic bag, combine the oil, vinegar, garlic and salt; add the tomatoes, mushrooms and cheese. Seal bag and toss to coat. Refrigerate for at least 4 hours before serving. Drain and discard marinade.

YIELD: 12-14 SERVINGS.

Kim Marie Van Rheenen, Mendota, Illinois

I like to serve these savory mushrooms alongside sliced baguettes and crackers. They're colorful and so versatile. You might like to vary the cheese or add olives, artichokes or a little basil.

garlic tomato bruschetta

¼ cup olive oil

3 tablespoons chopped fresh basil

3 to 4 garlic cloves, minced

½ teaspoon salt

¼ teaspoon pepper

4 medium tomatoes, diced

2 tablespoons grated Parmesan cheese

1 loaf (1 pound) unsliced French bread

1 In a bowl, combine the oil, basil, garlic, salt and pepper. Add tomatoes and toss gently. Sprinkle with cheese. Refrigerate for at least 1 hour.

2 Bring to room temperature before serving. Cut bread into 24 slices; toast under broiler until lightly browned. Top with tomato mixture. Serve immediately.

YIELD: 12 SERVINGS.

Jean Franzoni, Rutland, Vermont

Bruschetta is a popular snack because it is made with fresh and flavorful ingredients and is so tasty.

cucumber whimsies

2 cans (6 ounces *each*) crabmeat, drained, flaked and cartilage removed

¼ cup mayonnaise

1 small tomato, chopped

2 tablespoons snipped fresh dill

1 green onion, chopped

1 teaspoon grated lemon peel

⅛ teaspoon cayenne pepper

Dash salt

3 medium cucumbers, cut into ¼-inch slices

Lemon-pepper seasoning

Dill sprigs

1 In a large bowl, combine the first eight ingredients. Cover and chill for 1 hour.

2 Sprinkle the cucumber slices with lemon-pepper. Top each with about 1½ teaspoons crab mixture; garnish with a dill sprig. Refrigerate until serving.

YIELD: 5 DOZEN.

Cheryl Stevens, Carrollton, Texas

During the heat of summer, it's nice to offer lighter fare. These cold snacks are a great addition to a picnic buffet.

smoked salmon new potatoes

36 small red potatoes (about 1½ pounds)

1 package (8 ounces) reduced-fat cream cheese, cubed

2 packages (3 ounces *each*) smoked cooked salmon

2 tablespoons chopped green onion

2 teaspoons dill weed

2 teaspoons lemon juice

⅛ teaspoon salt

⅛ teaspoon pepper

Fresh dill sprigs

1 Place the potatoes in a large saucepan and cover with water. Bring to a boil. Reduce heat; simmer, uncovered, for 20-22 minutes or until tender.

2 Meanwhile, in a food processor or blender, combine the cream cheese, salmon, onion, dill, lemon juice, salt and pepper. Cover and process until smooth; set aside.

3 Drain potatoes and immediately place in ice water. Drain and pat dry with paper towels. Cut a thin slice off the bottom of each potato to allow it to sit flat. With a melon baller, scoop out a small amount of potato (discard or save for another use). Pipe or spoon salmon mixture into potatoes. Garnish with dill sprigs.

YIELD: 3 DOZEN.

Taste of Home Test Kitchen

This recipe proves that delicious party food and healthy eating are compatible. Plus, you're bound to get rave reviews when guests devour these baby stuffed potatoes. If you're in a hurry, you can serve the cream cheese mixture as a spread with whole wheat crackers.

tangy mozzarella bites

¼ cup olive oil

1 to 2 teaspoons balsamic vinegar

1 garlic clove, minced

1 teaspoon dried basil

1 teaspoon coarsely ground pepper

1 pound part-skim mozzarella cheese, cut into ½-inch cubes

In a bowl, combine the oil, vinegar, garlic, basil and pepper. Add cheese; toss to coat. Cover and refrigerate for at least 1 hour.

YIELD: ABOUT 3 CUPS.

Julie Wasem, Aurora, Nebraska

I adapted this recipe from one I found years ago, substituting ingredients most people have on hand. I like to serve it with crackers or small bread slices.

marinated cheese

2 blocks (8 ounces *each*) white cheddar cheese

2 packages (8 ounces *each*) cream cheese, softened

¾ cup chopped roasted sweet red peppers

½ cup olive oil

¼ cup white wine vinegar

¼ cup balsamic vinegar

3 tablespoons chopped green onions

3 tablespoons minced fresh parsley

2 tablespoons minced fresh basil

1 tablespoon sugar

3 garlic cloves, minced

½ teaspoon salt

½ teaspoon pepper

Toasted sliced French bread *or* assorted crackers

Laurie Casper, Coraopolis, Pennsylvania
This special appetizer always makes it to our neighborhood parties and is the first to disappear at the buffet table. It's attractive, delicious—and easy!

1 Slice each block of cheddar cheese into twenty ¼-in. slices. Cut each block of cream cheese into 18 slices; sandwich between cheddar slices, using a knife to spread evenly. Create four 6-in.-long blocks of cheese; place in a 13-in. x 9-in. dish.

2 In a small bowl, combine the roasted peppers, oil, vinegars, onions, herbs, sugar, garlic, salt and pepper; pour over cheese.

3 Cover and refrigerate overnight, turning once. Drain excess marinade. Serve cheese with bread or crackers.

YIELD: ABOUT 2 POUNDS.

salmon salad-stuffed endive leaves

1 salmon fillet (6 ounces), cooked
and flaked

1/4 cup tartar sauce

2 teaspoons capers

1 teaspoon snipped fresh dill

1/4 teaspoon lemon-pepper
seasoning

1 head Belgian endive (about
5 ounces), separated into leaves

Additional snipped fresh dill, optional

In a small bowl, combine the salmon, tartar sauce, capers, dill and lemon-pepper. Spoon about 2 teaspoonfuls onto each endive leaf. Garnish with additional dill if desired. Refrigerate until serving.

YIELD: 14 APPETIZERS.

Melissa Carafa, Broomall, Pennsylvania
Salmon creates an elegant party starter in this vibrant recipe idea. It's simple to prepare and can even be made ahead of time.

chilled raspberry soup

1/3 cup cranberry juice

1/3 cup sugar

5 1/3 cups plus 12 fresh raspberries,
divided

1 1/3 cups plus 2 tablespoons sour
cream, *divided*

1 In a blender, combine the cranberry juice, sugar and 5 1/3 cups raspberries; cover and process until blended. Strain and discard seeds. Stir in 1 1/3 cups sour cream. Cover and refrigerate for at least 2 hours.

2 To serve, pour 1/4 cup of soup into 12 cordial glasses. Top each with a raspberry and 1/2 teaspoon sour cream.

YIELD: 12 SERVINGS.

Amy Wenger, Severance, Colorado
Family and friends enjoy sipping this lovely, chilled soup. I often use sugar substitute and reduced-fat sour cream to make it a little lighter.

classic antipasto platter

Weda Mosellie, Phillipsburg, New Jersey

This is a real favorite at our parties. The large, colorful platter of sardines, anchovy fillets, cheese, olives and vegetables disappears quickly.

1 pound fresh mozzarella cheese, sliced

1 jar (16 ounces) pickled pepper rings, drained

1 jar (10 ounces) colossal Sicilian olives, drained

4 large tomatoes, cut into wedges

6 hard-cooked eggs, sliced

1 medium cucumber, sliced

1 medium sweet red pepper, julienned

1 can (3¾ ounces) sardines, drained

1 can (2 ounces) anchovy fillets, drained

¼ cup olive oil

1 teaspoon grated Parmesan cheese

1 teaspoon minced fresh oregano

⅛ teaspoon salt

⅛ teaspoon pepper

On a large serving platter, arrange the first nine ingredients. In a small bowl, whisk the oil, cheese, oregano, salt and pepper; drizzle over antipasto.

YIELD: 14-16 SERVINGS.

all wrapped up

100

116

No fork or knife are required for these festive, finger foods! Delicious, savory fillings are packaged in an assortment of easy-to-find pastry doughs and wrappers. Your menu options range from Chorizo-Queso Egg Rolls (p. 95) and Southwestern Appetizer Triangles (p. 100) to Vegetable Spiral Sticks (p. 116).

For large gatherings, why not make a double batch? Then place one tray out and keep a second tray either in a warm oven or in the refrigerator, ready to go!

mushroom puffs

4 ounces cream cheese, cubed

1 can (4 ounces) mushroom stems and pieces, drained

1 tablespoon chopped onion

⅛ teaspoon hot pepper sauce

1 tube (8 ounces) refrigerated crescent rolls

1 In a blender or food processor, combine the cream cheese, mushrooms, onion and hot pepper sauce; cover and process until blended. Unroll crescent dough; separate into four rectangles. Press perforations to seal. Spread mushroom mixture over dough.

2 Roll up jelly-roll style, starting with a long side. Cut each roll into five slices; place on an ungreased baking sheet. Bake at 425° for 8-10 minutes or until puffed and golden brown.

YIELD: 20 APPETIZERS.

Marilin Rosborough, Altoona, Pennsylvania

You can assemble these attractive appetizers in a jiffy with refrigerated crescent roll dough. The tasty little spirals disappear fast at parties!

chicken salad cups

1 package (15 ounces) refrigerated pie pastry

2 cups diced cooked chicken

1 can (8 ounces) unsweetened crushed pineapple, drained

1/2 cup slivered almonds

1/2 cup chopped celery

1/2 cup shredded cheddar cheese

1/2 cup mayonnaise

1/2 teaspoon salt

1/2 teaspoon paprika

TOPPING:

1/2 cup sour cream

1/4 cup mayonnaise

1/2 cup shredded cheddar cheese

1 Cut each sheet of pie pastry into 4 1/2-in. circles; reroll scraps and cut out additional circles. Press pastry onto the bottom and up the sides of 14 ungreased muffin cups. Bake at 450° for 6-7 minutes or until golden brown. Cool on a wire rack.

2 In a bowl, combine the chicken, pineapple, almonds, celery, cheese, mayonnaise, salt and paprika; refrigerate until chilled.

3 Just before serving, spoon two rounded tablespoonfuls of chicken salad into each pastry cup. Combine sour cream and mayonnaise; spoon over filling. Sprinkle with cheese.

YIELD: 14 APPETIZERS.

Lois Holdson, Millersville, Maryland

Pineapple and almonds enhance the creamy chicken salad in these cute tartlets made from convenient refrigerated pie pastry.

mozzarella tomato tartlets

Amy Golden, East Aurora, New York

Convenient frozen phyllo shells add to this impressive appetizer's easy preparation. Although I make them year-round, they're especially tasty with garden-fresh tomatoes.

1 garlic clove, minced

1 tablespoon olive oil

1½ cups seeded chopped tomatoes

¾ cup shredded part-skim mozzarella cheese

½ teaspoon dried basil

Pepper to taste

24 frozen miniature phyllo tart shells

6 pitted ripe olives, quartered

Grated Parmesan cheese

1 In a small skillet, saute garlic in oil for 1 minute. Add the tomatoes; cook until the liquid has evaporated. Remove from the heat; stir in the mozzarella cheese, basil and pepper.

2 Spoon 1 teaspoonful into each tart shell. Top each with a piece of olive; sprinkle with Parmesan cheese. Place on an ungreased baking sheet. Bake at 450° for 5-8 minutes or until bubbly.

YIELD: 2 DOZEN.

petite sausage quiches

1 cup butter, softened

2 packages (3 ounces *each*) cream cheese, softened

2 cups all-purpose flour

FILLING:

6 ounces bulk Italian sausage

1 cup (4 ounces) shredded Swiss cheese

1 tablespoon minced chives

2 eggs

1 cup half-and-half cream

1/4 teaspoon salt

Dash cayenne pepper

1 In a mixing bowl, beat the butter, cream cheese and flour until smooth. Shape tablespoonfuls of dough into balls; press onto the bottom and up the sides of greased miniature muffin cups.

2 In a skillet, cook sausage over medium heat until no longer pink; drain. Sprinkle sausage, Swiss cheese and chives into muffin cups. In a bowl, beat eggs, cream, salt and cayenne. Pour into shells.

3 Bake at 375° for 28-30 minutes or until browned. Serve warm.

YIELD: 3 DOZEN.

Dawn Stitt, Hesperia, Michigan

You won't be able to eat just one of these cute mini quiches. Filled with savory sausage, Swiss cheese and a dash of cayenne, the mouthwatering morsels add something special to buffet tables.

chorizo-queso egg rolls

½ cup mayonnaise

½ cup sour cream

2 ounces cream cheese, softened

2 tablespoons minced fresh cilantro

1 tablespoon chipotle peppers in adobo sauce

6 ounces uncooked chorizo or bulk spicy pork sausage

2 cups crumbled queso fresco

¼ cup enchilada sauce

¼ cup chopped green chilies

1 package (12 ounces) wonton wrappers

Oil for frying

1 For dipping sauce, in a small bowl, combine the mayonnaise, sour cream, cream cheese, cilantro and chipotle peppers. Cover and refrigerate until serving.

2 In a large skillet, cook chorizo over medium heat until no longer pink; drain. Stir in the queso fresco, enchilada sauce and chilies.

3 Position a wonton wrapper with one point toward you. Place 2 teaspoons filling in the center. (Keep wrappers covered with a damp paper towel until ready to use.) Fold bottom corner over filling; fold sides toward center over filling. Roll toward remaining point. Moisten top corner with water; press to seal. Repeat with remaining wrappers and filling.

4 In an electric skillet, heat 1 in. of oil to 375°. Fry egg rolls in batches for 1-2 minutes on each side or until golden brown. Drain on paper towels. Serve warm with dipping sauce.

YIELD: 4 DOZEN.

Kari Wheaton, Beloit, Wisconsin

Little bites deliver big flavor in this combination of tangy sausage and creamy cheese in crisp wontons. The recipe is an appetizing take-off on my favorite Mexican entree.

asparagus ham spirals

8 fresh asparagus spears, trimmed

1 tube (8 ounces) refrigerated crescent rolls

1 carton (8 ounces) spreadable chive-and-onion cream cheese

4 thin rectangular slices deli ham

2 tablespoons butter, melted

¼ teaspoon garlic powder

1 Place asparagus in a skillet; add ½ in. of water. Bring to a boil. Reduce the heat; cover and simmer for 3-5 minutes or until crisp-tender. Drain and set aside.

2 Separate crescent dough into four rectangles; seal perforations. Spread cream cheese over each rectangle to within ¼ in. of edges. Top each with ham, leaving ¼ in. uncovered on one long side. Place two asparagus spears along the long side with the ham; roll up and press seam to seal.

3 Cut each roll into seven pieces. Place cut side down 1 in. apart on greased baking sheets. Combine butter and garlic powder; brush over spirals. Bake at 375° for 10-12 minutes or until golden brown.

YIELD: 28 APPETIZERS.

Linda Fischer, Stuttgart, Arkansas

These appealing appetizers are sure to be a hit at your next party. I'm on the arts council in our small town, so I came up with this snack recipe to serve at some of the events we cater. People will think you really fussed with these yummy bites!

korean wontons

2 cups shredded cabbage

1 cup canned bean sprouts

1/2 cup shredded carrots

1 1/2 teaspoons plus 2 tablespoons vegetable oil, *divided*

1/3 pound ground beef

1/3 cup sliced green onions

1 1/2 teaspoons sesame seeds, toasted

1 1/2 teaspoons minced fresh gingerroot

3 garlic cloves, minced

1 1/2 teaspoons sesame oil

1/2 teaspoon salt

1/2 teaspoon pepper

1 package (12 ounces) wonton wrappers

1 egg, lightly beaten

3 tablespoons water

1 In a wok or large skillet, stir-fry cabbage, bean sprouts and carrots in 1 1/2 teaspoons oil until tender; set aside. In a skillet, cook beef over medium heat until no longer pink; drain. Add to vegetable mixture. Stir in onions, sesame seeds, ginger, garlic, sesame oil, salt and pepper.

2 Place about 1 tablespoon of filling in the center of each wonton wrapper. (Keep wrappers covered with a damp paper towel until ready to use.) Combine egg and water. Moisten wonton edges with egg mixture; fold opposite corners over filling and press to seal.

3 Heat remaining vegetable oil in a large skillet. Cook the wontons in batches for 1-2 minutes on each side or until golden brown, adding additional oil if needed.

YIELD: 5 DOZEN.

EDITOR'S NOTE: Fill wonton wrappers a few at a time, keeping the others covered with a damp paper towel until ready to use.

Christy Lee, Horsham, Pennsylvania

Korean wontons are not hot and spicy like many of the traditional Korean dishes. The fried dumplings, filled with vegetables and beef, are very easy to prepare, and the ingredients are inexpensive.

onion brie appetizers

2 medium onions, thinly sliced

3 tablespoons butter

2 tablespoons brown sugar

½ teaspoon white wine vinegar

1 sheet frozen puff pastry, thawed

4 ounces Brie *or* Camembert, rind removed, softened

1 to 2 teaspoons caraway seeds

1 egg

2 teaspoons water

1 In a large skillet, cook the onions, butter, brown sugar and vinegar over medium-low heat until onions are golden brown, stirring frequently. Remove with a slotted spoon; cool to room temperature.

2 On a lightly floured surface, roll puff pastry into an 11-in. x 8-in. rectangle. Spread Brie over pastry. Cover with the onions; sprinkle with caraway seeds.

3 Roll up one long side to the middle of the dough; roll up the other side so the two rolls meet in the center. Using a serrated knife, cut into ½-in. slices. Place on parchment paper-lined baking sheets; flatten to ¼-in. thickness. Refrigerate for 15 minutes.

4 In a small bowl, beat egg and water; brush over slices. Bake at 375° for 12-14 minutes or until puffed and golden brown. Serve warm.

YIELD: 1½ DOZEN.

Carole Resnick, Cleveland, Ohio

Guests will think you spent hours preparing these cute appetizers, but they're really easy to assemble, using purchased puff pastry. And the tasty combination of Brie, caramelized onions and caraway is terrific.

veggie wonton quiches

24 wonton wrappers

1 cup finely chopped fresh broccoli

¾ cup diced fresh mushrooms

½ cup diced sweet red pepper

¼ cup finely chopped onion

2 teaspoons vegetable oil

3 eggs

1 tablespoon water

2 teaspoons dried parsley flakes

¼ teaspoon salt

¼ teaspoon dried thyme

¼ teaspoon white pepper

Dash cayenne pepper

¾ cup shredded cheddar cheese

1 Gently press wonton wrappers into miniature muffin cups coated with nonstick cooking spray. Lightly coat wontons with nonstick cooking spray. Bake at 350° for 5 minutes. Remove wontons from cups; place upside down on baking sheets. Lightly coat with nonstick cooking spray. Bake 5 minutes longer or until light golden brown.

2 Meanwhile, in a nonstick skillet, cook the broccoli, mushrooms, red pepper and onion in oil over medium heat for 4-5 minutes or until crisp-tender. In a bowl, whisk eggs and water; stir in the parsley, salt, thyme, white pepper and cayenne. Add to vegetable mixture; cook over medium heat for 4-5 minutes or until eggs are completely set.

3 Remove from the heat; stir in cheese. Spoon about 1 tablespoonful into each wonton cup. Bake for 5 minutes or until filling is heated through. Serve warm.

YIELD: 2 DOZEN.

Taste of Home Test Kitchen

With green broccoli and red pepper, these mini quiches are a colorful finger food. Crispy wonton cups make a fun crust.

southwestern appetizer triangles

Shelia Pope, Preston, Idaho

A nifty cross between egg rolls and tacos, these triangles are fun to serve, especially at the holidays. My mom created the recipe years ago, much to the delight of my family. Since I began making them, my husband insists we have them on Sundays during football season as well as for holiday celebrations.

1 pound ground beef

1 medium onion, chopped

Salt and pepper to taste

1 can (16 ounces) refried beans

1½ cups (6 ounces) shredded cheddar cheese

1 cup salsa

1 can (4 ounces) diced jalapeno peppers, drained

2 packages (12 ounces *each*) wonton wrappers

Oil for deep-fat frying

Additional salsa

1 In a skillet, cook the beef, onion, salt and pepper over medium heat until meat is no longer pink; drain. Add the beans, cheese, salsa and jalapenos. Cook and stir over low heat until the cheese is melted. Remove from the heat; cool for 10 minutes.

2 Place a teaspoonful of beef mixture in the center of one wonton wrapper. (Keep wrappers covered with a damp paper towel until ready to use.) Moisten edges with water. Fold wontons in half, forming a triangle. Repeat.

3 In an electric skillet or deep-fat fryer, heat 1 in. of oil to 375°. Fry wontons, a few at a time, for 2-3 minutes or until golden brown. Drain on paper towels. Serve warm with salsa.

YIELD: ABOUT 7½ DOZEN.

mini sausage bundles

½ pound turkey Italian sausage links, casings removed

1 small onion, finely chopped

¼ cup finely chopped sweet red pepper

1 garlic clove, minced

½ cup shredded cheddar cheese

8 sheets phyllo dough (14 inches x 9 inches)

12 whole chives, optional

1 Crumble the sausage into a large nonstick skillet; add onion, red pepper and garlic. Cook over medium heat until meat is no longer pink; drain. Stir in cheese; cool slightly.

2 Place one sheet of phyllo dough on a work surface; coat with cooking spray. Cover with a second sheet of phyllo; coat with cooking spray. (Until ready to use, keep remaining phyllo covered with plastic wrap and a damp towel to prevent drying out.) Cut widthwise into three 4-in. strips, discarding trimmings. Top each with 2 rounded tablespoons of sausage mixture; fold bottom and side edges over the filling and roll up. Repeat with remaining phyllo and filling.

3 Place seam side down on an ungreased baking sheet. Bake at 425° for 5-6 minutes or until lightly browned. Tie a chive around each bundle if desired. Serve warm.

YIELD: 1 DOZEN.

Taste of Home Test Kitchen

These tasty hors d'oeuvres cut fat as well as cleanup by keeping the deep fryer at bay. The savory bundles are filled with turkey sausage, garlic and onion and baked.

sausage biscuit bites

1 tube (7½ ounces) refrigerated buttermilk biscuits

1 tablespoon butter, melted

4½ teaspoons grated Parmesan cheese

1 teaspoon dried oregano

1 package (8 ounces) brown-and-serve sausage links

1 On a lightly floured surface, roll out each biscuit into a 4-in. circle; brush with butter. Combine Parmesan cheese and oregano; sprinkle over butter. Place a sausage link in the center of each roll; roll up.

2 Cut each widthwise into four pieces; insert a toothpick into each. Place on an ungreased baking sheet. Bake at 375° for 8-10 minutes or until golden brown.

YIELD: 40 APPETIZERS.

Audrey Marler, Kokomo, Indiana

I sometimes bake these delightful little morsels the night before, refrigerate them, then put them in the slow cooker in the morning so my husband can share them with his co-workers. They're always gone in a hurry.

mozzarella puffs

1 tube (7½ ounces) refrigerated buttermilk biscuits

1 teaspoon dried oregano

1 block (2 to 3 ounces) mozzarella cheese

2 tablespoons pizza sauce

Make an indentation in the center of each biscuit; sprinkle with oregano. Cut the mozzarella into 10 cubes, ¾-in. each; place a cube in the center of each biscuit. Pinch dough tightly around cheese to seal. Place seam side down on an ungreased baking sheet. Spread pizza sauce over tops. Bake at 375° for 10-12 minutes or until golden brown. Serve warm. Refrigerate leftovers.

YIELD: 10 APPETIZERS.

Joan Mousley Dziuba, Waupaca, Wisconsin

These savory cheesy biscuits go over great at my house. Since they're so quick to make, I can whip up a batch anytime.

chili cheese snacks

2 packages (3 ounces *each*)
cream cheese, softened

1 cup (4 ounces) shredded
cheddar cheese

¼ cup chopped green chilies

¼ cup chopped ripe olives,
drained

2 teaspoons dried minced onion

¼ teaspoon hot pepper sauce

2 tubes (8 ounces *each*)
refrigerated crescent rolls

1 In a small mixing bowl, beat cream cheese. Add the cheddar cheese, chilies, olives, onion and hot pepper sauce. Separate each tube of crescent dough into four rectangles; press perforations to seal.

2 Spread cheese mixture over dough. Roll up jelly-roll style, starting with a long side. Cut each roll into 10 slices; place on greased baking sheets. Bake at 400° for 8-10 minutes or until golden brown.

YIELD: 80 APPETIZERS.

Carol Nelson, Cool, California

I've been collecting appetizer recipes for more than 20 years and have a host of tasty treats. These handheld morsels are perfect for parties because they allow folks to walk around and mingle.

artichoke wonton cups

1 cup grated Parmesan cheese

1 cup mayonnaise

$\frac{1}{2}$ teaspoon onion powder

$\frac{1}{2}$ teaspoon garlic powder

2 cups (8 ounces) shredded part-skim mozzarella cheese

1 can (14 ounces) water-packed artichoke hearts, rinsed, drained and chopped

1 package (12 ounces) wonton wrappers

1 In a small mixing bowl, combine the Parmesan cheese, mayonnaise, onion powder and garlic powder; mix well. Stir in the mozzarella cheese and artichokes; set aside.

2 Coat one side of each wonton wrapper with nonstick cooking spray; press greased side down into miniature muffin cups. Bake at 350° for 5 minutes or until edges are lightly browned.

3 Fill each cup with 1 tablespoon artichoke mixture. Bake 5-6 minutes longer or until golden brown. Serve warm.

YIELD: ABOUT 4 DOZEN.

Paige Scott, Murfreesboro, Tennessee

I came up with this hors d'oeuvre by combining several artichoke dip recipes. Wonton cups add a fancy look that's perfect for special occasions. If you're serving a large crowd, you may want to double the recipe.

sausage breadsticks

1 tube (11 ounces) refrigerated breadstick dough

8 smoked sausage links *or* hot dogs

1 Separate the dough into eight strips; unroll and wrap one strip around each sausage. Place on an ungreased baking sheet.

2 Bake at 350° for 15-17 minutes or until golden brown. Serve warm.

YIELD: 8 APPETIZERS.

Taste of Home Test Kitchen

Bring out the kid in everyone by preparing these snacks. This old-fashioned finger food is a fun addition to a breakfast buffet.

ham and cheese tarts

2 packages (3 ounces *each*) cream cheese, softened

1/2 cup French onion dip

1 tablespoon milk

1/4 teaspoon ground mustard

1/4 teaspoon grated orange peel

1/2 cup finely chopped fully cooked ham

1 tube (12 ounces) refrigerated buttermilk biscuits

1/4 teaspoon paprika

1 In a small mixing bowl, beat the cream cheese, onion dip, milk, mustard and orange peel until blended. Stir in the ham.

2 Split each biscuit into thirds; press into lightly greased miniature muffin cups. Spoon a scant tablespoonful of the ham mixture into each cup; sprinkle with paprika. Bake at 375° for 12-17 minutes or until golden brown. Serve warm.

YIELD: 2 1/2 DOZEN.

Delores Romyn, Stratton, Ontario

These savory tarts have been a family favorite for years. Make the ham mixture in advance to save time.

pizza rolls

4 cups (16 ounces) shredded pizza cheese blend *or* part-skim mozzarella cheese

1 pound bulk Italian sausage, cooked and drained

2 packages (3 ounces *each*) sliced pepperoni, chopped

1 medium green pepper, finely chopped

1 medium sweet red pepper, finely chopped

1 medium onion, finely chopped

2 jars (14 ounces *each*) pizza sauce

32 egg roll wrappers

Oil for frying

Additional pizza sauce for dipping, warmed, optional

1 In a large bowl, combine the cheese, sausage, pepperoni, peppers and onion. Stir in pizza sauce until combined. Place about ¼ cup filling in the center of each egg roll wrapper. (Keep wrappers covered with a damp paper towel until ready to use.) Fold bottom corner over filling; fold sides toward center over filling. Moisten remaining corner with water and roll up tightly to seal.

2 In an electric skillet, heat 1 in. of oil to 375°. Fry pizza rolls for 1-2 minutes on each side or until golden brown. Drain on paper towels. Serve with additional pizza sauce if desired.

YIELD: 32 ROLLS.

Julie Gaines, Normal, Illinois

This is my husband's version of store-bought pizza rolls, and our family loves them. Although they take some time to make, they freeze well. So when we're through, we get to enjoy the fruits of our labor for a long time!

veggie shrimp egg rolls

Carole Resnick, Cleveland, Ohio

These wonderful appetizers will be the hit of your next party. They're versatile in that you can also use cooked crab, lobster or chicken.

2 teaspoons minced fresh gingerroot

1 garlic clove, minced

3 tablespoons olive oil, *divided*

½ pound uncooked medium shrimp, peeled, deveined and chopped

2 green onions, finely chopped

1 medium carrot, finely chopped

1 medium sweet red pepper, finely chopped

1 cup canned bean sprouts, rinsed and finely chopped

2 tablespoons water

2 tablespoons reduced-sodium soy sauce

38 wonton wrappers

DIPPING SAUCE:

¾ cup apricot spreadable fruit

1 tablespoon water

1 tablespoon lime juice

1 tablespoon reduced-sodium soy sauce

1½ teaspoons Dijon mustard

¼ teaspoon minced fresh gingerroot

1 In a large skillet, saute ginger and garlic in 1 tablespoon oil over medium heat until tender. Add the shrimp, onions, carrot, red pepper, bean sprouts, water and soy sauce; cook and stir for 2-3 minutes or until vegetables are crisp-tender and shrimp turn pink. Reduce heat to low; cook for 4-5 minutes or until most of the liquid has evaporated. Remove from the heat; let stand for 15 minutes.

2 Place a tablespoonful of shrimp mixture in the center of a wonton wrapper. (Keep wrappers covered with a damp paper towel until ready to use.) Fold bottom corner over filling. Fold sides toward center over filling. Moisten remaining corner with water; roll up tightly to seal.

3 In a large skillet over medium heat, cook egg rolls, a few at a time, in remaining oil for 5-7 minutes on each side or until golden brown. Drain on paper towels.

4 In a blender or food processor, combine the sauce ingredients; cover and process until smooth. Serve with egg rolls.

YIELD: 38 EGG ROLLS.

gouda bites

1 tube (8 ounces) refrigerated reduced-fat crescent rolls

½ teaspoon garlic powder

5 ounces Gouda cheese, cut into 24 pieces

1 Unroll crescent dough into one long rectangle; seal the seams and perforations. Sprinkle with garlic powder. Cut into 24 pieces; lightly press onto the bottom and up the sides of ungreased miniature muffin cups.

2 Bake at 375° for 3 minutes. Place a piece of the cheese in each cup. Bake 8-10 minutes longer or until golden brown and cheese is melted. Serve warm.

YIELD: 2 DOZEN.

Phylis Behringer, Defiance, Ohio
I season refrigerated dough with garlic powder to create these golden, cheese-filled cups.

olive-cheese nuggets

2 cups (8 ounces) shredded cheddar cheese

1¼ cups all-purpose flour

½ cup butter, melted

½ teaspoon paprika

36 pimiento-stuffed olives

1 In a small mixing bowl, beat cheese, flour, butter and paprika until blended. Pat olives dry; shape 1 teaspoon of cheese mixture around each.

2 Place 2 in. apart on ungreased baking sheets. Bake at 400° for 12-15 minutes or until golden brown.

YIELD: 3 DOZEN.

Lavonne Hartel, Williston, North Dakota

More than 20 years ago, I tried these olive-stuffed treats for a holiday party. Friends are still asking me to bring them to get-togethers.

chili cheese tart

1 package (15 ounces) refrigerated pie pastry (2 sheets)

1 can (4 ounces) chopped green chilies, drained

1 cup (4 ounces) shredded cheddar cheese

1 cup (4 ounces) shredded Monterey Jack cheese

¼ teaspoon chili powder

Salsa and sour cream

1 Place one sheet of pie pastry on an ungreased pizza pan or baking sheet. Sprinkle chilies and cheeses over pastry to within ½ in. of edges. Top with remaining pastry; seal edges and prick top with a fork.

2 Sprinkle with chili powder. Bake at 450° for 10-15 minutes or until golden brown. Cool for 10 minutes before cutting into wedges. Serve with salsa and sour cream.

YIELD: 10-14 SERVINGS.

Rachel Nash, Pascagoula, Mississippi

When I fix this flavorful appetizer, I have to keep an eye out for sneaky fingers. My family just can't resist sampling the cheesy wedges.

pizza turnovers

3 tablespoons chopped fresh mushrooms

2 tablespoons chopped green pepper

2 tablespoons chopped onion

1 tablespoon butter

5 tablespoons tomato paste

2 tablespoons water

1/2 teaspoon dried oregano

1/8 teaspoon garlic powder

1/2 cup shredded part-skim mozzarella cheese

1 package (15 ounces) refrigerated pie pastry

1 egg, lightly beaten

1 In a small saucepan, saute the mushrooms, green pepper and onion in butter until tender. Add the tomato paste, water, oregano and garlic powder. Reduce heat to medium-low. Stir in cheese until melted. Remove from the heat.

2 Cut 3½-in. circles from pie pastry. Place 1 teaspoon filling in the center of each circle. Brush edges of dough with water. Fold each circle in half; seal edges with a fork. Brush the tops with beaten egg. Place the turnovers on a greased baking sheet.

3 Bake at 425° for 12-14 minutes or until golden brown.

YIELD: 14 TURNOVERS.

EDITOR'S NOTE: The turnovers may be frozen, unbaked, for up to 2 months. Before serving, bake at 425° for 16-18 minutes or until golden brown and heated through.

Janet Crouch, Three Hills, Alberta

These little pizza snacks are a real crowd-pleaser. Plus they can be made ahead and frozen, so you don't have to worry about last-minute preparation.

bite-size crab quiches

1 tube (16.3 ounces) large refrigerated buttermilk biscuits

1 can (6 ounces) crabmeat, drained, flaked and cartilage removed *or* 1 cup chopped imitation crabmeat

1/2 cup shredded Swiss cheese

1 egg

1/2 cup milk

1/2 teaspoon dill weed

1/4 teaspoon salt

1 Separate each biscuit into five equal pieces. Press onto the bottom and up the sides of 24 ungreased miniature muffin cups (discard remaining piece of dough). Fill each cup with 2 teaspoons crab and 1 teaspoon Swiss cheese. In a small bowl, combine the egg, milk, dill and salt; spoon about 1 1/2 teaspoons into each cup.

2 Bake at 375° for 15-20 minutes or until edges are golden brown. Let stand for 5 minutes before removing from pans. Serve warm.

YIELD: 2 DOZEN.

Virginia Ricks, Roy, Utah

These mouthwatering morsels make an appealing appetizer when you invite a few friends to your house after a movie or ball game.

creamy herb appetizer pockets

1 carton (4.4 ounces) reduced-fat garlic-herb cheese spread

4 ounces reduced-fat cream cheese

2 tablespoons half-and-half cream

1 garlic clove, minced

1 tablespoon dried basil

1 teaspoon dried thyme

1/2 teaspoon celery salt

1/4 teaspoon dill weed

1/4 teaspoon salt

1/4 teaspoon pepper

3 to 4 drops hot pepper sauce

1/2 cup chopped canned water-packed artichoke hearts

1/4 cup chopped roasted red peppers

2 tubes (8 ounces *each*) refrigerated reduced-fat crescent rolls

1 In a small mixing bowl, beat the cheese spread, cream cheese, cream and garlic until blended. Beat in the herbs, salt, pepper and hot pepper sauce. Fold in artichokes and red peppers. Cover and chill for at least 1 hour.

2 Unroll both tubes of crescent roll dough. On a lightly floured surface, form each tube of dough into a long rectangle; seal the seams and perforations. Roll each into a 16-in. x 12-in. rectangle. Cut lengthwise into four strips and widthwise into three strips; separate squares.

3 Place 1 rounded tablespoon of filling in the center of each square. Fold in half, forming triangles. Crimp edges to seal; trim if necessary. Place on ungreased baking sheets. Bake at 375° for 10-15 minutes or until golden brown. Serve warm.

YIELD: 2 DOZEN.

EDITOR'S NOTE: This recipe was tested with Bourisn Light Cheese Spread with garlic and fine herbs. One carton contains about 7 tablespoons of cheese spread.

Tina Scarpaci, Chandler, Arizona

I combined a creamy cheese sauce and an artichoke dip to come up with these bite-size morsels. The filling is tucked into triangles made from crescent roll dough— it's the perfect no-mess appetizer!

party pesto pinwheels

1 tube (8 ounces) refrigerated crescent rolls

1/3 cup prepared pesto sauce

1/4 cup roasted sweet red peppers, drained and chopped

1/4 cup grated Parmesan cheese

1 cup pizza sauce, warmed

1 Unroll crescent dough into two long rectangles; seal seams and perforations. Spread each with pesto; sprinkle with red peppers and Parmesan cheese.

2 Roll each up jelly-roll style, starting with a short side. With a sharp knife, cut each roll into 10 slices. Place cut side down 2 in. apart on two ungreased baking sheets.

3 Bake at 400° for 8-10 minutes or until golden brown. Serve warm with pizza sauce.

YIELD: 20 APPETIZERS.

Kathleen Farrell, Rochester, New York

I took a couple of my favorite recipes and combined them into these delicious hors d'oeuvres. The easy-to-make pinwheels are impressive.

vegetable spiral sticks

Teri Albrecht, Mt. Airy, Maryland

I love to serve these savory wrapped vegetable sticks for parties or special occasions. They're a simple but impressive appetizer. They even make for a tasty change-of-pace side dish.

3 medium carrots

12 fresh asparagus spears, trimmed

1 tube (11 ounces) refrigerated breadsticks

1 egg white, beaten

¼ cup grated Parmesan cheese

½ teaspoon dried oregano

1 Cut carrots lengthwise into quarters. In a large skillet, bring 2 in. of water to a boil. Add carrots; cook for 3 minutes. Add asparagus; cook 2-3 minutes longer. Drain and rinse with cold water; pat dry.

2 Cut each piece of breadstick dough in half. Roll each piece into a 7-in. rope. Wrap one rope in a spiral around each vegetable. Place on a baking sheet coated with cooking spray; tuck ends of dough under vegetables to secure.

3 Brush with egg white. Combine the Parmesan cheese and oregano; sprinkle over sticks. Bake at 375° for 12-14 minutes or until golden brown. Serve warm.

YIELD: 2 DOZEN.

crispy crab rangoon

1 package (3 ounces) cream cheese, softened

2 green onions, finely chopped

¼ cup finely chopped imitation crabmeat

1 teaspoon minced garlic

16 wonton wrappers

Oil for frying

Sweet-and-sour sauce

1 In a small mixing bowl, beat cream cheese until smooth. Add the onions, crab and garlic; mix well.

2 Place about 1½ teaspoons in the center of each wonton wrapper. (Keep wrappers covered with a damp paper towel until ready to use.) Moisten edges with water; fold opposite corners over filling and press to seal.

3 In an electric skillet, heat 1 in. of oil to 375°. Fry wontons for 1-2 minutes or until golden brown, turning once. Drain on paper towels. Serve with sweet-and-sour sauce.

YIELD: 16 APPETIZERS.

Cathy Blankman, Warroad, Minnesota

My husband loved the appetizers we ordered at a Chinese restaurant so much that I was determined to make them at home. After two more trips to the restaurant to taste them again and about four home trials, I had them perfected. I often make the filling earlier in the day to save time later.

mini bacon quiches

1 package (15 ounces) refrigerated pie pastry

½ pound sliced bacon, cooked and crumbled

½ cup ricotta cheese

½ cup shredded cheddar cheese

½ cup shredded part-skim mozzarella cheese

1 egg, lightly beaten

1 small onion, finely chopped

¼ teaspoon garlic powder

⅛ teaspoon salt

Dash pepper

Dash cayenne pepper

2 teaspoons all-purpose flour

1 Let pastry stand at room temperature for 15-20 minutes.

2 In a bowl, combine the bacon, cheeses, egg, onion, garlic powder, salt, pepper and cayenne.

3 Sprinkle each pastry crust with 1 teaspoon flour; place floured side down on a lightly floured surface. Cut 12 circles from each crust, using a 2½-in. round biscuit cutter.

4 Press dough onto the bottom and up the sides of lightly greased miniature muffin cups. Fill each with about 1 tablespoon of bacon mixture. Bake at 400° for 16-18 minutes or until filling is set. Cool for 5 minutes before removing from pans to a wire rack. Serve warm.

YIELD: 2 DOZEN.

Julie Nowakowski, LaSalle, Illinois
Brimming with bacon and cheese, these melt-in-your-mouth tidbits are easy for guests to handle, and they look so colorful on a buffet. Nobody can stop at just one.

spreads & dips

127

140

Warm from the oven or straight from the refrigerator, spreads and dips are guaranteed crowd-pleasers. Just choose from Baked Onion Brie Spread (p. 128), Mixed Fruit Salsa (p. 127) or Crabmeat Appetizer Cheesecake (p. 140).

Because many take just minutes to whip up, spreads and dips are classic must-haves for any celebration…whether formal or casual. When time's tight, serve them alongside store-bought dippers, such as crackers, bagel chips, potato chips or tortilla chips. For more nutritious options, cut up an assortment of fresh fruits and vegetables.

brie with apricot topping

½ cup chopped dried apricots

2 tablespoons brown sugar

2 tablespoons water

1 teaspoon balsamic vinegar

Dash salt

½ to 1 teaspoon minced fresh
  rosemary or ¼ teaspoon dried
  rosemary, crushed

1 round Brie cheese (8 ounces)

Assorted crackers

1 In a small saucepan, combine the apricots, brown sugar, water, vinegar and salt. Bring to a boil. Reduce heat to medium; cook and stir until slightly thickened. Remove from the heat; stir in rosemary.

2 Remove the rind from the top of the cheese. Place in an ungreased ovenproof serving dish. Spread apricot mixture over cheese. Bake, uncovered, at 400° for 10-12 minutes or until cheese is softened. Serve with crackers.

YIELD: 6-8 SERVINGS.

Taste of Home Test Kitchen

Folks will think you fussed over this pretty spread, but it takes
only minutes to top a round of smooth and creamy brie
with warm, sweet apricots. This is one easy appetizer
certain to make any occasion special.

sun-dried tomato-flavored hummus

1 can (15 ounces) garbanzo beans or chickpeas, rinsed and drained

1/3 cup reduced-fat mayonnaise

1 tablespoon sun-dried tomato pesto sauce mix

1 teaspoon lemon juice

Assorted crackers

In a food processor or blender, combine the beans, mayonnaise, sauce mix and lemon juice; cover and process until blended. Transfer mixture to a small bowl. Serve with crackers. Store hummus in the refrigerator.

YIELD: 1 1/4 CUPS.

EDITOR'S NOTE: This recipe was tested with Knorr Sun-Dried Tomato Pesto Sauce.

Kathleen Tribble, Buellton, California

I didn't like the hummus I bought in refrigerated tubs, so I made my own version using a pesto sauce. My husband and I enjoy it in sandwiches, but it's great on crackers, too. We like it so much that we eat any leftovers with a spoon!

walnut chicken spread

1 3/4 cups finely chopped cooked chicken

1 cup finely chopped walnuts

2/3 cup mayonnaise

1 celery rib, finely chopped

1 small onion, finely chopped

1 teaspoon salt

1/2 teaspoon garlic powder

Assorted crackers

In a bowl, combine the chicken, walnuts, mayonnaise, celery, onion, salt and garlic powder. Serve with crackers.

YIELD: 2 1/2 CUPS.

Joan Whelan, Green Valley, Arizona

It's a breeze to stir together this fun chicken spread. We enjoy the mild combination of chicken, crunchy walnuts, onion and celery. It's a perfect addition to any party.

calico corn salsa

Jennifer Gardner, Sandy, Utah

A friend gave me the recipe for this colorful salsa, and when I took it to a luncheon, everyone loved it. This recipe makes 4 cups, but is easily doubled for larger gatherings.

1½ cups frozen corn, thawed

1 cup frozen peas, thawed

½ teaspoon ground cumin

⅛ teaspoon dried oregano

1 tablespoon olive oil

1 can (15 ounces) black beans, rinsed and drained

1 medium tomato, chopped

⅓ cup chopped red onion

¼ cup lime juice

1 tablespoon Dijon mustard

1 garlic clove, minced

½ teaspoon salt

2 tablespoons minced fresh cilantro

Tortilla chips

1 In a large bowl, combine the corn and peas. In a nonstick skillet, cook cumin and oregano in oil over medium heat for 2 minutes. Pour over corn mixture; stir to coat evenly. Stir in the beans, tomato and onion.

2 In a small bowl, whisk the lime juice, mustard, garlic and salt. Stir in cilantro. Pour over corn mixture and stir to coat. Serve with tortilla chips. Refrigerate leftovers.

YIELD: 4 CUPS.

festive vegetable dip

1 cup mayonnaise

½ cup sour cream

2 tablespoons minced fresh parsley

1 tablespoon minced chives

1 teaspoon dried minced onion

½ teaspoon lemon juice

½ teaspoon Worcestershire sauce

¼ teaspoon salt

¼ teaspoon paprika

⅛ teaspoon curry powder

⅛ teaspoon pepper

1 medium green pepper

1 medium sweet red pepper

Assorted raw vegetables

1 In a large bowl, combine the first 11 ingredients. Cover and refrigerate for at least 1 hour.

2 Lay green pepper on its side; with a sharp knife, make a horizontal slice just above stem. Remove top piece; save for another use. Remove membrane and seeds. Repeat with red pepper. Fill peppers with dip. Serve with vegetables.

YIELD: 1½ CUPS.

Mary Pollard, Crossville, Tennessee

I like to serve this well-seasoned dip with veggies. It rounds out a holiday snack buffet in a festive way when it's served in hollowed-out green and red bell peppers.

mixed fruit salsa

1 package (16 ounces) mixed frozen berries, thawed and chopped

2 medium peaches, diced

2 medium kiwifruit, peeled and diced

3 tablespoons sugar

2 tablespoons lemon juice

1½ teaspoons grated lime peel

CINNAMON TORTILLA CHIPS:

8 flour tortillas (7 inches)

3 tablespoons butter, melted

3 tablespoons sugar

1½ teaspoons ground cinnamon

1 In a large bowl, combine the first six ingredients; set aside. Brush both sides of tortillas with butter. Combine the sugar and cinnamon; sprinkle over both sides of tortilla. Cut each into six wedges.

2 Place on ungreased baking sheets. Bake at 400° for 6-8 minutes on each side or until crisp. Drain salsa; serve with tortilla chips.

YIELD: 6-8 SERVINGS.

Laura Loncour, Milwaukee, Wisconsin

For a unique salsa, this recipe tosses frozen berries with fresh peaches and kiwifruit. You can use canned peaches instead of fresh. It's a terrific snack or dessert alongside homemade cinnamon tortilla chips.

baked onion brie spread

1 large onion, chopped

2 tablespoons minced garlic

2 tablespoons butter

1 round (8 ounces) Brie *or* Camembert cheese, rind removed and cubed

1 package (8 ounces) cream cheese, cubed

¾ cup sour cream

2 teaspoons brown sugar

2 teaspoons lemon juice

1 teaspoon Worcestershire sauce

⅛ teaspoon salt

⅛ teaspoon pepper

1 round loaf (1 pound) sourdough bread

Paprika

Fresh vegetables

1 In a large skillet, cook onion and garlic in butter over medium heat for 8-10 minutes or until onion is golden brown, stirring frequently. Remove from the heat; set aside.

2 Place Brie and cream cheese in a microwave-safe dish. Microwave, uncovered, until softened. Whisk in the sour cream, brown sugar, lemon juice, Worcestershire sauce, salt, pepper and onion mixture.

3 Cut top off loaf of bread; set aside. Hollow out loaf, leaving a ¾-in. shell. Cut removed bread into cubes. Fill shell with cheese mixture; replace top. Wrap in a large piece of heavy-duty foil (about 18 in. square). Place on a baking sheet.

4 Bake at 400° for 1 hour or until spread is bubbly. Remove top of bread. Sprinkle paprika over spread. Serve with bread cubes and fresh vegetables.

YIELD: 2¾ CUPS.

Lori Adams, Mooresville, Indiana

The buttery brie-and-onion flavor of this spread just melts in your mouth. Plus, you can even eat the bread bowl, which my husband says is the best part!

caramel peanut butter dip

30 caramels

1 to 2 tablespoons water

¼ cup plus 2 tablespoons creamy peanut butter

¼ cup finely crushed peanuts, optional

Sliced apples

In a microwave-safe bowl, microwave the caramels and water on high for 1 minute; stir. Microwave 1 minute longer or until smooth. Add peanut butter and mix well; microwave for 30 seconds or until smooth. Stir peanuts if desired. Serve warm with apples.

YIELD: 1 CUP.

Sandra McKenzie, Braham, Minnesota

When crisp autumn apples are available, I quickly use them up when I serve this delicious dip.

chutney cheddar spread

4 ounces cheddar cheese, cubed

¼ cup chutney

2 tablespoons butter, softened

1 tablespoon finely chopped onion

¼ teaspoon Worcestershire sauce

Dash hot pepper sauce

Assorted crackers

In a food processor, combine the first six ingredients; cover and process until mixture achieves spreading consistency. Refrigerate until serving. Serve with crackers.

YIELD: ABOUT 1 CUP.

Regina Costlow, East Brady, Pennsylvania

This appetizer can be whipped together in minutes with ingredients I have on hand in the kitchen.

cider cheese fondue

¾ cup apple cider *or* apple juice

2 cups (8 ounces) shredded
   cheddar cheese

1 cup (4 ounces) shredded
   Swiss cheese

1 tablespoon cornstarch

⅛ teaspoon pepper

1 loaf (1 pound) French bread,
   cut into cubes

In a large saucepan, bring the cider to a boil. Reduce the heat to medium-low. Toss the cheeses with cornstarch and pepper; stir into cider. Cook and stir for 3-4 minutes or until cheese is melted. Transfer to a small ceramic fondue pot or slow cooker; keep warm. Serve with bread cubes.

YIELD: 2⅔ CUPS.

Kim Marie Van Rheenen, Mendota, Illinois

Cheese lovers are sure to enjoy dipping into this creamy, quick-to-fix fondue that has just a hint of apple flavor. Apple or pear wedges also make fabulous dippers.

sweet cheese ball

2 packages (8 ounces *each*) cream cheese, softened

1/2 cup confectioners' sugar

2/3 cup flaked coconut

8 maraschino cherries, finely chopped

3/4 cup finely chopped pecans

Assorted fresh fruit

In a small mixing bowl, beat cream cheese and confectioners' sugar until smooth. Beat in the coconut and cherries. Shape into a ball; roll in pecans. Cover and refrigerate until serving. Serve with fruit.

YIELD: 1 CHEESE BALL (3½ CUPS).

Melissa Friend, Oakland, Maryland

You'll need only a few items for this unique cheese ball. Coconut comes through in the cherry-flecked mixture that's coated in pecans. It looks pretty and tastes delicious served with apple slices, pineapple wedges, berries and other fresh fruit.

baked spinach dip in bread

Shauna Dittrick, Leduc, Alberta

This is the only way my kids will eat spinach! The dip can be made ahead and chilled. Place in the bread shell and bake just before your company arrives.

2 packages (8 ounces *each*) cream cheese, softened

1 cup mayonnaise

1 package (10 ounces) frozen chopped spinach, thawed and squeezed dry

1 cup (4 ounces) shredded cheddar cheese

1 pound sliced bacon, cooked and crumbled

1/4 cup chopped onion

1 tablespoon dill weed

1 to 2 garlic cloves, minced

1 round loaf (1 pound) unsliced sourdough bread

Assorted fresh vegetables

1 In a large mixing bowl, beat the cream cheese and mayonnaise until blended. Stir in the spinach, cheese, bacon, onion, dill and garlic; set aside.

2 Cut a 1½-in. slice off top of bread; set aside. Carefully hollow out bottom, leaving a ½-in. shell. Cube removed bread and place on a baking sheet. Broil 3-4 in. from the heat for 1-2 minutes or until golden brown; set aside.

3 Fill bread shell with spinach dip; replace top. Place any dip that doesn't fit in shell in a greased baking dish. Wrap filled bread in a large piece of heavy-duty foil (about 18 in. square). Place on a baking sheet.

4 Bake at 350° for 1 hour or until dip is heated through. Cover and bake additional dip for 40-45 minutes or until heated through. Open foil carefully. Serve dip warm with vegetables and reserved bread cubes.

YIELD: 4 CUPS.

EDITOR'S NOTE: Fat-free cream cheese and mayonnaise are not recommended for this recipe.

beer cheese

⅓ cup beer *or* nonalcoholic beer

4 ounces cream cheese, cubed

3 ounces crumbled blue cheese

¼ cup Dijon mustard

2 tablespoons grated onion

½ to 1 teaspoon hot pepper sauce

1 garlic clove, minced

3 cups (12 ounces) shredded cheddar cheese

Assorted crackers

1 In a small saucepan, bring beer to a boil. Remove from the heat and cool to room temperature.

2 In a food processor, combine the beer, cream cheese, blue cheese, mustard, onion, hot pepper sauce and garlic. Add cheddar cheese; cover and process until well blended. Transfer to a bowl. Cover and refrigerate overnight.

3 Let cheese stand at room temperature for 30 minutes before serving with crackers.

YIELD: 3 CUPS.

Pat Wartman, Bethlehem, Pennsylvania

I like to serve this zesty cheese spread with crackers. It's terrific to take along to picnics or to tailgates.

roasted eggplant dip

1 medium eggplant (about 1 pound)

9 green onions (white portion only)

3 tablespoons reduced-fat plain yogurt

1 tablespoon lemon juice

1 tablespoon olive oil

$1/2$ teaspoon salt

$1/4$ teaspoon pepper

3 tablespoons minced chives, *divided*

Pita breads (6 inches), cut into 6 wedges

Carrot sticks, optional

1 Pierce eggplant several times with a fork. Place eggplant and onions in a shallow foil-lined baking pan. Bake at 400° for 25-30 minutes or until tender. Cool. Peel and cube the eggplant.

2 In a blender or food processor, combine the yogurt, lemon juice, oil, salt, pepper, eggplant and onions. Cover and process until almost smooth. Add 2 tablespoons chives; cover and process until blended.

3 Transfer to a serving bowl; sprinkle with remaining chives. Serve with pita wedges and carrots if desired.

YIELD: 1$1/2$ CUPS.

Nina Hall, Spokane, Washington

Here's a fun way to use some of your garden-fresh eggplant crop. This chunky guacamole-like dip—seasoned with lemon juice, onions and chives—goes great with pita wedges or melba toast.

ham cream cheese balls

2 packages (8 ounces *each*) cream cheese, softened

1 package (2½ ounces) thinly sliced deli ham, finely chopped

3 green onions, finely chopped

2 tablespoons Worcestershire sauce

1 cup finely chopped peanuts

Crackers and raw vegetables

In a bowl, combine the cream cheese, ham, onions and Worcestershire sauce; mix well. Shape into ¾-in. balls. Roll in peanuts. Cover and refrigerate until serving. Serve with crackers and vegetables.

YIELD: ABOUT 5 DOZEN.

Jill Kirby, Calhoun, Georgia

It seems like I'm always hosting a shower, birthday or other celebration. I can depend on these individual cheese balls to please party-goers.

hot and spicy cranberry dip

1 can (16 ounces) jellied cranberry sauce

2 to 3 tablespoons prepared horseradish

2 tablespoons honey

1 tablespoon Worcestershire sauce

1 tablespoon lemon juice

1 garlic clove, minced

1/4 to 1/2 teaspoon ground cayenne pepper

Dippers: pineapple chunks, orange sections and warmed mini fully cooked sausages

In a medium saucepan, combine first seven ingredients. Bring to a boil. Reduce heat; cover and simmer for 5 minutes. Serve warm with the pineapple, oranges and sausages.

YIELD: 2 CUPS.

Dorothy Pritchett, Wills Point, Texas

This savory dipping sauce has a festive red color and is packed with lots of zesty flavor.

chorizo cheese dip

1/2 pound uncooked chorizo, casings removed

1 small green pepper, chopped

1 small sweet red pepper, chopped

1 small onion, chopped

3 garlic cloves, minced

1 tablespoon vegetable oil

1/2 teaspoon cayenne pepper

2 cartons (12 ounces *each*) white Mexican dipping cheese

Tortilla chips

1 In a large skillet, cook chorizo over medium heat until no longer pink; drain. Remove and set aside. In the same skillet, saute the peppers, onion and garlic in oil until tender. Stir in cayenne and chorizo; heat through.

2 Heat cheese according to package directions; stir into meat mixture. Serve warm with tortilla chips. Refrigerate leftovers.

YIELD: 4 CUPS.

Taste of Home Test Kitchen

Guests will wipe the bowl clean when you set out this spicy favorite. Serve it with tortilla chips or even vegetable dippers.

texas caviar

1 can (15½ ounces) black-eyed peas, rinsed and drained

¾ cup chopped sweet red pepper

¾ cup chopped green pepper

1 medium onion, chopped

3 green onions, chopped

¼ cup minced fresh parsley

1 jar (2 ounces) diced pimientos, drained

1 garlic clove, minced

1 bottle (8 ounces) fat-free Italian salad dressing

Tortilla chips

In a large bowl, combine the peas, peppers, onions, parsley, pimientos and garlic. Pour salad dressing over pea mixture; stir gently to coat. Cover and refrigerate at least 24 hours. Serve with tortilla chips.

YIELD: 4 CUPS.

Kathy Faris, Lytle, Texas

My neighbor gave me a container of this zippy, tangy salsa one Christmas and I had to have the recipe. I fix it regularly for potlucks and get-togethers and never have any left over. I bring copies of the recipe with me whenever I take it.

hot seafood spread

1 package (8 ounces) cream cheese, softened

2 cups (8 ounces) shredded cheddar cheese

1 cup mayonnaise

1 can (4¼ ounces) tiny shrimp, rinsed and drained

¾ cup imitation crabmeat, chopped

½ cup chopped green onions

¼ cup grated Parmesan cheese

2 teaspoons dill weed

2 teaspoons minced fresh parsley

1 round loaf (1½ pounds) unsliced bread

Assorted fresh vegetables

1 In a mixing bowl, combine the first nine ingredients. Cut the top fourth off the loaf of bread; carefully hollow out bottom, leaving a ½-in. shell. Cube removed bread; set aside. Fill bread shell with seafood mixture.

2 Place on an ungreased baking sheet. Cover top edges loosely with foil. Bake at 350° for 25 minutes. Remove foil; bake 25-35 minutes longer or until crust is golden brown and spread is heated through. Serve with vegetables and bread cubes.

YIELD: 4 CUPS.

EDITOR'S NOTE: Fat-free cream cheese and mayonnaise are not recommended for this recipe.

Linda Doll, St. Albert, Alberta

This creamy, flavorful dip is sure to be popular at parties. Bake it in a hollowed-out pumpernickel or white round bread loaf. Serve it with bread cubes, pita bread or assorted raw veggies. Sometimes I use canned crab instead of the imitation crabmeat.

crabmeat appetizer cheesecake

Andrea MacIntire, Delaware Water Gap, Pennsylvania

I found a lobster cheesecake recipe and decided to come up with my own version using crabmeat instead. It tastes great, so now I make it often.

½ cup seasoned bread crumbs

½ cup grated Parmesan cheese

¼ cup butter, melted

FILLING:

¼ cup *each* chopped sweet red, yellow and green pepper

¼ cup chopped onion

¼ cup butter

4 packages (three 8 ounces, one 3 ounces) cream cheese, softened

3 eggs, lightly beaten

2 cups heavy whipping cream

2 cups canned crabmeat, drained, flaked and cartilage removed

2 cups (8 ounces) shredded Swiss cheese

½ teaspoon salt

1 In a bowl, combine the bread crumbs, Parmesan cheese and butter. Press onto the bottom of a 10-in. springform pan; set aside. In a skillet, saute the peppers and onion in butter until tender; set aside.

2 In a mixing bowl, beat cream cheese until smooth. Add eggs; beat on low speed just until combined. Stir in the cream, crab, Swiss cheese, pepper mixture and salt. Pour over crust.

3 Place pan on a baking sheet. Bake at 325° for 60-65 minutes or until center is almost set. Cool on a wire rack for 10 minutes. Carefully run a knife around edge of pan to loosen. Cool cheesecake for 1 hour longer. Refrigerate overnight.

4 Remove sides of pan. Let stand at room temperature for 30 minutes before serving. Refrigerate leftovers.

YIELD: 16-18 SERVINGS.

ten-minute zesty salsa

1 can (10 ounces) diced tomatoes and green chilies, undrained

1 tablespoon seeded chopped jalapeno pepper

1 tablespoon chopped red onion

1 tablespoon minced fresh cilantro

1 garlic clove, minced

1 tablespoon olive oil

Dash salt

Dash pepper

Tortilla chips

In a small bowl, combine the tomatoes, jalapeno, onion, cilantro, garlic, oil, salt and pepper. Refrigerate until serving. Serve with tortilla chips.

YIELD: 1½ CUPS.

EDITOR'S NOTE: When cutting or seeding hot peppers, use rubber or plastic gloves to protect your hands. Avoid touching your face.

Kim Morin, Lake George, Colorado

The view from our mountain home includes Pikes Peak, so we frequently eat on our wraparound porch when the weather is good. We savor this zippy salsa with chips while we feast on the natural beauty all around us.

lobster spread

1 package (8 ounces) cream cheese, softened

1 tablespoon milk

1½ cups flaked lobster *or* crabmeat

2 tablespoons chopped onion

½ teaspoon horseradish

¼ teaspoon salt

Dash pepper

Paprika

¼ cup sliced almonds

Assorted crackers

In a bowl, combine the cream cheese and milk until smooth. Add the lobster, onion, horseradish, salt and pepper. Spread into a greased 8-in. ovenproof dish. Sprinkle with the paprika and almonds. Bake at 375° for about 15 minutes until bubbly. Serve warm with assorted crackers.

YIELD: 2¾ CUPS.

Jeff and Judi Burke, Isle au Haut, Maine

We like to enjoy this with crispy whole wheat crackers. It's always a hit when we serve it, and it takes only a few minute to whip up.

feta olive dip

4 ounces reduced-fat cream cheese

½ cup crumbled feta cheese

½ cup reduced-fat sour cream

¼ cup sliced ripe olives

2 garlic cloves, minced

2 teaspoons dried oregano

1 teaspoon minced fresh parsley

¼ teaspoon salt

¼ to ½ teaspoon hot pepper sauce

Baked pita chips

In a food processor or blender, combine the first nine ingredients; cover and process until blended. Transfer to a bowl. Cover and refrigerate for at least 1 hour before serving. Serve with pita chips.

YIELD: ABOUT 1½ CUPS.

Debbie Burton, Callander, Ontario

Feta cheese, garlic and ripe olives, along with a hint of hot sauce, give a Greek salad-like flavor to this distinctive dip. Besides pita chips, it's terrific with crackers, tortilla chips, pita bread, pretzels and carrot and celery sticks.

six-layer dip

2 medium ripe avocados, peeled and sliced

2 tablespoons lemon juice

1/2 tablespoon garlic salt

1/8 teaspoon hot pepper sauce

1 cup (8 ounces) sour cream

1 can (2 1/4 ounces) chopped ripe olives, drained

1 jar (16 ounces) thick and chunky salsa, drained

2 medium tomatoes, seeded and chopped

1 cup (8 ounces) shredded cheddar cheese

Tortilla chips

In a large bowl, mash the avocados with lemon juice, garlic salt and hot pepper sauce. Spoon into a deep-dish 10-in. pie plate or serving bowl. Layer with the sour cream, olives, salsa, tomatoes and cheese. Cover and refrigerate for at least 1 hour. Serve with chips.

YIELD: 2 1/2 CUPS.

Etta Gillespie, San Angelo, Texas

Tortilla chips make great scoopers for this dip, which is a family favorite. Sometimes I serve it in a glass bowl—just to show off the pretty layers.

raspberry cheese spread

4 ounces cream cheese, softened

1 cup mayonnaise

2 cups (8 ounces) shredded part-skim mozzarella cheese

2 cups (8 ounces) shredded cheddar cheese

3 green onions, finely chopped

1 cup chopped pecans

¼ cup seedless raspberry preserves

Assorted crackers

1 In a small mixing bowl, beat the cream cheese and mayonnaise until blended. Beat in cheeses and onions. Stir in pecans. Spread into a plastic wrap-lined 9-in. round dish. Refrigerate until set, about 1 hour.

2 Invert onto a serving plate; spread with preserves. Serve with crackers.

YIELD: ABOUT 3½ CUPS.

Jane Montgomery, Hilliard, Ohio

A party guest brought this attractive appetizer to our home, and we fell in love with it. Now I often make it myself when we have company.

tiered cheese slices

1 package (8 ounces) cream cheese, softened

1/2 teaspoon hot pepper sauce

1/4 teaspoon salt

1/4 cup chopped pecans

1/4 cup dried cranberries

2 packages (8 ounces *each*) deli-style cheddar cheese slices (about 3 inches square)

Assorted crackers

1 In a mixing bowl, combine the cream cheese, hot pepper sauce and salt. Stir in pecans and cranberries.

2 On a 12-in. square of aluminum foil, place two slices of cheese side by side; spread with 2-3 tablespoons cream cheese mixture. Repeat layers six times. Top with two cheese slices. (Save remaining cheese slices for another use.)

3 Fold foil around cheese and seal tightly. Refrigerate for 8 hours or overnight. Cut in half lengthwise and then widthwise into 1/4-in. slices. Serve with crackers.

YIELD: ABOUT 4 DOZEN.

Diane Benjaminson, Coleville, Saskatchewan

I can't tell you how many times I've made this recipe and been asked to share it! Guests always think I fussed, but the simple ingredients go together in minutes using presliced cheese. For busy hostesses, it's a do-ahead delight.

dijon chicken liver pate

½ pound bulk pork sausage

1 small onion, chopped

½ pound chicken livers, cut in half

⅓ cup milk

2 tablespoons Dijon mustard

1 package (8 ounces) cream cheese, softened

½ teaspoon garlic powder

¼ teaspoon *each* minced chives, dried parsley flakes, tarragon and marjoram

Assorted crackers

1 In a large skillet, cook sausage and onion over medium heat until meat is no longer pink; remove with a slotted spoon and set aside. In the drippings, cook the chicken livers over medium heat for 6-8 minutes or until no longer pink. Drain; cool for 10 minutes.

2 Place chicken livers, milk and mustard in a blender or food processor; cover and process. Add the sausage mixture, cream cheese and seasonings; cover and process until nearly smooth.

3 Pour into a 3-cup serving bowl. Cover and refrigerate for 6 hours or overnight. Serve with crackers.

YIELD: 3 CUPS.

Katherine Wells, Brodhead, Wisconsin

I first served this pate at a holiday party quite a few years ago, and it was a real hit.

salsa guacamole

6 small ripe avocados, halved, pitted and peeled

¼ cup lemon juice

1 cup salsa

2 green onions, finely chopped

¼ teaspoon salt *or* salt-free seasoning blend

¼ teaspoon garlic powder

Tortilla chips

In a bowl, mash avocados with lemon juice. Stir in the salsa, onions, salt and garlic powder. Serve immediately with tortilla chips.

YIELD: 4 CUPS.

Lauren Heyn, Oak Creek, Wisconsin

I've never tasted better guacamole than this. If there's time, I make homemade tortilla chips by frying 1-inch strips of flour tortillas in oil.

warm asparagus-crab spread

Camille Wisniewski, Jackson, New Jersey

When my children entertain, I like to help them with the cooking. This warm and flavorful dip is a favorite contribution of mine. Cashew nuts give the creamy mixture a nice crunch.

1 medium sweet red pepper, chopped

3 green onions, sliced

2 medium jalapeno peppers, seeded and finely chopped

2 teaspoons vegetable oil

1 can (15 ounces) asparagus spears, drained and chopped

2 cans (6 ounces *each*) crabmeat, drained, flaked and cartilage removed

1 cup mayonnaise

1/2 cup grated *or* shredded Parmesan cheese

1/2 cup chopped cashews

Assorted crackers

1 In a large skillet, saute the red pepper, onions and jalapenos in oil until tender. Add the asparagus, crab, mayonnaise and Parmesan cheese; mix well.

2 Transfer to a greased 1-qt. baking dish. Sprinkle with cashews. Bake, uncovered, at 375° for 20-25 minutes or until bubbly. Serve with crackers.

YIELD: 3 CUPS.

EDITOR'S NOTE: Reduced-fat or fat-free mayonnaise is not recommended for this recipe. When cutting or seeding hot peppers, use rubber or plastic gloves to protect your hands. Avoid touching your face.

hot artichoke spread

1 can (14 ounces) water-packed artichoke hearts, rinsed, drained and chopped

1 cup mayonnaise

1 cup grated Parmesan cheese

1 can (4 ounces) chopped green chilies, drained

1 garlic clove, minced

1 cup chopped fresh tomatoes

3 green onions, thinly sliced

Crackers *or* pita bread

1 In a large bowl, combine the first five ingredients. Spread into a 1-qt. baking dish or 9-in. pie plate.

2 Bake, uncovered, at 350° for 20-25 minutes or until top is lightly browned. Sprinkle with tomatoes and onions. Serve with crackers or pita bread.

YIELD: 4½ CUPS.

EDITOR'S NOTE: Reduced-fat or fat-free mayonnaise is not recommended for this recipe.

Victoria Casey, Coeur d'Alene, Idaho

Green chilies add a bit of zip to this rich cracker spread. I serve it often at parties because it makes a lot, is quick to prepare and looks so pretty with the red tomatoes and green onions on top.

orange chocolate fondue

½ cup milk chocolate chips

3 squares (1 ounce *each*)
bittersweet chocolate

½ cup heavy whipping cream

3 tablespoons orange juice
concentrate

1 frozen pound cake (16 ounces),
thawed and cut into 1-inch
cubes

Sliced bananas and star fruit, orange
segments, sweet cherries *or*
strawberries *or* fruit of your choice

In a heavy saucepan, cook and stir the chocolate chips, bittersweet chocolate and cream over low heat until smooth. Stir in the orange juice concentrate. Transfer to a fondue pot and keep warm. Serve with cake and fruit.

YIELD: 1⅓ CUPS.

Mary Jean DeVries, Grandville, Michigan

Invite your family and friends to dip cubes of cake and
pieces of fruit into this rich, luscious
fondue for a special treat.

hearty cheese spread

1 Gouda cheese round in red wax covering (7 ounces), room temperature

1 package (2½ ounces) thinly sliced smoked beef, finely chopped

¼ cup sour cream

2 tablespoons sweet pickle relish

2 teaspoons prepared horseradish

Apple slices *or* crackers

1 Carefully slice through wax and cheese to within 1 in. of the bottom, forming eight pie-shaped wedges. Carefully fold wax back to expose cheese; remove cheese.

2 In a mixing bowl, beat the cheese until creamy. Add the beef, sour cream, relish and horseradish; mix well. Spoon into wax shell. Chill. Serve with apple slices or crackers.

YIELD: 1½ CUPS.

Fernie Nicolaisen, Cherokee, Iowa

Here's a cheese spread that will please a hungry crowd with its bold taste. Prepare this spread early in the day, spoon it into the cheese's wax shell and refrigerate until you are ready to serve.

guacamole dip

1 large ripe avocado, peeled

¼ cup plain yogurt

2 tablespoons picante sauce *or* salsa

1 tablespoon finely chopped onion

⅛ teaspoon salt

2 to 3 drops hot pepper sauce, optional

Tortilla chips

In a bowl, mash avocado until smooth. Stir in the yogurt, picante sauce, onion, salt and hot pepper sauce if desired. Cover and refrigerate until serving. Serve with tortilla chips.

YIELD: ¾ CUP.

Virginia Burwell, Dayton, Texas
Since guacamole is a favorite in this area, I decided to create my own recipe. I serve it as a dip for chips, with baked chicken or to top off a bed of lettuce.

handheld snacks

158

180

When the gang is hungry, surprise them with these pizzas, sandwiches and more. Each recipe is perfect when you want a lot of satisfaction in each bite. Check out all the delicious options such as Italian Subs (p. 165), Spicy Summer Sub (p. 158) and Double Sausage Pizza (p. 180).

These snacks are ideal for portion control, too! When offering a variety of foods, cut these into smaller pieces for just a taste. Or, serve larger pieces when they are your main menu attraction.

baked deli sandwich

1 loaf (1 pound) frozen bread dough, thawed

2 tablespoons butter, melted

$\frac{1}{4}$ teaspoon garlic salt

$\frac{1}{4}$ teaspoon dried basil

$\frac{1}{4}$ teaspoon dried oregano

$\frac{1}{4}$ teaspoon pizza seasoning

$\frac{1}{4}$ pound sliced deli ham

6 thin slices mozzarella cheese

$\frac{1}{4}$ pound sliced deli smoked turkey breast

6 thin slices cheddar cheese

Pizza sauce, warmed, optional

1 On a baking sheet coated with cooking spray, roll dough into a small rectangle. Let rest for 5-10 minutes.

2 In a small bowl, combine the butter and seasonings. Roll out dough into a 14-in. x 10-in. rectangle. Brush with half of the butter mixture. Layer the ham, mozzarella cheese, turkey and cheddar cheese lengthwise over half of the dough to within $\frac{1}{2}$ in. of edges. Fold the dough over and pinch firmly to seal. Brush with the remaining butter mixture.

3 Bake at 400° for 10-12 minutes or until golden brown. Cut into 1-in. slices. Serve immediately with pizza sauce if desired.

YIELD: 6-10 SERVINGS.

Sandra McKenzie, Braham, Minnesota

Frozen bread dough, fast assembly and quick baking time make this stuffed sandwich an appetizer I rely on often and one of my most-requested recipes. It's easy to double for a crowd or to experiment with different meats and cheeses.

southwestern chicken pizza

1 medium onion, julienned

1 medium green pepper, julienned

¼ cup water

1 tube (10 ounces) refrigerated pizza crust

1¼ cups salsa

2 packages (6 ounces *each*) ready-to-use Southwestern chicken strips

2 cups (8 ounces) shredded Mexican cheese blend

¼ teaspoon garlic powder

¼ teaspoon dried cilantro flakes

1 In a microwave-safe bowl, combine the onion, green pepper and water. Cover and microwave on high for 2-4 minutes or until vegetables are crisp-tender; drain well.

2 Unroll pizza crust onto a greased baking sheet, stretching gently to form a 14-in. x 10-in. rectangle. Spread with salsa. Top with chicken and onion mixture. Sprinkle with cheese, garlic powder and cilantro. Bake at 400° for 15-20 minutes or until crust is golden and cheese is melted. Cut into squares.

YIELD: 8 SLICES.

EDITOR'S NOTE: This recipe was tested in a 1,100-watt microwave.

Robin Poust, Stevensville, Maryland

Our family loves Mexican food and pizza, so I combined the two. It's easy to cook the pepper and onion in the microwave. Salsa, prepared chicken and other convenience items hurry along the rest of the recipe. The final result is fantastic!

spicy summer sub

Barb McMahan, Fenton, Missouri

A few years back, I served this sandwich to friends and family who came to help with our garage sale. Everyone was impressed with the preparation and combination of flavors.

1 round loaf (1½ pounds) rye bread

1 cup mayonnaise

2 tablespoons Dijon mustard

1 jar (2 ounces) diced pimientos, drained

¼ to ½ teaspoon hot pepper sauce

½ pound sliced provolone cheese

¼ pound sliced fully cooked ham

¼ pound sliced cooked turkey

¼ pound sliced Genoa salami

¼ pound sliced mozzarella cheese

1 Cut bread in half horizontally; hollow out top and bottom, leaving a ¾-in. shell. (Discard removed bread or save for another use.)

2 In a small bowl, combine the mayonnaise, mustard, pimientos and hot pepper sauce; spread ¼ cup in the bottom bread shell. Layer with a fourth of the provolone, ham, turkey, salami and mozzarella. Spread with more of the mayonnaise mixture. Repeat layers three times (you may not use up all of the mayonnaise mixture). Replace bread top and wrap tightly with plastic wrap. Chill for at least 3 hours.

3 Remove from the refrigerator 30 minutes before serving. Cut into wedges; serve with remaining mayonnaise mixture if desired.

YIELD: 6-8 SERVINGS.

tomato rosemary focaccia

1 tube (13.8 ounces) refrigerated pizza crust

2 tablespoons olive oil

2 garlic cloves, minced

¼ teaspoon salt

1 tablespoon minced fresh rosemary *or* 1 teaspoon dried rosemary, crushed, *divided*

2 to 3 plum tomatoes, thinly sliced

1 small red onion, thinly sliced

Unroll pizza crust onto a greased baking sheet. Combine the oil, garlic, salt and half of the rosemary; spread over crust. Top with tomatoes and onion; sprinkle with remaining rosemary. Bake at 425° for 12-15 minutes or until golden. Cut into rectangles.

YIELD: 6 SERVINGS.

Dorothy Smith, El Dorado, Arkansas

This quick Italian flat bread is a delicious savory snack and is also good with soup or a salad.

turkey roll-ups

1 package (8 ounces) fat-free cream cheese

½ cup reduced-fat mayonnaise

¼ teaspoon dried basil

¼ teaspoon dried oregano

¼ teaspoon dill weed

¼ teaspoon garlic powder

10 flour tortillas (6 inches), warmed

1 medium onion, chopped

10 slices deli turkey breast

Shredded lettuce

In a small mixing bowl, combine the first six ingredients; beat until smooth. Spread over the tortillas. Sprinkle with onion; top with turkey and lettuce. Roll up tightly jelly-roll style. Cut wraps in half; serve immediately.

YIELD: 20 SERVINGS.

Paula Alf, Cincinnati, Ohio

Whether cut into bite-size appetizers or served whole for lunch, these light wraps are always a hit. We prefer this blend of herbs, but feel free to use any combination you'd like.

party pitas

1 package (8 ounces) cream cheese, softened

½ cup mayonnaise

½ teaspoon dill weed

¼ teaspoon garlic salt

8 mini pita breads (4 inches)

16 fresh spinach leaves

¾ pound shaved fully cooked ham

½ pound thinly sliced Monterey Jack cheese

1 In a large mixing bowl, beat the cream cheese, mayonnaise, dill and garlic salt until blended.

2 Cut each pita in half horizontally; spread 1 tablespoon cream cheese mixture on each cut surface. On eight pita halves, layer spinach, ham and cheese. Top with remaining pita halves. Cut each pita into four wedges; secure with a toothpick.

YIELD: 32 PIECES.

Janette Root, Ellensburg, Washington

Whenever the ladies of our church host a bridal shower, these pita sandwiches are on the menu. Not only are they easy and tasty, they look nice on the table.

mediterranean pizza

2 jars (6½ ounces *each*) marinated artichoke hearts

1 loaf (1 pound) frozen bread dough, thawed

1 teaspoon dried basil

1 teaspoon dried oregano

½ teaspoon dried thyme

2 cups (8 ounces) shredded Monterey Jack cheese, *divided*

¼ pound thinly sliced deli ham, julienned

1 cup halved cherry tomatoes

1 cup chopped ripe olives

¼ cup crumbled feta cheese

1 Drain artichokes, reserving marinade. Chop artichokes; set aside. On a floured surface, roll bread dough into a 15-in. circle. Transfer to a greased 14-in. pizza pan; build up edges slightly. Brush the dough lightly with reserved marinade.

2 Combine the basil, oregano and thyme; sprinkle over marinade. Sprinkle with 1 cup Monterey Jack cheese, ham, artichokes, tomatoes, olives and feta cheese. Sprinkle with remaining Monterey Jack cheese. Bake at 400° for 20-25 minutes or until crust and cheese are lightly browned.

YIELD: 8-10 SLICES.

Pamela Brooks, South Berwick, Maine

Tangy marinated artichokes add flavor to both the crust and the topping of this delicious specialty pizza.

reuben roll-ups

1 tube (13.8 ounces) refrigerated pizza crust

1 cup sauerkraut, well drained

1 tablespoon Thousand Island salad dressing

4 slices corned beef, halved

4 slices Swiss cheese, halved

1 Roll the dough into a 12-in. x 9-in. rectangle. Cut into eight 3-in. x 4½-in. rectangles. Combine sauerkraut and salad dressing. Place a slice of beef on each rectangle. Top with about 2 tablespoons sauerkraut mixture and a slice of cheese. Roll up.

2 Place with seam side down on a greased baking sheet. Bake at 425° for 12-14 minutes or until golden.

YIELD: 8 ROLL-UPS.

Patty Kile, Greentown, Pennsylvania
This recipe turns the popular Reuben sandwich into an interesting and hearty appetizer. We love these roll-ups at our house.

sausage pizza loaf

1 pound bulk Italian sausage

¼ cup *each* chopped onion, sweet red pepper and green pepper

2 packages (6½ ounces *each*) pizza crust mix

1 cup (4 ounces) shredded part-skim mozzarella cheese

½ cup chopped pepperoni

1 egg, lightly beaten

2 tablespoons grated Parmesan cheese

1 teaspoon dried oregano

¼ teaspoon garlic powder

1 In a large skillet, cook the sausage, onion and peppers over medium heat until the meat is no longer pink; drain. Combine crust mixes; prepare according to package directions. With greased fingers, press onto the bottom of a greased 15-in. x 10-in. x 1-in. baking pan.

2 Combine the sausage mixture, mozzarella cheese, pepperoni and egg; spread over dough to within ½ in. of the edges. Sprinkle with the Parmesan cheese, oregano and garlic powder.

3 Roll up jelly-roll style, starting with a long side; pinch seams to seal. Arrange seam side down on pan and shape into a crescent. Bake at 400° for 30 minutes or until golden brown.

YIELD: 15 SERVINGS.

Pat Coon, Ulster, Pennsylvania

Savory slices of this bread make a popular Saturday night meal for my family. Just like pizza, it can be eaten as a fun finger food. Guests can't stop nibbling when I serve it at parties. Plus, it's good warm or cold.

italian subs

1/3 cup olive oil

4 1/2 teaspoons white wine vinegar

1 tablespoon dried parsley flakes

2 to 3 garlic cloves, minced

1 can (2 1/4 ounces) sliced ripe olives, drained

1/2 cup chopped stuffed olives

1 loaf (1 pound, 20 inches) French bread, unsliced

24 thin slices hard salami

24 slices provolone cheese

24 slices fully cooked ham

Lettuce leaves, optional

1 In a bowl, combine the oil, vinegar, parsley and garlic. Stir in olives. Cover and refrigerate for 8 hours or overnight.

2 Cut bread in half lengthwise. Place olive mixture on the bottom of bread. Top with the salami, cheese and ham; add lettuce if desired. Replace top. Cut into 2-in. slices. Insert a toothpick in each slice.

YIELD: 10 SERVINGS.

Delores Christner, Spooner, Wisconsin

Olive lovers are sure to rejoice over this stacked sandwich! Stuffed and ripe olives are marinated in white wine vinegar and garlic before being used to flavor speedy subs showcasing salami, ham and provolones.

chicago-style pan pizza

Nikki MacDonald, Sheboygan, Wisconsin

I developed a love for Chicago's deep-dish pizzas while attending college in the Windy City. This simple recipe relies on frozen bread dough, so I can indulge in the mouthwatering sensation without leaving home.

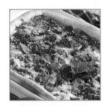

1 loaf (1 pound) frozen bread dough, thawed

1 pound bulk Italian sausage

2 cups (8 ounces) shredded part-skim mozzarella cheese

½ pound sliced fresh mushrooms

1 small onion, chopped

2 teaspoons olive oil

1 can (28 ounces) diced tomatoes, drained

¾ teaspoon dried oregano

½ teaspoon salt

½ teaspoon fennel seed, crushed

¼ teaspoon garlic powder

½ cup grated Parmesan cheese

1 Press dough onto the bottom and up the sides of a greased 13-in. x 9-in. baking dish. In a large skillet, cook sausage over medium heat until no longer pink; drain. Sprinkle over dough. Top with mozzarella cheese.

2 In a skillet, saute mushrooms and onion in oil until onion is tender. Stir in the tomatoes, oregano, salt, fennel seed and garlic powder. Spoon over mozzarella cheese. Sprinkle with Parmesan cheese. Bake at 350° for 25-35 minutes or until crust is golden brown.

YIELD: 12 SLICES.

curried chicken tea sandwiches

2 cups cubed cooked chicken

1 medium unpeeled red apple, chopped

¾ cup dried cranberries

½ cup thinly sliced celery

¼ cup chopped pecans

2 tablespoons thinly sliced green onions

¾ cup mayonnaise

2 teaspoons lime juice

½ to ¾ teaspoon curry powder

12 slices bread

Lettuce leaves

1 In a bowl, combine the first six ingredients. Combine mayonnaise, lime juice and curry powder; add to chicken mixture and stir to coat. Cover and refrigerate until ready to serve.

2 Cut each slice of bread with a 3-in. heart-shaped cookie cutter if desired. Top with lettuce and chicken salad.

YIELD: 6 SERVINGS.

Robin Fuhrman, Fond du Lac, Wisconsin

At a Victorian-theme bridal shower I hosted, I spread this dressed-up chicken salad on bread triangles. Apples and dried cranberries add color and tang.

italian cheese loaf

1 loaf (1 pound) French bread

2 cups diced fresh tomatoes

1 cup (4 ounces) shredded part-skim mozzarella cheese

1 cup (4 ounces) shredded cheddar cheese

1 medium onion, finely chopped

¼ cup grated Romano cheese

¼ cup chopped ripe olives

¼ cup Italian salad dressing

1 teaspoon chopped fresh basil

1 teaspoon chopped fresh oregano

1 Cut top half off loaf of bread; set aside. Carefully hollow out bottom of loaf, leaving a ½-in. shell (discard removed bread or save for another use).

2 In a bowl, combine the remaining ingredients. Spoon into bread shell; replace top. Wrap in foil. Bake at 350° for 25 minutes or until cheese is melted. Slice and serve warm.

YIELD: 12 SERVINGS.

Mary Ann Marino, West Pittsburg, Pennsylvania
Here's a deliciously different sandwich. It's yummy warm from the oven or off the grill at a cookout. The cheesy filling is complemented by a mix of garden-fresh tomatoes and herbs and by crusty bread.

turkey tortilla spirals

¾ pound thinly sliced deli turkey

6 flour tortillas (8 inches)

1 package (8 ounces) fat-free cream cheese

6 tablespoons finely chopped pecans

1 can (16 ounces) whole-berry cranberry sauce, *divided*

¼ cup chopped celery

2 green onions, thinly sliced

1 Place turkey on tortillas to within ¼ in. of edge. Spread cream cheese over turkey; sprinkle with pecans. Spread each with 2 tablespoons cranberry sauce. Roll up jelly-roll style; wrap tightly in plastic wrap. Refrigerate for 1 hour or until firm.

2 Just before serving, cut each roll into six pieces. In a small bowl, combine the celery, onions and remaining cranberry sauce. Serve with tortilla spirals.

YIELD: 3 DOZEN.

Peggy Grieme, Pinehurst, North Carolina
No one suspects that these addictive pinwheels are light.
People are always surprised by how easy they are to make.

garlic-cheese flat bread

1 tube (13.8 ounces) refrigerated pizza crust

¼ cup butter, melted

4 garlic cloves, minced

1 tablespoon minced fresh basil

1 cup (4 ounces) shredded cheddar cheese

½ cup grated Romano cheese

¼ cup grated Parmesan cheese

Press dough into a greased 15-in. x 10-in. x 1-in. baking pan. In a small bowl, combine butter, garlic and basil; drizzle over dough. Sprinkle with the cheeses. Bake at 400° for 10-12 minutes or until crisp. Cut into squares. Serve warm.

YIELD: 12-15 SERVINGS.

Tom Hilliker, Lake Havasue City, Arizona

I use refrigerated pizza dough to create savory squares with Italian flair. Serve them with spaghetti sauce for dipping.

onion brie pizza

6 medium sweet onions, thinly sliced

¼ cup butter

1 package (16 ounces) hot roll mix

1¼ cups warm water (110° to 115°)

2 tablespoons olive oil

8 ounces Brie cheese, rind removed, and cut into small pieces

⅓ cup sliced almonds

1 In a large skillet, cook onions in butter over medium-low heat for 25 minutes or until golden brown, stirring occasionally.

2 Meanwhile, prepare hot roll mix according to package directions, using the warm water and oil. Place dough in a greased bowl, turning once to grease top. Cover and let stand for 5 minutes.

3 Roll out the dough to a 14-in. circle; transfer to a greased 14-in. pizza pan. Top with the onions, Brie and almonds. Bake at 400° for 18-20 minutes or until golden brown. Let stand for 10 minutes before cutting.

YIELD: 8 SLICES.

Cindy Bedell, West Layfayette, Indiana

This pizza is elegant enough for guests yet easy enough for family suppers.

beef 'n' cheese tortillas

1/2 cup garlic-herb cheese spread

4 flour tortillas (10 inches)

3/4 pound thinly sliced cooked roast beef

20 to 25 whole spinach leaves

11 to 12 sweet banana peppers

Spread about 2 tablespoons cheese spread over each tortilla. Layer with roast beef and spinach. Remove seeds from peppers and slice into thin strips; arrange over spinach. Roll up each tortilla tightly; wrap in plastic wrap. Refrigerate until ready to serve.

YIELD: 8 SERVINGS.

Myra Innes, Auburn, Kansas

I like to take these sandwiches along on our many outings. They can be made in advance and don't get soggy. You'll appreciate the convenience, and your family and friends will love the great taste!

chicken french bread pizza

1 loaf (1 pound) French bread

½ cup butter, softened

½ cup shredded cheddar cheese

⅓ cup grated Parmesan cheese

1 garlic clove, minced

¼ teaspoon Italian seasoning

1 can (10 ounces) chunk white chicken, drained and flaked

1 cup (4 ounces) shredded part-skim mozzarella cheese

½ cup chopped sweet red pepper

½ cup chopped green onions

1 Cut bread in half lengthwise, then in half widthwise. Combine the butter, cheddar, Parmesan, garlic and Italian seasoning; spread over bread. Top with the remaining ingredients. Place on a baking sheet.

2 Bake at 350° for 10-12 minutes or until cheese is melted. Cut into smaller pieces if desired.

YIELD: 8 SERVINGS.

Laura Mahaffey, Annapolis, Maryland
This pizza makes a hearty snack for a game
night with friends or as an after-school treat.

ham and cheese bread

1 package (16 ounces) frozen chopped broccoli

2 loaves (1 pound *each*) frozen bread dough, thawed

3 cups (12 ounces) shredded cheese (cheddar, Swiss *and/or* Monterey Jack)

2 cups finely chopped fully cooked ham

2 tablespoons butter, melted

1 teaspoon poppy seeds

1 Cook broccoli according to package directions. Drain and cool.

2 Roll each loaf of dough into a 15-in. x 10-in. rectangle. Place one in a greased 15-in. x 10-in. x 1-in. baking pan. Sprinkle with the broccoli, cheese and ham to within 1/2 in. of edges. Place second rectangle on top, sealing edges.

3 Brush the top with butter; sprinkle with poppy seeds. Bake at 350° for 35-40 minutes or until golden brown. Serve warm.

YIELD: 10-12 SERVINGS.

Marian Christensen, Sumner, Michigan

Ham and cheese baked inside bread dough makes a hearty appetizer. The broccoli adds a bit of color.

tree and star crab sandwiches

¾ cup mayonnaise

¾ cup shredded sharp cheddar cheese

1 can (6 ounces) crabmeat, drained, flaked and cartilage removed

2 tablespoons prepared French salad dressing

½ teaspoon prepared horseradish

Dash hot pepper sauce

48 bread slices

Fresh dill sprigs

In a bowl, combine the first six ingredients; set aside. Using 2½-in. cookie cutters, cut stars and Christmas trees out of bread (two stars or trees from each slice). Spread half of the cutouts with crab mixture; top with remaining cutouts. Garnish with dill.

YIELD: 4 DOZEN.

Karen Gardiner, Eutaw, Alabama

To cool off during summer—or any season at all—try a finger food that starts with a flavorful crab filling. I regularly serve the spread at Christmas get-togethers. It's a hit every time. For man-size sandwiches, there's no need to use cookie cutters.

chicken quesadillas

4 cups all-purpose flour

1½ teaspoons salt

½ teaspoon baking powder

1 cup shortening

1¼ cups warm water

1 cup *each* shredded cheddar, part-skim mozzarella and pepper Jack cheese

2 cups diced cooked chicken

1 cup sliced green onions

1 cup sliced ripe olives

1 can (4 ounces) chopped green chilies, drained

Salsa and sour cream

1 In a bowl, combine the flour, salt and baking powder. Cut in shortening until crumbly. Add enough warm water, stirring until mixture forms a ball. Let stand for 10 minutes. Divide into 28 portions.

2 On a lightly floured surface, roll each portion into a 7-in. circle. Cook on a lightly greased griddle for 1½ to 2 minutes on each side, breaking any bubbles with a toothpick if necessary. Keep warm.

3 In a bowl, combine the cheeses. For each quesadilla, place a tortilla on the griddle; sprinkle with about 2 tablespoons cheese mixture, 2 tablespoons chicken, 1 tablespoon onions, 1 tablespoon olives and 1 teaspoon chilies. Top with 1 tablespoon cheese mixture and another tortilla. Cook for 30-60 seconds; turn and cook 30 seconds longer or until cheese is melted. Cut into wedges. Serve with the salsa and sour cream.

YIELD: 14 QUESADILLAS.

Linda Miller, Klamath Falls, Oregon

Tender homemade tortillas make this savory snack, filled with chicken and melted cheese, extra-special.

ham buns

½ cup butter, softened

1 small onion, grated

1 tablespoon poppy seeds

2 teaspoons Worcestershire sauce

2 teaspoons prepared mustard

1¼ cups finely chopped fully cooked ham (about 8 ounces)

1 cup (4 ounces) shredded Swiss cheese

16 to 20 mini buns, split

1 In a bowl, combine the butter, onion, poppy seeds, Worcestershire sauce and mustard. Add ham and cheese; mix well. Divide evenly among buns.

2 Place in a shallow baking pan and cover with foil. Bake at 350° for 15 to 20 minutes or until hot.

YIELD: 16-20 APPETIZERS.

Esther Shank, Harrisonburg, Virginia

These tasty sandwiches are a great way to use leftover ham. Friends with whom I've shared the recipe tell me they disappear fast at potlucks. Use 6-8 hamburger buns for an easy meal.

mozzarella pepperoni bread

1 loaf (1 pound) French bread

3 tablespoons butter, melted

3 ounces sliced turkey pepperoni

1½ cups (6 ounces) shredded part-skim mozzarella cheese

3 tablespoons minced fresh parsley

1 Cut loaf of bread in half widthwise; cut into 1-in. slices, leaving slices attached at bottom. Brush butter on both sides of each slice. Arrange pepperoni between slices; sprinkle with cheese and parsley.

2 Place on an ungreased baking sheet. Bake at 350° for 12-15 minutes or until cheese is melted.

YIELD: 24 SLICES.

Terri Toti, San Antonio, Texas

My family enjoys this tempting bread as an appetizer whenever we have company and as a quick dinner on hectic evenings.

pepper-crusted tenderloin crostini

2 large onions, thinly sliced

6 tablespoons butter, softened, *divided*

2 teaspoons sugar

1 tablespoon olive oil

1 beef tenderloin roast (1½ pounds)

2 to 3 teaspoons coarsely ground pepper

2 garlic cloves, minced

¾ teaspoon salt

2 teaspoons prepared horseradish

1 French bread baguette (10½ ounces), cut into 30 slices

Minced fresh parsley

1 In a large skillet over medium-low heat, cook onions in 3 tablespoons butter for 5 minutes or until tender. Add sugar; cook over low heat for 30-40 minutes longer or until onions are golden brown, stirring frequently.

2 Meanwhile, rub oil over tenderloin. Combine the pepper, garlic and salt; rub over beef. In a large skillet, brown beef on all sides. Transfer to a baking sheet. Bake at 425° for 20-25 minutes or until meat reaches desired doneness (for medium-rare, a meat thermometer should read 145°; medium, 160°; well-done, 170°). Let stand for 10 minutes.

3 In a small bowl, beat horseradish and remaining butter until blended. Spread over bread slices. Place on a baking sheet. Broil 3-4 in. from heat for 2-3 minutes or until lightly golden brown.

4 Thinly slice the beef; place on toasted bread. Top with caramelized onions. Garnish with parsley.

YIELD: 2½ DOZEN.

Taste of Home Test Kitchen

Caramelized onions add a touch of sweetness to this elegant hors d'oeuvre.

artichoke veggie pizza

1 tube (13.8 ounces) refrigerated pizza crust

1 package (8 ounces) cream cheese, softened

1/2 cup sun-dried tomato spread

1 can (14 ounces) water-packed artichoke hearts, rinsed, drained and finely chopped

1/2 cup chopped sweet onion

1 can (4 1/4 ounces) chopped ripe olives, drained

3/4 cup sliced carrots

3/4 cup chopped green pepper

1 1/2 cups fresh broccoli florets, chopped

1 cup (4 ounces) shredded Italian cheese blend

1 Press pizza dough into a greased 15-in. x 10-in. x 1-in. baking pan. Prick dough thoroughly with a fork. Bake at 400° for 13-15 minutes or until golden brown. Cool.

2 In a small mixing bowl, beat cream cheese and tomato spread until blended. Stir in the artichokes. Spread over the crust. Sprinkle with the onion, olives, carrots, green pepper, broccoli and cheese; press down lightly. Refrigerate for 1 hour. Cut the pizza into squares. Refrigerate leftovers.

YIELD: 36 SERVINGS.

Taste of Home Test Kitchen

A sun-dried tomato spread is used as the base for this vegetable-laden appetizer.

double sausage pizza

1 package (16 ounces) hot roll mix

2 tablespoons garlic powder

2 tablespoons dried oregano

2 tablespoons Italian seasoning

1¼ cups warm water (120° to 130°)

2 tablespoons vegetable oil

1 can (15 ounces) pizza sauce

½ cup grated Parmesan cheese

1 pound bulk pork sausage, cooked and crumbled

½ pound sliced fresh mushrooms

1 package (8 ounces) sliced pepperoni

4 cups (28 ounces) shredded part-skim mozzarella cheese

1 In a large bowl, combine the hot roll mix, contents of yeast packet, garlic powder, oregano and Italian seasoning. Stir in water and oil until dough pulls away from sides of bowl. Turn dough onto a lightly floured surface. Shape into a ball. Knead for 5 minutes or until smooth. Cover and let stand for 5 minutes.

2 Divide dough in half. With greased hands, press dough onto two greased 12-in. pizza pans. Prick dough thoroughly with a fork. Spread crusts with pizza sauce. Top with the Parmesan cheese, sausage, mushrooms, pepperoni and mozzarella cheese. Bake at 425° for 18-20 minutes or until cheese is melted.

YIELD: 2 PIZZAS (8-10 SLICES EACH).

Emalee Satoski, Union Mills, Indiana

This recipe has been in the family since I was a kid. It was a Sunday night ritual then, and remains one today in my home. A dressed-up hot roll mix gives us enough dough for two flavorful crusts, so there is plenty of sausage-pepperoni pizza to serve guests at a party.

kielbasa bundles

½ pound fully cooked kielbasa *or* Polish sausage, chopped

1 small onion, chopped

¼ cup chopped green pepper

1 garlic clove, minced

1 tablespoon butter

⅓ cup barbecue sauce

2 tubes (8 ounces *each*) refrigerated crescent rolls

4 slices process American cheese, halved

1 egg white

1 tablespoon water

Sesame seeds

1 In a large skillet, cook sausage for 5-8 minutes; drain. Add the onion, green pepper, garlic and butter; cook until vegetables are tender. Stir in barbecue sauce; heat through.

2 Unroll crescent roll dough and separate into eight rectangles; seal perforations. Place a cheese slice on half of each rectangle; top with 2 tablespoons sausage mixture. Fold dough over filling and pinch edges to seal; fold seam under. Beat egg white and water; brush over dough. Sprinkle with sesame seeds.

3 Place bundles seam side down on greased baking sheets. Bake at 350° for 15-18 minutes or until golden brown.

YIELD: 8 SERVINGS.

Robin Touchey, San Angelo, Texas
My family really enjoys these flavorful sandwiches.
They make great, hearty additions to buffet tables.

herbed onion focaccia

Melanie Eddy, Manhattan, Kansas

This recipe makes three savory flat breads, but don't be surprised to see them all disappear from the table!

1 tablespoon active dry yeast

1 teaspoon sugar

1½ cups warm water (110° to 115°), *divided*

6 tablespoons olive oil, *divided*

2 teaspoons salt

4 to 4½ cups all-purpose flour

3 tablespoons finely chopped green onions

1½ teaspoons minced fresh rosemary *or* ½ teaspoon dried rosemary, crushed

1½ teaspoons small fresh sage leaves *or* ½ teaspoon rubbed sage

1½ teaspoons minced fresh oregano plus ½ teaspoon dried oregano

Seasoned olive oil *or* additional olive oil, optional

1 In a large mixing bowl, dissolve yeast and sugar in ½ cup warm water; let stand for 5 minutes. Add 4 tablespoons oil, salt, 2 cups flour and remaining water. Beat until smooth. Stir enough remaining flour to form a soft dough.

2 Turn onto a floured surface; knead until smooth and elastic, about 6-8 minutes. Place in a greased bowl, turning once to grease top. Cover and let rise in a warm place until doubled, about 1 hour.

3 Punch dough down. Divide into three portions. Cover and let rest for 10 minutes. Shape each portion into an 8-in. circle; place on greased baking sheets. Cover and let rise until doubled, about 30 minutes.

4 Using the end of a wooden spoon handle, make several ¼-in. indentations in each loaf. Brush with remaining oil. Sprinkle with green onions, rosemary, sage and oregano. Bake at 400° for 20-25 minutes or until golden brown. Remove to wire racks. Serve with olive oil for dipping if desired.

YIELD: 3 LOAVES.

cranberry camembert pizza

1 tube (13.8 ounces) refrigerated pizza crust

8 ounces Camembert *or* Brie cheese, rind removed and cut into ½-inch cubes

¾ cup whole-berry cranberry sauce

½ cup chopped pecans

1 Unroll crust onto a lightly greased 12-in. pizza pan; flatten dough and build up edges slightly. Bake at 425° for 10-12 minutes or until light golden brown.

2 Sprinkle cheese over crust. Spoon cranberry sauce evenly over crust; sprinkle with pecans. Bake 8-10 minutes longer or until the cheese is melted and crust is golden brown. Cool for 5 minutes before cutting.

YIELD: 12-14 SLICES.

Heidi Mellon, Waukesha, Wisconsin
After I'd tasted this quick, yummy pizza at a party, I just knew I had to have the recipe. I've been serving it in my household for years, and it always disappears in minutes.

guacamole turkey subs

1 package (3 ounces) cream cheese, softened

1/3 cup prepared guacamole

1/4 cup picante sauce

3 submarine sandwich buns (about 8 inches), split

1 1/2 cups shredded lettuce

1 medium tomato, thinly sliced

9 slices smoked deli turkey

9 bacon strips, cooked and drained

In a bowl, combine the cream cheese, guacamole and picante sauce; spread over cut side of buns. On bun bottoms, layer half of the lettuce, all of the tomato, turkey and bacon, then remaining lettuce. Replace tops. Cut sandwiches in half; wrap in plastic wrap. Refrigerate until serving.

YIELD: 6 SERVINGS.

Marci McDonald, Amarillo, Texas

This may sound like a strange combination, but it is without a doubt the best sandwich you'll ever eat!

salsa strips

1 tube (8 ounces) refrigerated crescent rolls

2 tablespoons Dijon mustard

3/4 cup salsa

1 cup (4 ounces) shredded part-skim mozzarella cheese

Minced fresh cilantro

1 Unroll crescent roll dough and separate into four rectangles. Place on greased baking sheets. Spread mustard and salsa on each rectangle.

2 Bake at 350° for 10 minutes. Sprinkle with cheese; bake 8-10 minutes longer or until golden brown. Cool for 10 minutes. Cut each into four strips; sprinkle with cilantro.

YIELD: 16 APPETIZERS.

Joann Woloszyn, Fredonia, New York

Refrigerated crescent rolls make these crisp Southwestern appetizers a breeze to prepare. Choose mild, medium or hot salsa to suit your taste.

game day faves

194

206

Getting together to watch the game? You can't go wrong with these snacks. Be sure to have plenty of napkins on hand when you serve these saucy specialties, including Orange-Glazed Chicken Wings (p. 203), Glazed Meatballs (p. 195), Stuffed Butterflied Shrimp (p. 194) and Chicken Bacon Bites (p. 206).

To make last-minute preparations simple, choose recipes you can whip up the day before and just reheat when the gang arrives.

cranberry meatballs and sausage

1 egg, beaten

1 small onion, finely chopped

¾ cup dry bread crumbs

1 tablespoon dried parsley flakes

1 tablespoon Worcestershire sauce

¼ teaspoon salt

1 pound bulk pork sausage

1 can (16 ounces) jellied cranberry sauce

3 tablespoons cider vinegar

2 tablespoons brown sugar

1 tablespoon prepared mustard

1 package (1 pound) miniature smoked sausage links

1 In a large bowl, combine the first six ingredients. Crumble bulk sausage over the mixture and mix well. Shape into 1-in. balls. In a large skillet, cook meatballs over medium heat until browned; drain.

2 In a large saucepan, combine the cranberry sauce, vinegar, brown sugar and mustard. Cook and stir over medium heat until cranberry sauce is melted. Add the meatballs and sausage links. Bring to a boil. Reduce heat; simmer, uncovered, for 10-15 minutes or until meatballs are no longer pink and sauce is slightly thickened.

YIELD: 14-16 SERVINGS.

Marybell Lintott, Vernon, British Columbia
Years ago, I found a version of this recipe in a cookbook. At first taste, my family judged it a keeper. The tangy, saucy meatballs are requested by our friends whenever I host a party. The bites are great when camping, too.

bandito chicken wings

12 whole chicken wings
   (about 2 pounds)

½ teaspoon salt

⅛ teaspoon pepper

½ cup butter, *divided*

2 tablespoons vegetable oil

½ cup taco sauce

¼ cup barbecue sauce

¼ cup French salad dressing

1 teaspoon Worcestershire sauce

⅛ teaspoon hot pepper sauce

1 Cut chicken wings into three sections; discard wing tips. Sprinkle wings with salt and pepper. In a skillet, melt 2 tablespoons butter with oil over medium. Fry chicken until brown, about 6-8 minutes on each side. Place in a greased 13-in. x 9-in. baking dish.

2 In a saucepan, combine the taco sauce, barbecue sauce, French dressing, Worcestershire sauce, hot pepper sauce and the remaining butter; cook and stir over medium heat until butter is melted and sauce is blended. Pour ½ cup over the chicken wings.

3 Bake, uncovered, at 325° for 15-20 minutes or until chicken juices run clear. Serve with the remaining sauce.

YIELD: 8-10 SERVINGS.

EDITOR'S NOTE: This recipe was prepared with the first and second sections of the chicken wings.

Gloria Jarrett, Loveland, Ohio
These fantastic wings make a mouthwatering,
hot and spicy appetizer.

buffalo chicken-topped potatoes

Michelle Gauer, Spicer, Minnesota

If your favorite appetizers are cheesy potato skins and buffalo chicken wings, you'll find this recipe one to cheer about. Loaded with cheese, sour cream and chicken, these hearty stuffed potatoes get a sassy bite from mild wing sauce.

4 medium potatoes (about 1½ pounds)

¾ cup shredded cheddar cheese, *divided*

½ cup sour cream

2 tablespoons buffalo wing sauce, *divided*

1 pound boneless skinless chicken breasts, cubed

¼ teaspoon salt

¼ teaspoon chili powder

1 tablespoon canola oil

2 tablespoons white vinegar

2 tablespoons butter

Additional sour cream and chopped green onions

1 Scrub and pierce potatoes. Bake at 375° for 1 hour or until tender. When cool enough to handle, cut each potato in half lengthwise. Scoop out the pulp, leaving thin shells.

2 In a large bowl, mash the pulp with 1/2 cup cheese, sour cream and 1 tablespoon buffalo wing sauce. Spoon the mixture into potato shells. Sprinkle with remaining cheese.

3 Place on a baking sheet. Bake 8-12 minutes longer or until heated through. Meanwhile, sprinkle chicken with salt and chili powder.

4 In a large skillet, cook chicken in oil over medium heat for 6-8 minutes or until no longer pink. Stir in the vinegar, butter and remaining buffalo wing sauce; cook and stir 2-3 minutes longer.

5 Spoon chicken mixture over potatoes. Serve with additional sour cream and onions.

YIELD: 8 SERVINGS.

mini chimichangas

1 pound ground beef

1 medium onion, chopped

1 envelope taco seasoning

¾ cup water

3 cups (12 ounces) shredded Monterey Jack cheese

1 cup (8 ounces) sour cream

1 can (4 ounces) chopped green chilies, drained

1 package (1 pound) egg roll wrappers (14 count)

1 egg white, lightly beaten

Oil for deep-fat frying

Salsa and additional sour cream

1 In a large skillet, cook beef and onion over medium heat until meat is no longer pink; drain. Stir in taco seasoning and water. Bring to a boil. Reduce heat; simmer, uncovered, for 5 minutes, stirring occasionally. Remove from the heat; cool slightly.

2 In a large bowl, combine the cheese, sour cream and chilies. Stir in beef mixture. Place an egg roll wrapper on work surface with one point facing you. Place ⅓ cup filling in center. Fold bottom third of wrapper over filling; fold in sides.

3 Brush top point with egg white; roll up to seal. Repeat with remaining wrappers and filling. (Keep remaining egg roll wrappers covered with waxed paper to avoid drying out.)

4 In a large saucepan, heat 1 in. of oil to 375°. Fry chimichangas for 1½ minutes on each side or until golden brown. Drain on paper towels. Serve warm with salsa and sour cream.

YIELD: 14 SERVINGS.

Kathy Rogers, Hudson, Ohio

Welcome your gang with this south-of-the-border specialty! Hearty enough to serve as a meal, these flavorful and filling chimichangas draw raves whenever I serve them.

party time cheeseburgers

1 egg, lightly beaten

2 tablespoons dill pickle relish

2 tablespoons ketchup

2 teaspoons Worcestershire sauce

2 teaspoons prepared mustard

¼ cup quick-cooking oats

¼ teaspoon pepper

⅛ teaspoon garlic powder

1 pound ground beef

3 slices process American cheese

10 dinner rolls, split

1 In a large bowl, combine the first eight ingredients. Crumble beef over mixture and mix well. Shape into 10 patties. Broil 3-4 in. from the heat for 4-6 minutes on each side or until a meat thermometer reads 160° and juices run clear.

2 Meanwhile, using a 1-in. round cookie cutter, cut out 10 shapes from cheese slices. Immediately place on burgers; serve on rolls.

YIELD: 10 SERVINGS.

Taste of Home Test Kitchen

Kids of all ages love the taste of these moist and mouthwatering mini burgers. Juiced up with pickle relish and topped with cheese slices, these "sliders" will disappear before halftime.

stuffed butterflied shrimp

24 uncooked unpeeled large shrimp

1 cup Italian salad dressing

1½ cups seasoned bread crumbs

1 can (6½ ounces) chopped clams, drained and minced

6 tablespoons butter, melted

1½ teaspoons minced fresh parsley

1 Peel shrimp, leaving tail section on. Make a deep cut along the top of each shrimp (do not cut all the way through); remove the vein. Place shrimp in a shallow dish; add salad dressing. Set aside for 20 minutes.

2 Meanwhile, in a large bowl, combine the bread crumbs, clams, butter and parsley. Drain shrimp, discarding salad dressing. Arrange in a greased 13-in. x 9-in. baking dish. Open shrimp and press flat; fill each with 1 tablespoon of crumb mixture. Bake, uncovered, at 350° for 20-25 minutes or until shrimp turn pink.

YIELD: 2 DOZEN.

Joan Elliott, Deep River, Connecticut

These flavorful shrimp make a great appetizer or even an entree. I've handed out this recipe to many friends and family members.

glazed meatballs

2 eggs

²/₃ cup milk

1¼ cups soft bread crumbs

1 tablespoon prepared horseradish

1½ pounds ground beef

1 cup water

½ cup chili sauce

½ cup ketchup

¼ cup maple syrup

¼ cup soy sauce

1½ teaspoons ground allspice

½ teaspoon ground mustard

1 In a bowl, beat eggs and milk. Stir in bread crumbs and horseradish. Crumble beef over mixture and mix well. Shape into 1½-in. balls.

2 Place in a lightly greased 15-in. x 10-in. x 1-in. baking pan. Bake at 375° for 15-20 minutes or until meat is no longer pink.

3 In a large saucepan, combine the remaining ingredients. Bring to a boil; add the meatballs. Reduce heat; cover and simmer for 15 minutes or until heated through, stirring occasionally.

YIELD: ABOUT 3½ DOZEN.

Nancy Horsburgh, Everett, Ontario

Allspice adds a bit of a twist to the barbecue-style sauce used in this recipe.

garlic-cheese chicken wings

2 large whole garlic bulbs

1 tablespoon plus ½ cup olive oil, *divided*

½ cup butter, melted

1 teaspoon hot pepper sauce

1½ cups seasoned bread crumbs

¾ cup grated Parmesan cheese

¾ cup grated Romano cheese

½ teaspoon pepper

15 whole chicken wings (about 3 pounds)

1 Remove papery outer skin from garlic (do not peel or separate cloves). Cut top off garlic bulbs. Brush with 1 tablespoon oil. Wrap each bulb in heavy-duty foil. Bake at 425° for 30-35 minutes or until softened. Cool for 10-15 minutes.

2 Squeeze the softened garlic into a blender or food processor. Add butter, hot pepper sauce and remaining oil; cover and process until smooth. Pour into a shallow bowl. In another shallow bowl, combine the bread crumbs, cheeses and pepper.

3 Cut chicken wings into three sections; discard wing tip section.

4 Dip chicken wings into the garlic mixture, then coat with crumb mixture. Place on a greased rack in a 15-in. x 10-in. x 1-in. baking pan; drizzle with any remaining garlic mixture. Bake, uncovered, at 350° for 50-55 minutes or until chicken juices run clear.

YIELD: 2½ DOZEN.

EDITOR'S NOTE: 3 pounds of uncooked chicken wing sections (wingettes) may be substituted for the whole chicken wings. Omit the third step.

Donna Pierce, Lady Lake, Florida

I developed this recipe several years ago using chicken breasts, then decided to try it on wings as an appetizer. It was a hit! If you like garlic, you're sure to enjoy these tender, zesty bites.

flavorful sausage balls

1 pound bulk pork sausage

1 egg, beaten

1/2 cup dry bread crumbs

3/4 cup ketchup

1/4 cup packed brown sugar

2 tablespoons white vinegar

2 tablespoons soy sauce

1 In a bowl, combine sausage and egg. Sprinkle with bread crumbs; mix well. Shape into 1-in. balls.

2 In a skillet, brown meatballs; drain. Combine remaining ingredients; pour over meatballs. Simmer for 10 minutes or until meat is no longer pink.

YIELD: 2 1/2 DOZEN.

Olive Lamb, Cushing, Oklahoma

I whip up a batch of these meatballs in a matter of minutes. They're a great treat on busy days when you need something fast that's full of flavor.

three-cheese dunk

2 cups (16 ounces) 4% cottage cheese, drained

3 tablespoons mayonnaise

1 tablespoon prepared horseradish

1 tablespoon spicy brown mustard

1/4 teaspoon salt

1/8 teaspoon pepper

1 cup (4 ounces) finely shredded cheddar cheese

1/2 cup crumbled blue cheese

3 green onions, finely chopped

Sliced fresh pears *or* apples, assorted vegetables *or* crackers

1 In a food processor, combine the cottage cheese, mayonnaise, horseradish, mustard, salt and pepper; cover and process until blended.

2 Transfer to a small bowl. Fold in the cheddar cheese, blue cheese and onions. Cover and refrigerate for 1 hour or until chilled. Serve with pears, apples, vegetables or crackers.

YIELD: 3 CUPS.

Ms. Bibs Orr, Oceanside, California

Cottage cheese lends to the creaminess of this versatile dip.

touchdown cookies

1 cup butter, softened

1 cup sugar

2 eggs

1 teaspoon vanilla extract

3 cups all-purpose flour

2 teaspoons cream of tartar

1 teaspoon baking soda

GLAZE:

2 cups confectioners' sugar

4 to 5 tablespoons hot water

3 to 4 teaspoons baking cocoa

1 In a large bowl, cream butter and sugar until light and fluffy. Add eggs, one at a time, beating well after each addition. Beat in vanilla. Combine the flour, cream of tartar and baking soda; gradually add to creamed mixture and mix well. Cover and refrigerate for 3 hours or until easy to handle.

2 On a lightly floured surface, roll out dough to 1/8-in. thickness. Cut with a football-shaped cookie cutter. Place 2 in. apart on ungreased baking sheets.

3 Bake at 350° for 8-10 minutes or until lightly browned. Remove to wire racks to cool.

4 In a large bowl, combine confectioners' sugar and enough hot water to achieve spreading consistency; beat until smooth. Place 3 tablespoons glaze in a small bowl; set aside.

5 Add cocoa to the remaining glaze; stir until smooth. Spread the brown glaze over cookies. Pipe white glaze onto the cookies to form football laces.

YIELD: 4½ DOZEN.

Sister Judith LaBrozzi, Canton, Ohio

With some simple sweet touches, you can transform regular sugar cookies into a special treat for football fans.

nuggets with chili sauce

1 cup chicken broth

2 cans (4 ounces *each*) chopped green chilies

2 medium onions, diced

3 tablespoons butter

1 tablespoon chili powder

2 teaspoons ground cumin

2 garlic cloves, minced

¼ cup packed brown sugar

¼ cup orange juice

¼ cup ketchup

2 tablespoons lemon juice

CHICKEN NUGGETS:

½ cup cornmeal

1 tablespoon chili powder

2 teaspoons ground cumin

¼ teaspoon salt

1½ pounds boneless skinless chicken breasts, cut into 1-inch cubes

3 tablespoons vegetable oil

1 In blender or food processor, combine broth and chilies; cover and process until pureed. Set aside. In a large skillet, saute onions in butter until tender. Stir in the chili powder, cumin, garlic and pureed mixture. Bring to a boil. Reduce heat to low; simmer, uncovered, for 20 minutes, stirring occasionally.

2 Add the brown sugar, orange juice, ketchup and lemon juice. Cook and stir over low heat for 15 minutes or until thickened; keep warm.

3 For nuggets, combine the cornmeal, chili powder, cumin and salt in a large resealable plastic bag. Add chicken pieces, a few at a time; shake to coat. Heat oil in skillet; cook chicken for 6-8 minutes or until juices run clear, turning frequently. Serve with sauce.

YIELD: 4 SERVINGS.

Diane Hixon, Niceville, Florida

These crisp golden bites of chicken taste better than the fast-food versions. The chili sauce really sets them apart from any others.

crowd-pleasing ravioli nachos

1 package (25 ounces) frozen cheese ravioli

1 package (25 ounces) frozen sausage ravioli

3 eggs, lightly beaten

2 cups seasoned bread crumbs

2 tablespoons grated Parmesan cheese

1/4 teaspoon crushed red pepper flakes

1/4 teaspoon pepper

1/8 teaspoon garlic salt

Oil for deep-fat frying

3/4 cup Alfredo sauce

3/4 cup spaghetti sauce

2 cups (8 ounces) shredded cheddar cheese

5 green onions, sliced

1 can (3.8 ounces) sliced ripe olives, drained

Additional spaghetti sauce, optional

1 Cook ravioli according to package directions. Drain and pat dry. Place eggs in a shallow bowl. In another shallow bowl, combine the bread crumbs, Parmesan cheese, pepper flakes, pepper and garlic salt. Dip ravioli in the eggs, then bread crumb mixture.

2 In an electric skillet or deep-fat fryer, heat oil to 375°. Fry ravioli, a few at a time, for 1-2 minutes on each side or until golden brown. Drain on paper towels.

3 Arrange ravioli in an ungreased 15-in. x 10-in. x 1-in. baking pan. Spoon sauces over ravioli; sprinkle with cheddar cheese.

4 Bake at 350° for 3-5 minutes or until cheese is melted. Sprinkle with onions and olives. Serve immediately with additional spaghetti sauce if desired.

YIELD: 6½ DOZEN.

Robert Doornbos, Jenison, Michigan

Lightly breaded and deep-fried, ravioli goes to a new level in this hearty appetizer. Kids and grown-ups can't get enough of the crispy, cheesy snacks.

savory coconut bites

2 cups flaked coconut

1 egg

2 tablespoons milk

¾ pound boneless skinless chicken breasts, cut into ¾-inch pieces

½ cup all-purpose flour

Oil for deep-fat frying

1 teaspoon celery salt

½ teaspoon garlic powder

½ teaspoon ground cumin

1 In a blender or food processor, process coconut until finely chopped. Transfer to a bowl and set aside. In another bowl, combine egg and milk. Toss chicken with flour; dip in egg mixture, then in coconut. Place in a single layer on a baking sheet. Refrigerate for 30 minutes.

2 In an electric skillet or deep-fat fryer, heat 2 in. of oil to 375°. Fry chicken, a few pieces at time, for 1½ minutes on each side or until golden brown. Drain on paper towels; place in a bowl. Sprinkle with celery salt, garlic powder and cumin; toss to coat. Serve warm.

YIELD: 3 DOZEN.

Linda Schwarz, Bertrand, Nebraska
These tender nuggets are great for nibbling, thanks to the coconut and seasonings. I've served the bites several times at parties, and everyone always enjoys them.

chicken meatball appetizers

2½ cups minced cooked chicken breast

3 tablespoons finely chopped onion

3 tablespoons finely chopped celery

2 tablespoons finely chopped carrot

2 tablespoons dry bread crumbs

1 egg white

½ teaspoon poultry seasoning

Pinch pepper

In a bowl, combine all ingredients; mix well. Shape into ¾-in. balls; place on a baking sheet that has been coated with cooking spray. Bake at 400° for 8-10 minutes or until lightly browned.

YIELD: ABOUT 2½ DOZEN.

Norma Snider, Chambersburg, Pennsylvania
Here's a crowd-pleasing change of pace on the appetizer tray. Try these chicken meatballs plain or dipped in mustard.

pizza fondue

½ pound ground beef

1 cup chopped fresh mushrooms

1 medium onion, chopped

1 garlic clove, minced

1 tablespoon cornstarch

1½ teaspoons fennel seed

1½ teaspoons dried oregano

¼ teaspoon garlic powder

2 cans (15 ounces *each*) pizza sauce

2½ cups (10 ounces) shredded cheddar cheese

1 cup (4 ounces) shredded part-skim mozzarella cheese

2 tablespoons chopped ripe olives

Breadsticks, bagel chips, baked pita chips *and/or* tortilla chips

1 In a large skillet, cook the beef, mushrooms and onion over medium heat until meat is no longer pink. Add garlic; cook 1 minute longer. Drain. Stir in the cornstarch, fennel, oregano and garlic powder until blended. Stir in pizza sauce.

2 Bring to a boil; cook and stir for 1-2 minutes or until thickened. Gradually stir in cheeses until melted. Stir in olives. Keep warm. Serve with breadsticks, bagel chips, pita chips and/or tortilla chips.

YIELD: 5½ CUPS.

Margaret Schissler, Milwaukee, Wisconsin
Great for a game-day gathering or any party, this hearty appetizer can also be made with Italian sausage instead of ground beef. Add a little more pizza sauce if the mixture seems too thick.

orange-glazed chicken wings

15 whole chicken wings (about 3 pounds)

1½ cups soy sauce

1 cup orange juice

1 teaspoon garlic powder

1 Cut chicken wings into three sections; discard wing tips. In a large resealable plastic bag, combine the soy sauce, orange juice and garlic powder; add wings. Seal bag and turn to coat; refrigerate wings overnight.

2 Drain and discard marinade. Place chicken wings in a greased foil-lined 15-in. x 10-in. x 1-in. baking pan. Bake at 350° for 1 hour or until juices run clear and glaze is set, turning twice.

YIELD: 2½ DOZEN.

EDITOR'S NOTE: 3 pounds of uncooked chicken wingettes may be substituted for the whole chicken wings. Omit the first step.

Holly Mann, Amherst, New Hampshire
I normally don't care for wings, but after trying this recipe from a co-worker, I changed my mind. The tangy glaze is finger-licking-good!

pigskin sandwiches

1 package (¼ ounce) active
   dry yeast

½ cup sugar, *divided*

2 cups warm water (110° to 115°),
   divided

½ cup plus 2 tablespoons butter,
   softened, *divided*

1½ teaspoons salt

1 egg, lightly beaten

6½ to 7 cups all-purpose flour

Mayonnaise *or* mustard, optional

Lettuce leaves and sliced tomatoes

18 slices process American cheese

2½ pounds sliced deli ham

4 ounces cream cheese, softened

1 In a large bowl, dissolve yeast and 2 teaspoons sugar in ¼ cup warm water. Let stand for 5 minutes. Add ½ cup butter, salt, egg, 4 cups flour and remaining sugar and water. Beat until smooth. Stir in enough remaining flour to form a soft dough.

2 Turn onto a floured surface; knead until smooth and elastic, about 6-8 minutes. Place in a greased bowl, turning once to grease top. Cover and let rise in a warm place until doubled, about 1 hour.

3 Punch dough down. Turn onto a lightly floured surface; divide into 18 pieces. Shape into ovals; place 2 in. apart on greased baking sheets. Cover and let rise until doubled, about 30 minutes.

4 Bake at 350° for 18-23 minutes or until golden. Melt remaining butter; brush over buns. Remove from pans to wire racks to cool.

5 Split buns. Spread with mayonnaise or mustard if desired. Top with lettuce, tomato, cheese and ham. Replace tops. Place cream cheese in a plastic bag; cut a small hole in the corner of the bag. Pipe football laces on sandwiches.

YIELD: 18 SERVINGS.

Sister Judith LaBrozzi, Canton, Ohio

Guests won't need much coaching to run for sandwiches when they're served on tasty, homemade football buns.

sweet-and-sour sausages

2 packages (16 ounces *each*) miniature smoked sausages

2 tablespoons butter

1 can (15¼ ounces) sliced peaches, drained and halved

1 cup chili sauce

¾ cup sugar

½ cup ketchup

1 teaspoon dried minced onion

1 teaspoon curry powder

1 In a large skillet, brown sausages in butter. In a large bowl, combine the remaining ingredients; stir in the sausages. Transfer to a greased 2-qt. baking dish.

2 Bake, uncovered, at 350° for 30 minutes. Stir; bake 15 minutes longer or until bubbly.

YIELD: 18 SERVINGS.

Dorothy Anderson, Langley, British Columbia

A perfect buffet appetizer, these zesty links also make a great main course. I've prepared them so often that I can recite the recipe from memory.

skewered shrimp

3 tablespoons soy sauce

2 tablespoons lemon juice

1 tablespoon chili sauce

1 tablespoon minced fresh gingerroot

1 pound uncooked medium shrimp, peeled and deveined

1 In a bowl, combine the soy sauce, lemon juice, chili sauce and ginger; mix well. Pour half into a large resealable plastic bag; add the shrimp. Seal bag and turn to coat; refrigerate for 2 hours. Cover and refrigerate remaining marinade.

2 Drain and discard marinade from shrimp. Thread onto metal or soaked wooden skewers. Grill, uncovered, over medium heat for 6-8 minutes or until shrimp turn pink, turning once. Serve with reserved marinade.

YIELD: 4 SERVINGS.

Joan Morris, Lillian, Alabama

A ginger mixture is used as both a marinade and a sauce for these barbecued shrimp. Serve them with toothpicks as an appetizer or stir into pasta for an entree.

chicken bacon bites

Betty Pierson, Wellington, Florida

Ginger and orange marmalade give these rumaki-style snacks wonderful flavor. I marinate the wrapped chicken earlier in the day and broil them when guests arrive.

12 bacon strips, halved

10 ounces boneless skinless chicken breasts, cut into 24 cubes

1 can (8 ounces) sliced water chestnuts, drained

½ cup orange marmalade

¼ cup soy sauce

2 garlic cloves, minced

1 teaspoon grated fresh gingerroot

1 Place bacon on a broiler rack. Broil 4 in. from the heat for 1-2 minutes on each side or until partially cooked; cool.

2 Wrap a piece of bacon around a chicken cube and water chestnut slice; secure with a toothpick. In a resealable plastic bag, combine the marmalade, soy sauce, garlic and ginger. Add wrapped chicken; carefully turn to coat. Seal and refrigerate for 2 hours.

3 Drain and discard marinade. Broil chicken for 3-4 minutes on each side or until juices run clear and bacon is crisp. Serve warm.

YIELD: 2 DOZEN.

fiery potato chips

4 medium unpeeled potatoes

4 teaspoons salt, *divided*

4 cups ice water

1 tablespoon chili powder

1 teaspoon garlic salt

1 teaspoon dried parsley flakes

¼ to ½ teaspoon cayenne pepper

Oil for deep-fat frying

1 Using a vegetable peeler or metal cheese slicer, cut potatoes into very thin lengthwise strips. Place in a large bowl; add 3 teaspoons salt and ice water. Soak for 30 minutes; drain.

2 Place potatoes on paper towels and pat dry. In a small bowl, combine the chili powder, garlic salt, parsley, cayenne and remaining salt; set aside.

3 In an electric skillet or deep-fat fryer, heat oil to 375°. Cook potatoes in oil in batches for 2-3 minutes or until deep golden brown, stirring frequently.

4 Remove with a slotted spoon; drain on paper towels. Immediately sprinkle with reserved seasoning mixture. Store in an airtight container.

YIELD: 10 CUPS.

Sue Murphy, Greenwood, Michigan

Seasoned with chili powder and cayenne pepper, these paper-thin chips are surefire crowd-pleasers.

golden seafood bites

1 can (6 ounces) crabmeat, drained, flaked and cartilage removed

¾ cup seasoned bread crumbs, *divided*

¼ cup finely chopped celery

¼ cup frozen cooked tiny shrimp, thawed

1 egg, lightly beaten

1 green onion, sliced

1 tablespoon chopped sweet red pepper

1 tablespoon milk

1 teaspoon garlic powder

½ teaspoon dried parsley flakes

½ teaspoon seafood seasoning

½ teaspoon pepper

1 cup crushed butter-flavored crackers (about 25 crackers)

1 egg white, lightly beaten

Oil for deep-fat frying

1 In a large mixing bowl, combine the crab, ¼ cup bread crumbs, celery, shrimp, egg, onion, red pepper, milk, garlic powder, parsley, seafood seasoning and pepper. Shape into 1-in. balls.

2 Place the cracker crumbs, egg white and remaining bread crumbs in separate shallow bowls. Roll balls in bread crumbs; dip in egg white, then roll in cracker crumbs.

3 In an electric skillet or deep-fat fryer, heat oil to 375°. Fry a few balls at a time for 1-2 minutes on each side or until golden brown. Drain on paper towels. Serve warm.

YIELD: 1½ DOZEN.

Helen McLain, Quinlan, Texas

After sampling a similar appetizer at a local restaurant, I went home to create my own. Family and friends like my version even better!

tijuana tidbits

12 cups popped popcorn

4 cups bite-size tortilla chips

3 cups Crispix

1 can (11½ ounces) mixed nuts

½ cup butter, cubed

½ cup light corn syrup

½ cup packed brown sugar

3 teaspoons chili powder

¼ teaspoon salt

⅛ to ¼ teaspoon cayenne pepper

⅛ teaspoon ground cinnamon

1 In a large greased roasting pan, combine the popcorn, tortilla chips, cereal and nuts.

2 In a small saucepan, combine the remaining ingredients. Bring to a boil, stirring constantly. Pour over popcorn mixture, toss to coat.

3 Bake, uncovered, at 250° for 1 hour, stirring every 20 minutes. Cool on waxed paper. Store in an airtight container.

YIELD: 4¾ QUARTS.

Beverly Phillips, Duncanville, Texas

Tortilla chips, chili powder and cayenne pepper lend to the Mexican flavor of this snack mix, while corn syrup and brown sugar add a bit of sweetness.

courtside caramel corn

6 quarts popped popcorn

2 cups packed brown sugar

1 cup butter, cubed

½ cup corn syrup

1 teaspoon salt

3 teaspoons vanilla extract

½ teaspoon baking soda

1 Place popcorn in a large bowl and set aside. In a large saucepan, combine the brown sugar, butter, corn syrup and salt; bring to a boil over medium heat, stirring constantly. Boil for 5 minutes, stirring occasionally.

2 Remove from the heat. Stir in vanilla and baking soda; mix well. Pour over popcorn and stir until well-coated. Pour into two greased 13-in. x 9-in. baking pans.

3 Bake, uncovered, at 250° for 45 minutes, stirring every 15 minutes. Cool completely. Store in airtight containers.

YIELD: ABOUT 5½ QUARTS.

Sharon Landeen, Tucson, Arizona

"I can't stop eating it!" is what guests say about my caramel corn. For a basketball party, I fixed enough to fill a big tin decorated with our team's logo.

chicken satay

Sue Gronholz, Beaver Dam, Wisconsin

These golden skewered chicken snacks are marinated and grilled, then served with a zesty Thai-style peanut butter sauce.

2 pounds boneless skinless chicken breasts

$\frac{1}{2}$ cup milk

6 garlic cloves, minced

1 tablespoon brown sugar

1 tablespoon *each* ground coriander, ground turmeric and ground cumin

1 teaspoon salt

1 teaspoon white pepper

$\frac{1}{8}$ teaspoon coconut extract

PEANUT BUTTER SAUCE:

$\frac{1}{3}$ cup peanut butter

$\frac{1}{3}$ cup milk

2 green onions, chopped

1 small jalapeno pepper, seeded and finely chopped

2 to 3 tablespoons lime juice

2 tablespoons soy sauce

1 garlic clove, minced

1 teaspoon sugar

1 teaspoon minced fresh cilantro

1 teaspoon minced fresh gingerroot

$\frac{1}{8}$ teaspoon coconut extract

1 Flatten chicken to $\frac{1}{4}$-in. thickness; cut lengthwise into 1-in.-wide strips. In a large resealable plastic bag, combine the milk, garlic, brown sugar, seasonings and extract. Add chicken; seal bag and turn to coat. Refrigerate for 8 hours or overnight.

2 In a bowl, whisk the sauce ingredients until blended. Cover and refrigerate until serving.

3 Drain and discard marinade from chicken. Thread two chicken strips onto each metal or soaked wooden skewer. Grill, uncovered, over medium-hot heat for 2-3 minutes on each side or until chicken juices run clear. Serve with peanut butter sauce.

YIELD: 8 SERVINGS (1 CUP SAUCE).

EDITOR'S NOTE: When cutting or seeding hot peppers, use rubber or plastic gloves to protect your hands. Avoid touching your face.

shrimp on rosemary skewers

8 fresh rosemary sprigs, about 6 inches long

½ cup orange marmalade

½ cup flaked coconut, chopped

¼ teaspoon crushed red pepper flakes

¼ teaspoon minced fresh rosemary

1½ pounds uncooked large shrimp, peeled and deveined

1 Soak rosemary sprigs in water for 30 minutes. In a small bowl, combine the marmalade, coconut, pepper flakes and minced rosemary; set aside ¼ cup for serving.

2 Coat grill rack with nonstick cooking spray before starting the grill. Thread shrimp onto rosemary sprigs. Grill for 4 minutes. Turn; baste with some of the remaining marmalade mixture. Grill 3-4 minutes longer or until shrimp turn pink; baste again. Serve with reserved marmalade mixture.

YIELD: 8 SERVINGS.

Amber Joy Newport, Hampton, Virginia
Fresh springs of rosemary are the clever skewers for these shrimp kabobs. You can serve this as an appetizer or as a main course.

pizza egg rolls

1 package (3½ ounces) sliced pepperoni, chopped

1 cup chopped fresh mushrooms

1 medium green pepper, chopped

½ cup grated Parmesan cheese

½ teaspoon pizza seasoning *or* Italian seasoning

14 egg roll wrappers

14 pieces string cheese

Oil for deep-fat frying

1 can (15 ounces) pizza sauce, warmed

1 In a small bowl, combine the pepperoni, mushrooms, green pepper, Parmesan cheese and pizza seasoning. Place an egg roll wrapper on a work surface with a point facing you; place a piece of string cheese near the bottom corner. Top with about 2 tablespoons pepperoni mixture.

2 Fold bottom corner over filling. Fold sides toward center over filling. Using a pastry brush, wet the top corner with water; roll up tightly to seal. Repeat with remaining wrappers, cheese and filling.

3 In an electric skillet or deep-fat fryer, heat oil to 375°. Fry egg rolls, a few at a time, for 1-2 minutes on each side or until golden brown. Drain on paper towels. Serve with pizza sauce.

YIELD: 14 EGG ROLLS.

Taste of Home Test Kitchen

We gave traditional pizza a twist by rolling up the usual toppings in egg roll wrappers, then deep-frying them. Yum!

horseradish cheese spread

1 package (16 ounces) process cheese (Velveeta), cubed

¾ cup mayonnaise

⅓ cup prepared horseradish

¼ cup milk

⅛ teaspoon hot pepper sauce

Baked soft pretzels, optional

In a heavy saucepan over low heat, combine the cheese, mayonnaise, horseradish, milk and pepper sauce. Cook and stir until cheese is melted and mixture is blended. Serve with pretzels if desired.

YIELD: 2½ CUPS.

Cathy Bodell, Frankfort, Michigan

Cheesy, thick and rich, this flavorful dip stays put on freshly baked soft pretzels. It's also delicious spread on slices of crusty French bread.

honey garlic ribs

6 pounds pork baby back ribs, cut into two-rib portions

2 cups water, *divided*

¾ cup packed brown sugar

2 tablespoons cornstarch

1 teaspoon garlic powder

¼ teaspoon ground ginger

½ cup honey

¼ cup soy sauce

1 Place ribs bone side down in a large roasting pan; pour 1 cup of water over ribs. Cover tightly and bake at 350° for 1½ hours.

2 In a small bowl, combine the brown sugar, cornstarch, garlic powder and ginger. Stir in the honey, soy sauce and remaining water until smooth. Drain fat from roasting pan; pour the sauce over the ribs.

3 Bake, uncovered, for 45 minutes or until meat is tender.

YIELD: 24 SERVINGS.

Lily-Michele Alexis, Louisville, Kentucky

When you want a real "meaty" appetizer for your game-day buffet, reach for these finger-licking-good ribs!

homemade crisp crackers

1¾ cups all-purpose flour

½ cup cornmeal

½ teaspoon baking soda

½ teaspoon sugar

½ teaspoon salt

½ teaspoon garlic powder

¼ teaspoon Italian seasoning

½ cup cold butter, cubed

1½ cups (6 ounces) shredded
   Colby-Monterey Jack cheese

½ cup plus 2 tablespoons
   cold water

2 tablespoons cider vinegar

1 In a large bowl, combine the first seven ingredients; cut in butter until crumbly. Stir in cheese. Gradually add water and vinegar, tossing with a fork until dough forms a ball. Wrap in plastic wrap and refrigerate for 1 hour or until firm.

2 Divide into six portions. On a lightly floured surface, roll each portion into an 8-in. circle. Cut into eight wedges and place on greased baking sheets.

3 Bake at 375° for 17-20 minutes or until edges are lightly browned. Cool on wire racks. Store in an airtight container.

YIELD: 4 DOZEN.

Taste of Home Test Kitchen
Store-bought crackers have nothing on these cheesy crisps. Make them in advance and keep them handy in an airtight container for anytime snacking.

cowboy beef dip

Jessica Klym, Killdeer, North Dakota

A group of us in a foods class developed this recipe for 1995's North Dakota State Beef Bash Competition. We won the contest, and now my family requests this dip for all our special gatherings!

1 pound ground beef

4 tablespoons chopped onion, *divided*

3 tablespoons chopped sweet red pepper, *divided*

2 tablespoons chopped green pepper, *divided*

1 can (10¾ ounces) condensed nacho cheese soup, undiluted

½ cup salsa

4 tablespoons sliced ripe olives, *divided*

4 tablespoons sliced pimiento-stuffed olives, *divided*

2 tablespoons chopped green chilies

1 teaspoon chopped seeded jalapeno pepper

¼ teaspoon dried oregano

¼ teaspoon pepper

¼ cup shredded cheddar cheese

2 tablespoons sour cream

2 to 3 teaspoons minced fresh parsley

Tortilla chips

1 In a large skillet, cook the beef, 3 tablespoons onion, 2 tablespoons red pepper and 1 tablespoon green pepper over medium heat until meat is no longer pink; drain. Stir in the soup, salsa, 3 tablespoons ripe olives, 3 tablespoons pimiento-stuffed olives, chilies, jalapeno, oregano and pepper. Bring to a boil. Reduce heat; simmer, uncovered, for 5 minutes.

2 Transfer to a serving dish. Top with the cheese, sour cream and parsley; sprinkle with the remaining onion, peppers and olives. Serve with tortilla chips.

YIELD: 3 CUPS.

EDITOR'S NOTE: When cutting hot peppers, disposable gloves are recommended. Avoid touching your face.

flavored oyster crackers

2 packages (10 ounces *each*)
  oyster crackers

½ cup canola oil

¼ cup grated Parmesan cheese

1 envelope savory herb with
  garlic soup mix

1 Place the crackers in a large bowl. Combine the oil, cheese and soup mix; pour over crackers and toss gently. Transfer to two ungreased 15-in. x 10-in. x 1-in. baking pans.

2 Bake at 350° for 5-7 minutes, stirring once. Let cool completely. Store in an airtight container.

YIELD: 12 CUPS.

Taste of Home Test Kitchen

These jazzed-up oyster crackers have such great flavor, we bet you'll have trouble not eating them all at once! With Parmesan cheese and seasoning from a soup mix, they're a sure-fire hit on game day.

crispy shrimp poppers

20 uncooked medium shrimp, peeled and deveined

4 ounces cream cheese, softened

10 bacon strips

1 cup all-purpose flour

2 eggs, lightly beaten

2 cups panko (Japanese) bread crumbs

Oil for deep-fat frying

1 Butterfly the shrimp along the outside curves. Spread about 1 teaspoon of cream cheese inside each shrimp. Cut the bacon strips in half lengthwise; wrap a piece of bacon around each shrimp and secure with toothpicks.

2 In three separate shallow bowls, place the flour, eggs and bread crumbs. Coat the shrimp with flour; dip into eggs, then coat with bread crumbs.

3 In an electric skillet or deep-fat fryer, heat oil to 375°. Fry shrimp, a few at a time, for 3-4 minutes or until golden brown. Drain on paper towels. Discard toothpicks before serving.

YIELD: 20 APPETIZERS.

Jacquelynne Stine, Las Vegas, Nevada

A crisp, golden coating surrounds these butterflied shrimp stuffed with bacon and cream cheese. You'll want to make a meal out of them!

grilled glazed drummies

1 cup ketchup

⅓ cup soy sauce

4 teaspoons honey

¾ teaspoon ground ginger

½ teaspoon garlic powder

3 pounds fresh *or* frozen chicken drumettes, thawed

1 In a small bowl, combine the first five ingredients. Pour 1 cup marinade into a large resealable plastic bag. Add the chicken; seal bag and turn to coat. Refrigerate for at least 4 hours or overnight. Cover and refrigerate remaining marinade for basting.

2 Drain chicken and discard marinade. Grill, covered, over medium heat for 15-20 minutes or until juices run clear, turning and basting occasionally with reserved marinade.

YIELD: ABOUT 2 DOZEN.

Laura Mahaffey, Annapolis, Maryland
It's nice to have a wing recipe you can prepare on the grill. My family actually prefers these mild-tasting snacks to traditional hot wings.

mexican chicken roll-ups

2½ teaspoons cornmeal, *divided*

2¼ cups cubed cooked chicken

1 cup (4 ounces) shredded cheddar cheese

½ cup sliced ripe olives

½ cup sour cream

1 can (4 ounces) chopped green chilies, drained

¼ cup chopped onion

2 tubes (8 ounces *each*) refrigerated crescent rolls

1 egg white

1 tablespoon water

Salsa

1 Grease a baking sheet and sprinkle with 1½ teaspoons cornmeal; set aside. In a large bowl, combine the chicken, cheese, olives, sour cream, chilies and onion; set aside.

2 Separate crescent dough into eight rectangles; firmly press perforations to seal. Spread ½ cup chicken mixture over each rectangle to within 1 in. of edges. Roll up, starting from long side. Place 1 in. apart on prepared pan.

3 In a small bowl, beat the egg white and water until foamy; brush over the roll-ups. Sprinkle with the remaining cornmeal. Bake at 375° for 20-25 minutes or until golden brown. Serve warm with salsa. Refrigerate leftovers.

YIELD: 8 SERVINGS.

Julie McDaniel, Batesville, Indiana

Refrigerated crescent rolls make these hearty appetizers easy to assemble. Keep the ingredients on hand for last-minute snacking.

hot mustard popcorn

1 teaspoon ground mustard

½ teaspoon dried thyme

½ teaspoon salt

¼ teaspoon pepper

Dash cayenne pepper

3 quarts freshly popped popcorn

Combine the first five ingredients. Place popcorn in a large bowl; add seasonings and toss to coat.

YIELD: 3 QUARTS.

Diane Hixon, Niceville, Florida

When friends pop over, I like to dish up yummy munchies like this one.

tex-mex dip

1 can (16 ounces) refried beans

¼ cup picante sauce

1½ cups prepared guacamole

½ cup sour cream

½ cup mayonnaise

4½ teaspoons taco seasoning

1 cup (4 ounces) shredded cheddar cheese

1 can (2¼ ounces) sliced ripe olives, drained

Chopped green onions, shredded lettuce and chopped tomatoes

Tortilla chips

1 In a small bowl, combine the beans and picante sauce. Spread onto a serving platter. Spread with guacamole.

2 In another small bowl, combine the sour cream, mayonnaise and taco seasoning; spread over guacamole. Sprinkle with cheese, olives, onions, lettuce and tomatoes. Refrigerate until serving. Serve with tortilla chips.

YIELD: 12-14 SERVINGS.

Terri Newton, Marshall, Texas

Perfect for a party, this dip is a real crowd-pleaser.
Ingredients in the recipe blend very well, and it makes
a large platter of dip.

spicy chicken appetizer pizza

½ cup rice vinegar

¼ cup reduced-sodium soy sauce

1 cup chopped green onions, *divided*

4 garlic cloves, minced

3 teaspoons olive oil, *divided*

½ teaspoon pepper

¼ teaspoon cayenne pepper

¾ pound boneless skinless chicken breasts, cut into ½-inch pieces

1 tablespoon cornstarch

1 prebaked 12-inch thin pizza crust

¼ cup shredded Monterey Jack cheese

¼ cup shredded part-skim mozzarella cheese

2 tablespoons sliced almonds

1 In a small bowl, combine the vinegar, soy sauce, ½ cup onions, garlic, 1 teaspoon oil, pepper and cayenne. Pour ½ cup into a large resealable plastic bag; add the chicken. Seal the bag and turn to coat; refrigerate for 30 minutes. Cover and refrigerate the remaining marinade.

2 Drain chicken, discarding marinade. In a large nonstick skillet over medium heat, cook chicken in remaining oil until no longer pink. Combine cornstarch and reserved marinade until blended; stir into skillet. Bring to a boil; cook and stir for 2 minutes or until thickened. Remove from the heat.

3 Place the crust on an ungreased baking sheet; top with chicken mixture. Sprinkle with cheeses. Bake at 400° for 12 minutes. Top with almonds and remaining onions. Bake 2-3 minutes longer or until cheese is golden brown.

YIELD: 12 SLICES.

Michelle Martin, Waterville, Ohio

This flavorful pizza uses marinated chicken and a surprise ingredient—almonds—to pack a tasty punch.

prosciutto chicken kabobs

¼ cup five-cheese Italian salad dressing

¼ cup lime juice

2 teaspoons white Worcestershire sauce for chicken

½ pound boneless skinless chicken breasts, cut into 3-in. x ½-in. strips

12 thin slices prosciutto

24 fresh basil leaves

AVOCADO DIP:

2 medium ripe avocados, peeled

¼ cup minced fresh cilantro

2 green onions, chopped

2 tablespoons lime juice

2 tablespoons mayonnaise

1½ teaspoons prepared horseradish

1 garlic clove, minced

¼ teaspoon salt

1 In a large resealable plastic bag, combine the salad dressing, lime juice and Worcestershire sauce; add chicken. Seal bag and turn to coat; refrigerate for 1 hour.

2 Drain and discard the marinade. Fold the prosciutto slices in half; top each with two basil leaves and a chicken strip. Roll up jelly-roll style, starting with a short side. Thread onto metal or soaked wooden skewers.

3 Grill, covered, over medium heat for 5 minutes on each side or until chicken is no longer pink.

4 Meanwhile, in a small bowl, mash the avocados. Stir in the cilantro, onions, lime juice, mayonnaise, horseradish, garlic and salt. Serve with the kabobs.

YIELD: 12 APPETIZERS.

Elaine Sweet, Dallas, Texas

Everyone will think you spent hours preparing these clever grilled wraps which are served with a guacamole-like dip. Basil gives the chicken a lovely, fresh herb flavor.

cashew brittle

1 cup sugar

½ cup light corn syrup

1 to 1½ cups salted cashew halves

1 teaspoon butter

1 teaspoon baking soda

1 teaspoon vanilla extract

1 In a microwave-safe bowl, combine the sugar and corn syrup. Microwave, uncovered, on high for 3 minutes; stir. Heat 2 minutes longer. Stir in the cashews and butter. Microwave on high for 20-50 seconds or until the mixture turns a light amber (the mixture will be very hot).

2 Quickly stir in baking soda and vanilla until light and foamy. Immediately pour onto a greased baking sheet and spread with a metal spatula. Chill for 20 minutes or until set; break into small pieces. Store in an airtight container.

YIELD: ¾ POUND.

EDITOR'S NOTE: This recipe was tested in a 1,100-watt microwave.

Rhonda Glenn, Prince Frederick, Maryland

I like this quick-and-easy recipe because it doesn't require a candy thermometer. It also makes a great gift.

pretzels with mustard

½ cup Dijon mustard

⅓ cup honey

1 tablespoon white wine vinegar

2 teaspoons sugar

Large soft pretzels, warmed

In a small bowl, whisk the mustard, honey, vinegar and sugar until blended. Serve with soft pretzels.

YIELD: ¾ CUP.

Taste of Home Test Kitchen

The sauce for this wonderful treat adds an almost-homemade note to appetizer buffets. It also makes a great after-school snack.

crunchy munchies

232

231

Let your guests nibble and nosh on crisp, flavorful treats of popcorn, snack mixes and seasoned nuts while you entertain. Sweet or savory—there's a lot to choose from, such as Deluxe Caramel Corn (p. 239), Harvest Snack Mix (p. 232) and Cinnamon 'n' Spice Pecans (p. 231).

Set out these easy-to-make snacks in bowls with scoops or serve them up in popcorn bags, large paper cups or small brown paper lunch bags. Kids and adults will love them! These recipes are also great on road trips, are perfect for tailgating and promise to bring big money at bake sales.

cajun party mix

6 cups miniature fish-shaped crackers

6 cups pretzel sticks

3 cups Rice Chex

3 cups Corn Chex

1 can (11½ ounces) mixed nuts

1 cup butter, melted

1 teaspoon garlic powder

½ to 1 teaspoon celery salt

½ teaspoon cayenne pepper

⅛ teaspoon hot pepper sauce

1 In a large roasting pan, combine the first five ingredients. Combine the butter, garlic powder, celery salt, cayenne and hot pepper sauce; pour over cereal mixture and stir to coat.

2 Bake, uncovered, at 250° for 35-40 minutes, stirring every 15 minutes. Cool completely. Store in airtight containers.

YIELD: ABOUT 5 QUARTS.

Twila Burkholder, Middleburg, Pennsylvania

I pack this mix in tins to give to friends and family. They can't seem to get enough—and it's so easy!

cinnamon 'n' spice pecans

⅓ cup butter, melted

2 teaspoons ground cinnamon

¾ teaspoon salt

½ teaspoon cayenne pepper

1 pound pecan halves

1 In a bowl, combine the butter, cinnamon, salt and cayenne. Stir in pecans until evenly coated.

2 Transfer to an ungreased 15-in. x 10-in. x 1-in. baking pan. Bake at 350° for 15-18 minutes or until pecans are toasted, stirring every 5 minutes. Cool completely. Store in an airtight container.

YIELD: 4 CUPS.

Terry Maly, Olathe, Kansas

Originally, these crunchy nuts were used to top a salad, but I adjusted the recipe so they could stand on their own as a snack. Cayenne pepper gives them a little kick, making the nuts a fun party starter.

harvest snack mix

Marlene Harguth, Maynard, Minnesota

Candy corn makes this a natural snack for fall gatherings. The sweet and salty flavors are irresistible to many.

2 cups pretzel sticks

1 cup mixed nuts

1/2 cup sunflower kernels

6 tablespoons butter, melted

1/2 teaspoon ground cinnamon

1/8 teaspoon ground cloves

8 cups popped popcorn

1 cup candy corn

1 cup chocolate bridge mix

1 In a large bowl, combine the pretzels, nuts and sunflower kernels. Combine the butter, cinnamon and cloves. Drizzle a third of butter mixture over pretzel mixture; toss to coat.

2 Transfer to a greased 15-in. x 10-in. x 1-in. baking pan. Bake at 300° for 15 minutes.

3 Place popcorn in a large bowl; drizzle with remaining butter mixture and toss to coat. Stir into pretzel mixture. Bake 15 minutes longer or until heated through. Cool; transfer to a large bowl. Add candy corn and bridge mix; toss to combine. Store in an airtight container.

YIELD: 3 QUARTS.

peanut butter chocolate pretzels

2 cups (12 ounces) semisweet chocolate chips

4 teaspoons vegetable oil, *divided*

35 to 40 large thin pretzel twists

½ cup peanut butter chips

1 In a microwave or heavy saucepan, melt chocolate chips and 3 teaspoons oil until smooth. Dip pretzels; shake off excess. Place on waxed paper-lined baking sheets to set.

2 Melt the peanut butter chips and remaining oil; transfer to a small resealable bag. Cut a small hole in the corner of bag; drizzle over half of the pretzels. Let dry. Store in an airtight container.

YIELD: ABOUT 3 DOZEN.

Marcia Porch, Winter Park, Florida

These treats are easy for any age to make but pretty enough to share with friends. You can add color sprinkles to customize them for any holiday or occasion.

honey snack mix

1 package (10 ounces) honey-flavored bear-shaped graham crackers (about 4 cups)

3 cups Honeycomb cereal

1½ cups Reese's Pieces

1 cup chocolate-covered raisins

In a large bowl, combine all of the ingredients. Store in an airtight container.

YIELD: 9 CUPS.

Taste of Home Test Kitchen

No one can resist gobbling up the crackers, cereal, raisins and candy in this sweet snack mix. It's perfet for children's birthday parties.

italian nut medley

2 tablespoons butter

4 cups mixed nuts

1 tablespoon soy sauce

1 envelope Italian salad dressing mix

In a skillet, melt the butter over medium heat. Add nuts; cook and stir constantly for 2 minutes. Stir in soy sauce. Sprinkle with salad dressing mix; stir to coat. Immediately transfer to a greased baking pan and spread in a single layer. Cool. Store in an airtight container.

YIELD: 4 CUPS.

Karen Riordan, Fern Creek, Kentucky

Italian salad dressing mix is my easy secret ingredient—it adds just the right zip to plain mixed nuts.

white chocolate party mix

16 cups popped popcorn

3 cups Frosted Cheerios

1½ cups pecan halves

1 package (14 ounces) milk chocolate M&M's

1 package (10 ounces) fat-free pretzel sticks

1 package English toffee bits (10 ounces) *or* almond brickle bits (7½ ounces)

2 packages (10 to 12 ounces *each*) vanilla *or* white chips

2 tablespoons vegetable oil

In a large bowl, combine the first six ingredients. In a microwave or heavy saucepan, melt the chips and oil; stir until smooth. Pour over the popcorn mixture and toss to coat. Immediately spread onto two baking sheets; let stand until dry, about 2 hours. Store in airtight containers.

YIELD: 9½ QUARTS.

Rose Wentzel, St. Louis, Missouri

I get rave reviews every time I prepare this tasty, crispy combination of cereal, popcorn, pretzels, nuts and candies. Coated in white chocolate, this mix is great for meetings, parties and gift giving.

cinnamon granola

2 cups old-fashioned oats

¾ cup whole unsalted nuts

⅔ cup flaked coconut

½ cup sunflower kernels

⅓ cup sesame seeds

⅓ cup toasted wheat germ

¼ cup oat bran

2 tablespoons cornmeal

2 tablespoons whole wheat flour

1 tablespoon ground cinnamon

½ cup honey

2 tablespoons vegetable oil

2 tablespoons vanilla extract

¼ teaspoon salt

1 cup golden raisins

1 In a large bowl, combine the first 10 ingredients; mix well. In a saucepan, heat honey and oil over medium heat for 4-5 minutes. Remove from the heat; stir in vanilla and salt. Pour over oat mixture and toss to coat.

2 Transfer to a greased 15-in. x 10-in. x 1-in. baking pan. Bake at 275° for 45-50 minutes or until golden brown, stirring every 15 minutes. Cool, stirring occasionally. Stir in raisins. Store in an airtight container.

YIELD: 7 CUPS.

Linda Agresta, Colorado Springs, Colorado
Although it's meant for breakfast, my family eats this
crunchy cereal by the handful all day long.

seasoned snack mix

3 cups Rice Chex

3 cups Corn Chex

3 cups Cheerios

3 cups pretzels

2 teaspoons Worcestershire sauce

2 teaspoons butter-flavored sprinkles

1/2 teaspoon garlic powder

1/2 teaspoon seasoned salt

1/2 teaspoon onion powder

1 In a 15-in. x 10-in. x 1-in. baking pan, combine cereals and pretzels. Lightly coat with nonstick cooking spray; drizzle with Worcestershire sauce. Combine remaining ingredients; sprinkle over cereal mixture.

2 Bake at 200° for 1 1/2 hours, stirring every 30 minutes. Cool completely. Store in an airtight container.

YIELD: 3 QUARTS.

Flo Burtnett, Gage, Oklahoma

You'll never miss the oil or nuts in this deliciously seasoned party mix. I keep some on hand for whenever the munchies strike.

tumbleweeds

1 can (12 ounces) salted peanuts

1 can (7 ounces) potato sticks

3 cups butterscotch chips

3 tablespoons peanut butter

1 Combine peanuts and potato sticks in a bowl; set aside. In a microwave, heat butterscotch chips and peanut butter at 70% power for 1-2 minutes or until melted, stirring every 30 seconds. Add to peanut mixture; stir to coat evenly.

2 Drop mixture by rounded tablespoonfuls onto waxed paper-lined baking sheets. Refrigerate until set, about 5 minutes. Store in an airtight container.

YIELD: ABOUT 4 1/2 DOZEN.

Victoria Johnson, Venice, Florida

I like making these crisp and creamy treats because they require only four ingredients. It's hard to stop eating them...they're irresistible!

deluxe caramel corn

4 quarts plain popped popcorn

5 cups mini pretzel twists

2 cups packed brown sugar

1 cup butter

½ cup dark corn syrup

½ teaspoon salt

½ teaspoon baking soda

1 cup salted peanuts

2 cups nonchocolate candy (Skittles, gumdrops, etc.)

1 Place popcorn and pretzels in a large bowl; set aside. In a large heavy saucepan, combine the brown sugar, butter, corn syrup and salt; cook over medium heat, stirring occasionally, until mixture comes to a rolling boil. Cook and stir until candy thermometer reads 238° (soft-ball stage). Remove from the heat; stir in baking soda. Quickly pour over popcorn and mix thoroughly; stir in peanuts.

2 Turn into two greased 13-in. x 9-in. baking pans. Bake at 200° for 20 minutes; stir. Bake 25 minutes longer. Remove from the oven; add the candy and mix well. Remove from the pans and place on waxed paper to cool. Break into clusters. Store in airtight containers or plastic bags.

YIELD: 6½ QUARTS.

EDITOR'S NOTE: You should test your candy thermometer each time you use it. To do this, simply place the thermometer in a saucepan of boiling water and wait for several minutes. If the thermometer reads 212° in boiling water, it is accurate. If it rises above 212° or does not reach 212°, add or subtract the difference to the temperature called for in the recipe you're making.

Lisa Claas, Watertown, Wisconsin
A batch of this colorful crunchy mix is perfect for serving at parties or movie nights.

spicy nuts

1 tablespoon vegetable oil

2 cups cashews *or* whole unblanched almonds

½ to 1 teaspoon cayenne pepper

½ teaspoon ground coriander

¼ teaspoon salt

Dash *each* ground cinnamon and cloves

1 In a heavy skillet, heat oil over medium heat; add nuts. Cook and stir for 3-5 minutes or until lightly browned; drain. Add the seasonings; stir to coat. Cool completely. Store in an airtight container. To serve warm, place in a baking pan. Heat at 300° for 5 minutes.

YIELD: 2 CUPS.

Laurene Nickel, Niagara on the Lake, Ontario

Cayenne pepper gives nuts a bit of a kick and a nice flavor contrast to the coriander, cinnamon and cloves. My son-in-law can't get enough of these crunchy treats.

zesty pretzel nuggets

4 packages (10 ounces *each*) pretzel nuggets

1 cup canola oil

1 envelope ranch salad dressing mix

1 tablespoon steak seasoning

2 to 3 teaspoons cayenne pepper

1 teaspoon dill weed

1 Place pretzels in a large bowl. In a small bowl, combine the oil, dressing mix, steak seasoning, cayenne and dill. Pour over pretzels; toss to coat evenly.

2 Transfer to two ungreased 15-in. x 10-in. x 1-in. baking pans. Bake at 250° for 50-60 minutes, stirring every 15 minutes. Cool. Store in an airtight container.

YIELD: 4 QUARTS.

EDITOR'S NOTE: This recipe was tested with McCormick's Montreal Steak Seasoning. Look for it in the spice aisle.

Joyce Daubert, Pine Grove, Pennsylvania

Ordinary pretzels just don't compare to these easily seasoned nuggets. I've been making them for guests for years and they never fail to please.

snackin' granola

2²/₃ cups flaked coconut

1 cup quick-cooking oats

¼ cup packed brown sugar

¼ cup raisins *or* chopped pitted dried plums

¼ cup chopped dried apricots

2 tablespoons sesame seeds

¼ cup vegetable oil

¼ cup honey

¼ cup semisweet chocolate chips *or* M&M's

1 In a large metal bowl, combine the first six ingredients. In a small saucepan, bring the oil and honey to just a boil. Immediately remove from the heat; pour over the coconut mixture, stirring to coat evenly.

2 Spread in an ungreased 13-in. x 9-in. baking pan. Bake at 325° for 25 minutes, stirring several times. Transfer to waxed paper to cool. Sprinkle with chocolate chips or M&M's. Store in an airtight container.

YIELD: 7 CUPS.

Marlene Mohr, Cincinnati, Ohio

Granola's a popular treat with children these days—and this one couldn't be more convenient to prepare. I flavor it with lots of tasty good-for-you ingredients. It's perfect to send in bag lunches or to serve after school. I've also used it as an in-the-car treat when we take family vacations.

sweet minglers

1 cup (6 ounces) semisweet chocolate chips

¼ cup creamy peanut butter

6 cups Corn or Rice Chex

1 cup confectioners' sugar

1 In a large microwave-safe bowl, melt chocolate chips on high for 1 minute. Stir; microwave 30 seconds longer or until the chips are melted. Stir in peanut butter. Gently stir in cereal until well coated; set aside.

2 Place confectioners' sugar in a 2-gallon plastic storage bag. Add cereal mixture and shake until well coated. Store in an airtight container in the refrigerator.

YIELD: ABOUT 6 CUPS.

Mary Obeilin, Selinsgrove, Pennsylvania

This mix is perfect for a late-night treat or a pick-me-up anytime of the day. I sometimes take a batch to work, and it's always eaten up quickly. It's slightly different because of the chocolate and peanut butter.

critter crunch

¼ cup butter

3 tablespoons brown sugar

1 teaspoon ground cinnamon

1½ cups Crispix

1½ cups Cherrios

1½ cups animal crackers

1½ cups honey-flavored bear-shaped graham crackers

1 cup bite-size Shredded Wheat

1 cup miniature pretzels

1 In a saucepan or microwave-safe bowl, heat the butter, brown sugar and cinnamon until butter is melted; mix well. In a large bowl, combine the remaining ingredients. Add butter mixture and toss to coat.

2 Place in a greased 15-in. x 10-in. x 1-in. baking pan. Bake, uncovered, at 300° for 30 minutes, stirring every 10 minutes. Store in an airtight container.

YIELD: ABOUT 8 CUPS.

Wilma Miller, Port Angeles, Washington

Young kids will enjoy this fun snack that features a variety of wild animals.

cheese ball snack mix

1½ cups salted cashews

1 cup crisp cheese balls snacks

1 cup Corn Chex

1 cup Rice Chex

1 cup miniature pretzels

1 cup chow mein noodles

½ cup butter, melted

1 tablespoon soy sauce

1 teaspoon Worcestershire sauce

½ teaspoon seasoned salt

¼ teaspoon chili powder

¼ teaspoon hot pepper sauce

1 In a bowl, combine the cashews, cheese balls, cereals, pretzels and chow mein noodles. In another bowl, combine all the remaining ingredients. Pour over cereal mixture and toss to coat.

2 Transfer to an ungreased 15-in. x 10-in. x 1-in. baking pan. Bake at 250° for 1 hour, stirring every 15 minutes. Cool completely. Store in an airtight container.

YIELD: ABOUT 6 CUPS.

EDITOR'S NOTE: This recipe was tested with Planter's Cheeze Balls.

Mary Detweiler, West Farmington, Ohio
Folks love the zippy burst of flavor in every bite
of this crunchy snack mix.

iced almonds

¼ cup butter

2½ cups whole unblanched almonds

1 cup sugar

1 teaspoon vanilla extract

1 In a heavy saucepan, melt butter over medium-high heat. Add almonds and sugar. Cook and stir constantly for 7-8 minutes or until syrup is golden brown. Remove from the heat; stir in vanilla.

2 Immediately drop by clusters or separate almonds on a greased baking pan. Cool. Store in an airtight container.

YIELD: 4 CUPS.

Susan Marie Taccone, Erie, Pennsylvania

These sweet almonds make a special nibble on their own. You can also use them to dress up a salad or to garnish a dessert.

pretzel snackers

2 packages (16 ounces *each*) sourdough pretzel nuggets

1 envelope ranch salad dressing mix

1½ teaspoons dried oregano

1 teaspoon lemon-pepper seasoning

1 teaspoon dill weed

½ teaspoon garlic powder

½ teaspoon onion powder

¼ cup olive oil

1 Place pretzels in a large bowl. In a small bowl, combine the dressing mix, oregano, lemon-pepper, dill weed, garlic powder and onion powder. Sprinkle over pretzels; toss gently to combine. Drizzle with oil; toss until well coated.

2 Spread in a 15-in. x 10-in. x 1-in. baking pan coated with nonstick cooking spray. Bake, uncovered, at 350° for 10 minutes. Stir and bake 5 minutes longer. Cool completely. Store in airtight containers.

YIELD: 10 CUPS.

Elissa Armbruster, Medford, New Jersey

I first served this when my husband's aunt came to visit and she asked for the recipe. She has since reported that all her friends enjoy it as much as we do! The recipe can easily be doubled or tripled.

cracker snack mix

12 cups original flavor Bugles

6 cups miniature pretzels

1 package (11 ounces) miniature butter-flavored crackers

1 package (10 ounces) Wheat Thins

1 package (9¼ ounces) Cheese Nips

1 package (7½ ounces) nacho cheese Bugles

1 package (6 ounces) miniature Parmesan fish-shaped crackers

1 cup mixed nuts *or* peanuts

1 bottle (10 *or* 12 ounces) butter-flavored popcorn oil

2 envelopes ranch salad dressing mix

1 In a very large bowl, combine the first eight ingredients. In a small bowl, combine oil and salad dressing mix. Pour over cracker mixture; toss to coat evenly.

2 Transfer to four ungreased 15-in. x 10-in. x 1-in. baking pans. Bake at 250° for 45 minutes, stirring every 15 minutes. Cool completely, stirring several times. Store in airtight containers.

YIELD: ABOUT 8 QUARTS.

Sharon Nichols, Brookings, South Dakota

Family and friends will munch this fun mix of crackers, nuts and ranch dressing by the handfuls! Everyone is sure to find something they like. If not, substitute other snack packages to vary the flavors.

chocolaty popcorn

12 cups butter-flavored microwave popcorn

1 package (12 ounces) semisweet chocolate chips

2 teaspoons shortening, *divided*

1 package (10 to 12 ounces) vanilla *or* white chips

2 cups coarsely chopped pecans, toasted

1 Place the popcorn in a greased 15-in. x 10-in. x 1-in. pan; set aside. Place semisweet chocolate chips and 1 teaspoon shortening in a microwave-safe bowl. Microwave, uncovered, at 70% power for 1 minute; stir until smooth. Drizzle over popcorn.

2 Place vanilla chips and remaining shortening in a microwave-safe bowl. Microwave, uncovered, at 70% power for 1 minute; stir until smooth. Drizzle over popcorn; toss gently to coat as much popcorn as possible. Sprinkle with pecans. Chill until firm before breaking into pieces. Store in airtight containers.

YIELD: 16 CUPS.

EDITOR'S NOTE: This recipe was tested in a 1,100-watt microwave.

Diane Halferty, Corpus Christi, Texas
Pack this irresistible sweet treat into wax or plastic bags and tie them shut with curling ribbons for a pretty presentation. You could also prepare a batch or two for a holiday bake sale. I guarantee it'll go quickly!

spiced pecans

Tari Ambler, Shorewood, Illinois

I usually make at least 2 batches of these nuts at a time and package in containers to give as hostess gifts.

2 tablespoons sugar

1 teaspoon pumpkin
pie spice

½ teaspoon salt

½ teaspoon ground ginger

2 tablespoons water

2 tablespoons honey

2 teaspoons canola oil

1¼ pounds pecan halves
(about 5 cups)

1 Combine the sugar, pie spice, salt and ginger; set aside. In a Dutch oven, bring the water, honey and oil to a boil. Add pecans; cook and stir until all of the liquid is evaporated, about 1 minute. Immediately sprinkle with reserved sugar mixture; toss to coat.

2 Transfer pecans to an ungreased 15-in. x 10-in. x 1-in. baking sheet. Bake at 325° for 15-20 minutes or until browned, stirring twice. Cool on a wire rack. Store in an airtight container.

YIELD: 5 CUPS.

striped popcorn mix

12 cups popped popcorn

2 cups miniature pretzels

1 cup pecan halves, toasted

1/4 cup butter, melted

4 ounces white candy coating, coarsely chopped

2 ounces milk chocolate candy coating, coarsely chopped

1 In a large bowl, combine the popcorn, pretzels and pecans. Drizzle with butter and toss; set aside.

2 In a microwave, melt white candy coating at 70% power for 1 minute; stir. Microwave at additional 10- to 20-second intervals, stirring until smooth. Drizzle over popcorn mixture; toss to coat. Spread on foil-lined baking sheets.

3 In a microwave, melt milk chocolate coating; stir until smooth. Drizzle over popcorn mixture. Let stand in a cool place until chocolate is set. Store in airtight containers.

YIELD: 17 CUPS.

EDITOR'S NOTE: This recipe was tested in a 1,100-watt microwave.

Mary Schmittinger, Colgate, Wisconsin
I'd seen chocolate popcorn in a candy shop and thought
I'd try making it. This recipe was a great success.

motoring munchies

1 package (18 ounces) granola without raisins

1 can (17 ounces) mixed nuts

1 package (15 ounces) raisins

1 package (14 ounces) milk chocolate M&M's

1 package (14 ounces) peanut M&M's

1 package (12¼ ounces) Honey-Nut Cheerios

1 package (8.9 ounces) Cheerios

In a large bowl, combine all ingredients. Store in an airtight container or large resealable plastic bags.

YIELD: 4½ QUARTS.

Nancy Schlinger, Middleport, New York
While taking a long car trip, we all snacked on these munchies and didn't even need to stop for dinner.

chocolate wheat cereal snacks

6 cups frosted bite-size Shredded Wheat

1 cup milk chocolate chips

¼ cup creamy peanut butter

1 cup confectioners' sugar

1 Place cereal in a large bowl; set aside. In a microwave, melt chocolate chips and peanut butter; stir until smooth. Pour over cereal and stir gently to coat. Let stand for 10 minutes.

2 Sprinkle with confectioners' sugar and toss to coat. Cool completely. Store in an airtight container.

YIELD: 6 CUPS.

Tracy Golder, Bloomsburg, Pennsylvania
This crunchy mix is great for any gathering or even a late night snack. The chocolate-peanut butter combination satisfies a sweet tooth.

vanilla caramel corn

3 packages (3.3 ounces *each*) butter-flavored microwave popcorn

1⅓ cups packed brown sugar

½ cup light corn syrup

⅔ cup sweetened condensed milk

½ cup butter, cubed

1 teaspoon vanilla extract

1 Pop popcorn according to manufacturer's directions. Transfer to two very large bowls; discard any unpopped kernels.

2 In a large heavy saucepan, combine brown sugar and corn syrup. Bring to a boil over medium heat; cook and stir for 3 minutes. Carefully stir in milk and butter; return to a boil.

3 Remove from the heat; stir in vanilla. Pour over popcorn and toss to coat. Spread in a single layer on greased 15-in. x 10-in. x 1-in. baking pans.

4 Bake at 250° for 40 minutes, stirring once. Remove from the pans and place on waxed paper to cool. Break into clusters. Store in airtight containers.

YIELD: 7 QUARTS.

Janel Andrews, Jerome, Idaho

This recipe gives a sweet and tasty twist to microwave popcorn. When I first tried it at a party, I couldn't stop eating it!

blizzard party mix

2 cups Corn Chex

2 cups miniature pretzels

1 cup dry roasted peanuts

20 caramels, coarsely chopped

1 package (10 to 12 ounces) vanilla *or* white chips

In a large bowl, combine the first four ingredients. In a microwave, melt chips; stir until smooth. Pour over cereal mixture; toss to coat. Immediately spread onto waxed paper-lined baking sheet; let stand until set, about 20 minutes. Break into pieces. Store in an airtight container.

YIELD: 4½ CUPS.

Kelley Scott, Parma, Ohio

This combo of flavors is sure to be popular. It's perfect for a potluck, munching at home or giving away as gifts.

fruity granola

3 cups old-fashioned oats

½ cup sliced almonds

1¼ cups honey

½ cup Grape-Nuts

1 tablespoon butter

1 teaspoon ground cinnamon

2½ cups Wheaties

½ cup dried cranberries

½ cup raisins

½ cup dried banana chips

1 In a large bowl, combine oats and almonds; spread evenly in a 15-in. x 10-in. x 1-in. baking pan coated with cooking spray. Bake at 325° for 15 minutes.

2 In a large bowl, combine the honey, Grape-Nuts, butter and cinnamon. Add oat mixture; stir to combine. Return mixture to the pan. Bake 15-20 minutes longer or until golden. Cool on wire rack.

3 When cool enough to handle, break granola into pieces. Place in a large bowl; stir in the Wheaties, cranberries, raisins and banana chips. Store in an airtight container in a cool dry place for up to 2 months.

YIELD: 10 CUPS.

Nancy Chapman, Center Harbor, New Hampshire

You'll love the chewy sweetness of this honey-flavored cereal, fruit and nut mixture. It's great to eat out of hand or to enjoy in a parfait glass layered with fruit and low-fat yogurt.

peanut butter popcorn crunch

12 cups popped popcorn

4 cups miniature pretzels

⅔ cup sugar

½ cup honey

½ cup light corn syrup

⅔ cup creamy peanut butter

1 teaspoon vanilla extract

4 cups chocolate-covered peanuts

1 In a large bowl, combine popcorn and pretzels; set aside. In a small saucepan, combine the sugar, honey and corn syrup. Bring to a boil; cook and stir for 2 minutes or until sugar is dissolved.

2 Remove from the heat. Stir in peanut butter and vanilla. Pour over the popcorn mixture and toss to coat. Pour into two greased 15-in. x 10-in. x 1-in. baking pans.

3 Bake, uncovered, at 250° for 1 hour, stirring every 15 minutes. Cool for 10 minutes. Break into clusters; place in a large bowl. Add chocolate-covered peanuts; mix well. Cool completely. Store in an airtight container.

YIELD: ABOUT 4 QUARTS.

LaVonne Smith, Kennebec, South Dakota

This sweet, crunchy mix makes a sensational snack to munch while watching movies.

sweet bites

262

258

Satisfy anyone's sweet tooth with one or two mini desserts. Individual sweets are a delectable complement to heartier appetizers. Let guests sample Cheese-Filled Shortbread Tarts (p. 260), French Vanilla Cream Puffs (p. 262), Sugared Raisin Pear Diamonds (p. 258) or one of the other sensational delights included here.

Before the party, just arrange on serving dishes and place them on the side. Halfway through the party, bring the desserts to the front of the buffet and serve with coffee.

sugared raisin pear diamonds

2½ cups plus 4½ teaspoons all-purpose flour, *divided*

¼ cup plus 6 tablespoons sugar, *divided*

½ teaspoon salt

¾ cup cold butter

½ teaspoon grated lemon peel

½ cup half-and-half cream

6 cups diced peeled ripe pears (about 7)

6 tablespoons golden raisins

¼ cup lemon juice

⅛ to ¼ teaspoon ground cinnamon

1 egg, lightly beaten

Additional sugar

1 In a bowl, combine 2½ cups flour, ¼ cup sugar and salt. Cut in butter and lemon peel until the mixture resembles coarse crumbs. Gradually add cream, tossing with a fork until dough forms a ball.

2 Divide in half. Roll out one portion of dough onto lightly floured waxed paper or pastry cloth into a 16-in. x 11½-in. rectangle. Transfer to an ungreased 15-in. x 10-in. x 1-in. baking pan.

3 Bake at 350° for 10-15 minutes or until lightly browned. Cool on a wire rack. Increase temperature to 400°.

4 In a bowl, combine the pears, raisins, lemon juice, cinnamon and remaining flour and sugar. Spread over crust. Roll out remaining dough into a 16-in. x 12-in. rectangle; place over filling. Trim and seal edges. Brush top with egg; sprinkle with additional sugar.

5 Bake for 30-34 minutes or until golden brown. Cool on a wire rack. Cut into diamond-shaped bars.

YIELD: ABOUT 2 DOZEN.

Jeanne Allen, Rye, Colorado

With their tender, golden crust and tempting pear and raisin filling, these fabulous bars stand out on any buffet table. Substitute apples for the pears, and you'll still get yummy results!

berry nut tarts

1/2 cup butter, softened

1 package (3 ounces) cream cheese, softened

1 cup all-purpose flour

FILLING:

1 1/2 cups packed brown sugar

2 tablespoons butter, melted

2 eggs, lightly beaten

2 teaspoons vanilla extract

2/3 cup finely chopped cranberries

1/3 cup chopped pecans

1 In a small mixing bowl, beat butter and cream cheese; add flour; mix well. Cover, refrigerate for 1 hour or until easy to handle.

2 Cut dough into 12 portions. Press onto the bottom and all the way up the sides of greased muffin cups. In a bowl, combine the brown sugar, butter, eggs and vanilla. Stir in the cranberries and pecans. Spoon into prepared crusts.

3 Bake at 350° for 25-30 minutes or until edges are golden brown. Cool for 5 minutes before removing from pan to a wire rack to cool completely. Store in the refrigerator.

YIELD: ABOUT 1 DOZEN.

Lena Ehlert, Vancouver, British Columbia

Cranberries are a delicious addition to this spin on individual pecan pies. Guests have a hard time eating just one!

cheese-filled shortbread tartlets

1 package (8 ounces) cream cheese, softened

1 cup sweetened condensed milk

1/3 cup lemon juice

1 teaspoon vanilla extract

1 cup butter, softened

1 1/2 cups all-purpose flour

1/2 cup confectioners' sugar

1 tablespoon cornstarch

Fresh raspberries and mint leaves for garnish

1 In a small mixing bowl, beat cream cheese until smooth. Gradually beat in the milk, lemon juice and vanilla. Cover and refrigerate for 8 hours or overnight.

2 In another mixing bowl, beat the butter, flour, confectioners' sugar and cornstarch until smooth. Roll into 1-in. balls. Place in greased miniature muffin cups; press onto the bottom and up the sides. Prick with a fork.

3 Bake at 325° for 20-25 minutes or until golden brown. Immediately run a knife around each tart to loosen. Cool in pans on wire racks.

4 Pipe or spoon 1 tablespoon filling into each tart shell. Cover and refrigerate until set. Just before serving, garnish as desired.

YIELD: 3 DOZEN.

Cathy Walerius, Mound, Minnesota

Bite-size treats are a nice addition to a dessert buffet. You can store cooled, baked tart shells in an airtight container at room temperature overnight or in the freezer for a few weeks.

caramel fondue

1 cup heavy whipping cream, *divided*

¾ cup sugar

½ cup light corn syrup

¼ cup butter

¼ teaspoon salt

½ teaspoon vanilla extract

Pound cake and assorted fresh fruit, cut into pieces

1 In a heavy saucepan, combine ½ cup cream, sugar, corn syrup, butter and salt. Bring to a boil over medium heat until a candy thermometer reads 234° (soft-ball stage), stirring constantly. Cool to 220°; stir in remaining cream. Bring to a boil. Remove from the heat; stir in vanilla.

2 Transfer to a fondue pot and keep warm. Serve with pound cake and fruit.

YIELD: 1¾ CUPS.

Leora Miller, Milford, Indiana

My brothers can't get enough of this caramel dip. We gather around the table, dipping pieces of pound cake and fruit until the fondue pot is clean.

marmalade turnovers

½ cup butter, softened

1 jar (5 ounces) sharp American cheese spread

1 cup all-purpose flour

⅓ cup marmalade

1 In a bowl, combine butter and cheese. Add flour; stir until mixture forms a ball. Cover and refrigerate for 1 hour. On a lightly floured surface, roll dough to ⅛-in. thickness; cut into 2¾-in. circles. Place ½ teaspoon marmalade on each circle. Fold pastry over and seal edges with a fork. Cut slits in top of pastry.

2 Place 2-in. apart on ungreased baking sheets. Bake at 350° for 5-9 minutes or until lightly browned. Remove to wire racks to cool.

YIELD: 2½ DOZEN.

Anna Jean Allen, West Liberty, Kentucky

A church friend prepares these delicate pastries for lots of gatherings.

french vanilla cream puffs

1 cup water

½ cup butter

1 cup all-purpose flour

¼ teaspoon salt

4 eggs

FILLING:

1½ cups cold milk

1 package (3.4 ounces) instant French vanilla pudding mix

1 cup whipped topping

1 package (12 ounces) miniature semisweet chocolate chips

Confectioners' sugar

1 In a saucepan, bring water and butter to a boil. Add flour and salt all at once; stir until a smooth ball forms. Remove from the heat; let stand for 5 minutes. Add eggs, one at a time, beating well after each addition. Beat until mixture is smooth and shiny.

2 Drop by rounded teaspoonfuls 2 in. apart onto greased baking sheets. Bake at 400° for 20-25 minutes or until golden brown. Remove puffs to wire racks. Immediately cut a slit in each for steam to escape. Cool. Split puffs and remove soft dough.

3 For filling, in a mixing bowl, whisk the milk and pudding mix for 2 minutes. Refrigerate for 5 minutes. Fold in whipped topping and chips. Fill cream puffs just before serving; replace tops. Dust with confectioners' sugar.

YIELD: ABOUT 2½ DOZEN.

Lean Haines, Lawrenceville, Georgia

French vanilla filling dotted with mini chocolate chips is sandwiched between puffy pastry in this elegantly sweet dessert. You could substitute white chocolate or chocolate pudding for the vanilla if you like.

brownie tarts

½ cup butter, softened

1 package (3 ounces) cream cheese, softened

1 cup all-purpose flour

FILLING:

½ cup semisweet chocolate chips

2 tablespoons butter

½ cup sugar

1 egg, beaten

1 teaspoon vanilla extract

½ cup chopped pecans, optional

Maraschino cherry halves, optional

1 In a mixing bowl, cream the butter and cream cheese. Add flour; mix well. Cover and refrigerate for 1 hour.

2 Shape into 1-in. balls. Place in ungreased miniature muffin cups; press into the bottom and up the sides to form a shell.

3 For filling, melt chocolate chips and butter in a small saucepan. Remove from the heat; stir in sugar, egg and vanilla. Add the pecans if desired. Spoon into shells.

4 Bake at 325° for 30-35 minutes or until a toothpick inserted near the center comes out clean. Cool for 10 minutes before removing from pans to wire racks. Garnish with cherries if desired.

YIELD: 2 DOZEN.

Sharon Wilkins, Grande Pointe, Ontario
I often take these chocolate goodies to potluck
dinners for our country dance club.

espresso panna cotta

1 envelope unflavored gelatin

1 cup milk

3 cups heavy whipping cream

½ cup sugar

2 tablespoons instant espresso powder *or* instant coffee granules

⅛ teaspoon salt

Dark and white chocolate curls

1 In a small saucepan, sprinkle the gelatin over milk; let stand for 1 minute. Heat over low heat, stirring until gelatin is completely dissolved. Stir in the cream, sugar, espresso powder and salt. Cook and stir until sugar is dissolved. Remove from the heat.

2 Pour into six dessert dishes. Cover and refrigerate for 1 hour, stirring every 20 minutes.

3 Refrigerate for at least 5 hours longer or until set. Just before serving, garnish with chocolate curls.

YIELD: 6 SERVINGS.

Nicole Clayton, Prescott, Arizona

Martini glasses make an elegant impression for such a luscious sweet treat. Best of all, guests can easily mingle while carrying the panna cotta.

apple walnut crescents

2 packages (8 ounces *each*) refrigerated crescent rolls

¼ cup sugar

1 tablespoon ground cinnamon

4 medium tart apples, peeled, cored and quartered

¼ cup chopped walnuts

¼ cup raisins, optional

¼ cup butter, melted

1 Unroll crescent roll dough and separate into 16 triangles. Combine sugar and cinnamon; sprinkle about ½ teaspoon on each triangle. Place an apple quarter near the short side and roll up. Place in a lightly greased 15-in. x 10-in. x 1-in. baking pan.

2 Press walnuts and raisins if desired into top of dough. Drizzle with butter. Sprinkle with the remaining cinnamon-sugar. Bake at 375° for 20-24 minutes or until golden brown. Serve warm.

YIELD: 16 SERVINGS.

Karen Petzold, Vassar, Michigan

A local apple orchard had a cook-off I wanted to enter, so I created these golden cinnamon treats. They're a snap to assemble with convenient crescent roll dough.

triple chocolate bundles

3 tablespoons semisweet chocolate chips

3 tablespoons vanilla *or* white chips

3 tablespoons milk chocolate chips

1 tube (8 ounces) refrigerated crescent rolls

Confectioners' sugar, optional

1 In a small bowl, combine the first three ingredients. Separate crescent dough into eight triangles. Place triangles on a work surface with the short edge toward you. For each bundle, place 1 tablespoon of chips in the center of each triangle. Bring top point over chips and tuck underneath dough. Fold side points over top, pressing to seal.

2 Place on an ungreased baking sheet. Bake at 375° for 10-12 minutes or until golden brown. Cool on a wire rack until serving. Sprinkle with sugar if desired.

YIELD: 8 BUNDLES.

Taste of Home Test Kitchen

No one will be able to resist three kinds of chocolate wrapped up in a fuss-free flaky dough. These are also delicious topped with a drizzle of melted chocolate.

puff pastry pillows

1 package (17.3 ounces) frozen puff pastry, thawed

1 egg

¼ cup milk

1 to 2 tablespoons coarse *or* granulated sugar

FILLING:

¼ cup all-purpose flour

1 cup milk

1 cup butter, softened

1 cup sugar

1 teaspoon vanilla extract

½ teaspoon almond extract

¼ teaspoon salt

1 Carefully open each puff pastry sheet. Cut each sheet of pastry at creases, forming 3 strips. Cut each strip widthwise into 7 pieces.

2 Combine egg and milk; lightly brush egg mixture over pastry. Sprinkle with sugar. Place on lightly greased baking sheets. Bake at 400° for 10-12 minutes or until golden brown. Remove to wire racks to cool. Split into top and bottom halves.

3 In a saucepan, combine the flour and milk until smooth. Bring to a boil over medium heat; cook and stir for 1 minute or until thickened. Cool.

4 Transfer to a mixing bowl; beat in the butter, sugar, vanilla, almond extract and salt until light and fluffy, about 10 minutes. Spread 1 tablespoonful on bottom half of each pastry; replace tops. Store in refrigerator.

YIELD: ABOUT 3½ DOZEN.

Robert Ryan, Newton, Iowa

My family and co-workers love these pretty, sweet treats. By using prepared puff pastry, you have a fun dessert without much fuss.

pretty petits fours

¼ cup butter, softened

¼ cup shortening

1 cup sugar

1 teaspoon vanilla extract

1⅓ cups all-purpose flour

2 teaspoons baking powder

½ teaspoon salt

⅔ cup milk

3 egg whites

GLAZE:

2 pounds confectioners' sugar

⅔ cup plus 2 tablespoons water

2 teaspoons orange extract

FROSTING:

6 tablespoons butter, softened

2 tablespoons shortening

½ teaspoon vanilla extract

3 cups confectioners' sugar

3 to 4 tablespoons milk

Pink and green gel, liquid *or* paste food coloring

1 In a large mixing bowl, cream the butter, shortening and sugar. Beat in vanilla. Combine the flour, baking powder and salt; add to creamed mixture alternately with milk. In a small mixing bowl, beat egg whites until soft peaks form; gently fold into batter.

2 Pour into a greased 9-in. square baking pan. Bake at 350° for 20-25 minutes or until a toothpick inserted near the center comes out clean. Cool for 10 minutes before removing from pan to a wire rack to cool completely.

3 Cut a thin slice off each side of cake. Cut cake into 1¼-in. squares. Place ½ in. apart on a rack in a 15-in. x 10-in. x 1-in. pan.

4 In a mixing bowl, combine glaze ingredients. Beat on low speed just until blended; beat on high until smooth. Apply glaze evenly over tops and sides of cake squares, allowing excess to drip off. Let dry. Repeat if necessary to thoroughly coat squares. Let dry completely.

5 For frosting, in a mixing bowl, cream the butter, shortening and vanilla. Beat in confectioners' sugar and enough milk to achieve desired consistency. Place ½ cup each in two bowls; tint one portion pink and one green.

6 Cut a small hole in the corner of a pastry or plastic bag; insert #104 tip. Fill with pink frosting; pipe a rosebud on each petit four. Insert #3 round tip into another pastry or plastic bag; fill with green frosting. Pipe a leaf under each rose.

YIELD: 2½ DOZEN (3 CUPS FROSTING).

Taste of Home Test Kitchen

Add a delicate touch to your dessert table with these bite-size cakes.

---

spicy ginger scones

2 cups biscuit/baking mix

2 tablespoons sugar

1 teaspoon ground cinnamon

¼ teaspoon ground ginger

¼ teaspoon ground nutmeg

⅔ cup half-and-half cream

½ cup golden raisins

2 tablespoons chopped crystallized ginger

Additional half-and-half cream and sugar

1 In a large bowl, combine the biscuit mix, sugar, cinnamon, ginger and nutmeg. Stir in cream just until moistened. Stir in raisins and ginger.

2 Turn onto a floured surface; knead 10 times. Transfer dough to a greased baking sheet. Pat into a 9-in. circle. Cut into eight wedges, but do not separate. Brush tops lightly with additional cream; sprinkle with additional sugar.

3 Bake at 425° for 12-15 minutes or until golden brown. Serve warm.

YIELD: 8 SCONES.

Rebecca Guffey, Apex, North Carolina

I created this recipe when we were having guests over Thanksgiving weekend. The candied ginger gives these scones a special zing!

miniature almond tarts

1 cup butter, softened

2 packages (3 ounces *each*) cream cheese, softened

2 cups all-purpose flour

FILLING:

6 ounces almond paste, crumbled

2 eggs, beaten

1/2 cup sugar

FROSTING:

1 1/2 cups confectioners' sugar

3 tablespoons butter, softened

4 to 5 teaspoons milk

Maraschino cherry halves (about 48)

1 In a mixing bowl, cream the butter and cream cheese. Add flour; mix well. Cover and refrigerate for 1 hour.

2 Shape into 1-in. balls. Place in ungreased miniature muffin cups; press into the bottom and up the sides to form a shell.

3 For filling, combine the almond paste, eggs and sugar in a mixing bowl. Beat on low speed until blended. Fill each shell with about 1 1/2 teaspoons filling.

4 Bake at 325° for 25-30 minutes or until edges are golden brown. Cool for 10 minutes before removing to wire racks to cool completely.

5 For frosting, combine the confectioners' sugar, butter and enough milk to achieve desired consistency. Pipe or spread over tarts. Top each with a cherry half.

YIELD: ABOUT 4 DOZEN.

Karen Van Den Berge, Holland, Michigan

My family requests these adorable little tarts at the holidays. I always enjoy making them since the almond paste in the filling reflects our Dutch heritage.

apricot crescents

1 cup cold butter

2 cups all-purpose flour

1 egg yolk

½ cup sour cream

½ cup apricot preserves

½ cup flaked coconut

¼ cup finely chopped pecans

Sugar

1 In a bowl, cut butter into flour until the mixture resembles coarse crumbs. Beat egg yolk and sour cream; add to crumb mixture and mix well. Cover and refrigerate for several hours or overnight.

2 Divide dough into fourths. On a sugared surface, roll each portion into a 10-in. circle. Turn dough over to sugar top side. Combine preserves, coconut and pecans; spread over circles. Cut each circle into 12 wedges and roll each wedge into a crescent shape, starting at the wide end. Sprinkle with sugar.

3 Place point side down 1 in. apart on ungreased baking sheets. Bake at 350° for 15-17 minutes or until set and very lightly browned. Immediately remove to wire racks to cool.

YIELD: 4 DOZEN.

Tamyra Vest, Scottsburg, Virginia

When I was in college, my roommate's mother sent these flaky horns in a holiday care package. I've been making them ever since. When I mail them to my parents, I put an equal number in two tins labeled "his" and "hers" so there's no squabbling over who gets more.

orange fantasy fudge

1½ teaspoons plus ½ cup butter, softened, *divided*

1½ cups sugar

1 can (5 ounces) evaporated milk

2 cups (12 ounces) semisweet chocolate chips

1 jar (7 ounces) marshmallow creme

3 teaspoons orange extract

1 teaspoon vanilla extract

1 Line a 9-in. square pan with foil; grease the foil with 1½ teaspoons butter and set aside. In a heavy saucepan, combine the sugar, milk and remaining butter. Cook and stir over medium heat until sugar is dissolved. Bring to a rapid boil; boil for 5 minutes; stirring constantly.

2 Reduce heat to low; stir in chocolate chips and marshmallow creme until melted and blended. Remove from the heat; stir in extracts. Pour into prepared pan. Refrigerate overnight or until firm.

3 Using foil, lift fudge out of pan; carefully peel off foil. Cut fudge into 1-in. squares. Store in the refrigerator.

YIELD: 2¼ POUNDS.

Marie Bickel, LaConner, Washington

Orange and chocolate team up in this full-flavored fudge. My daughter created the recipe when experimenting in the kitchen.

ice cream snowballs

½ gallon vanilla ice cream, softened

1 package (10 ounces) flaked coconut

Fresh mint, optional

Scoop ice cream into 12 balls. Place on a baking sheet and freeze until solid. Roll in coconut. Garnish with mint if desired.

YIELD: 12 SERVINGS.

Sister Judith LaBrozzi, Canton, Ohio

There's no better way to enjoy this festive ice cream delight than in the warm atmosphere of friends and family.

fluffy fruit dip

Sue Pence, Alexandria, Virginia

We've been making this sweet dip in my family for many generations. You can serve it throughout the year with whatever fresh fruits are in season. Best of all, you can prepare it ahead of time.

½ cup sugar

2 tablespoons all-purpose flour

1 cup unsweetened pineapple juice

1 tablespoon butter

1 egg, lightly beaten

1 cup heavy whipping cream, whipped

Assorted fresh fruit

1 In a small saucepan, combine sugar and flour. Gradually whisk in pineapple juice. Add butter. Cook and stir until butter is melted and mixture comes to a boil. Cook and stir for 1-2 minutes or until thickened.

2 Remove from the heat. Stir a small amount of hot mixture into egg; return all to the pan, stirring constantly. Bring to a gentle boil; cook and stir for 1 minute. Remove from the heat. Cool to room temperature, stirring several times.

3 Fold in whipped cream. Cover and refrigerate for at least 1 hour. Serve with fruit.

YIELD: ABOUT 2½ CUPS.

lemon tea cakes

1½ cups butter, softened

1 package (8 ounces) cream cheese, softened

2¼ cups sugar

6 eggs

3 tablespoons lemon juice

2 teaspoons lemon extract

1 teaspoon vanilla extract

1½ teaspoons grated lemon peel

3 cups all-purpose flour

GLAZE:

5¼ cups confectioners' sugar

½ cup plus 3 tablespoons 2% milk

3½ teaspoons lemon extract

1 In a large bowl, cream the butter, cream cheese and sugar until light and fluffy. Add eggs, one at a time, beating well after each addition. Beat in the lemon juice, extracts and lemon peel. Add flour; beat just until moistened.

2 Fill greased miniature muffin cups two-thirds full. Bake at 325° for 10-15 minutes or until a toothpick inserted near the center comes out clean. Cool for 5 minutes before removing from pans to wire racks to cool completely.

3 In a small bowl, combine glaze ingredients. Dip tops of cakes into glaze; place on waxed paper to dry.

YIELD: 8½ DOZEN.

Charlene Crump, Montgomery, Alabama
Whenever I serve these bite-size cakes, they get rave reviews…and I get requests for the recipe!

ginger chocolate temptation

2 cups heavy whipping cream

1 vanilla bean, split lengthwise

8 ounces bittersweet chocolate, chopped

6 egg yolks, lightly beaten

¼ cup minced crystallized ginger, *divided*

Heavy whipping cream, whipped, optional

1 In small heavy saucepan, combine cream and vanilla bean. Bring to a boil. Reduce heat; simmer, uncovered, for 5 minutes. Remove the vanilla bean and scrape the inside of the bean to remove the seeds; add seeds to the pan. Discard vanilla bean.

2 Stir in chocolate until melted. Stir ½ cup chocolate mixture into egg yolks; return all to the pan. Cook and stir until mixture reaches 160° and coats the back of a metal spoon. Remove from the heat. Stir in 2 tablespoons ginger.

3 Pour into 12 demitasse or espresso cups. Refrigerate for at least 1 hour. Just before serving, garnish with whipped cream and remaining ginger if desired.

YIELD: 12 SERVINGS.

Elise Lalor, Issaquah, Washington

Chocolate-covered candied ginger is one of my favorite treats, so I knew this recipe was for me. Every bite of this cool, creamy custard is rich, smooth and decadent.

banana-pecan sweet rolls

4¾ to 5 cups all-purpose flour

¼ cup sugar

2 packages (¼ ounce *each*)
  active dry yeast

1 teaspoon salt

1 cup milk

¼ cup butter, cubed

1 cup mashed ripe bananas
  (about 3 medium)

1 egg

1 teaspoon vanilla extract

FILLING:

3 tablespoons butter, melted

½ cup chopped pecans

¼ cup sugar

½ teaspoon ground allspice

ICING:

2 cups confectioners' sugar

1 tablespoon lemon juice

1 to 2 tablespoons milk

1 In a large bowl, combine 2 cups flour, sugar, yeast and salt. In a small saucepan, heat milk and butter to 120°-130°. Add to dry ingredients; beat just until moistened. Add the bananas, egg and vanilla; beat until smooth. Stir in enough remaining flour to form a soft dough (dough will be sticky).

2 Turn onto a floured surface; knead until smooth and elastic, about 6-8 minutes. Place in a greased bowl, turning once to grease top. Cover and let rise in a warm place until doubled, about 1 hour.

3 Punch dough down. Turn onto a lightly floured surface; divide in half. Roll each portion into a 16-in. x 6-in. rectangle. Brush with butter to within ½ in. of edges. Combine the pecans, sugar and allspice; sprinkle over dough to within ½ in. of edges.

4 Roll up jelly-roll style, starting with a long side; pinch seam to seal. Cut each into 16 slices. Place cut side up on greased baking sheets. Cover and let rise in a warm place until doubled, about 30 minutes.

5 Bake at 400° for 12-15 minutes or until golden brown. Remove from pans to wire racks. Combine icing ingredients; drizzle over rolls. Serve warm.

YIELD: 32 ROLLS.

Dorothy Pritchett, Wills Point, Texas
Banana adds fun flavor to these sweet bites that are
great for breakfast as well as for dessert.

wonton kisses

24 milk chocolate kisses

24 wonton wrappers

Oil for frying

Confectioners' sugar

1 Place a chocolate kiss in the center of a wonton wrapper. (Keep remaining wrappers covered with a damp paper towel until ready to use.) Moisten edges with water; fold opposite corners together over candy kiss and press to seal. Repeat.

2 In an electric skillet, heat 1 in. of oil to 375°. Fry wontons for 2½ minutes or until golden brown, turning once. Drain on paper towels. Dust with confectioners' sugar.

YIELD: 2 DOZEN.

Darlene Brenden, Salem, Oregon

These wrapped bundles are filled with a chocolate candy kiss and sure to delight guests at your next party.

sugar cookie fruit pizzas

Marge Hodel, Roanoke, Illinois

Purchased sugar cookies make a sweet crust for these colorful fruit pizzas. Make them throughout the year with a variety of fresh and canned fruits.

½ cup sugar

1 tablespoon cornstarch

½ cup unsweetened pineapple juice

¼ cup water

2 tablespoons lemon juice

4 ounces cream cheese, softened

¼ cup confectioners' sugar

1¾ cups whipped topping

12 sugar cookies (3 inches)

1 cup fresh blueberries

1 cup chopped peeled kiwifruit

½ cup chopped fresh strawberries

1 For glaze, in a small saucepan, combine the sugar, cornstarch, pineapple juice, water and lemon juice until smooth. Bring to a boil; cook and stir for 2 minutes or until thickened. Transfer to a small bowl; refrigerate until cooled but not set.

2 In a small bowl, beat cream cheese and confectioners' sugar until smooth; fold in whipped topping. Spread over tops of cookies. Arrange fruit on top; drizzle with glaze. Refrigerate for 1 hour or until chilled.

YIELD: 1 DOZEN.

apple cartwheels

¼ cup peanut butter

1½ teaspoons honey

½ cup miniature semisweet chocolate chips

2 tablespoons raisins

4 medium unpeeled Red Delicious apples, cored

1 In a small bowl, combine peanut butter and honey; fold in chocolate chips and raisins.

2 Fill centers of apples with peanut butter mixture; refrigerate for at least 1 hour. Cut into ¼-in. rings.

YIELD: ABOUT 2 DOZEN.

Miriam Miller, Thorp, Wisconsin

When you need to entertain a group of children, whip up these stuffed apple rings. The yummy filling is an irresistible combination of creamy peanut butter, sweet honey, miniature chocolate chips and raisins.

berry bruschetta

1 French bread baguette
   (1 pound)

2 tablespoons olive oil

1½ cups chopped fresh
   strawberries

¾ cup chopped peeled fresh
   peaches

1½ teaspoons minced fresh mint

½ cup Mascarpone cheese

1 Cut baguette into 32 slices, about ½ in. thick; place on ungreased baking sheets. Brush with the oil. Broil 6-8 in. from the heat for 1-2 minutes or until lightly toasted.

2 In a small bowl, combine the strawberries, peaches and mint. Spread each slice of bread with cheese; top with fruit mixture. Broil for 1-2 minutes or until the cheese is slightly melted. Serve immediately.

YIELD: 32 APPETIZERS.

Taste of Home Test Kitchen

Here's a tasty twist on the traditional variety of bruschetta, and it can be served as an appetizer or a dessert.

baklava tartlets

2 cups finely chopped walnuts

¾ cup honey

½ cup butter, melted

1 teaspoon ground cinnamon

1 teaspoon lemon juice

¼ teaspoon ground cloves

3 packages (1.9 ounces *each*) frozen miniature phyllo tart shells

In a small bowl, combine the first six ingredients; spoon 2 teaspoonfuls into each tart shell. Refrigerate until serving.

YIELD: 45 TARTLETS.

Ashley Eagon, Kettering, Ohio

Want a quick treat that's delicious and easy? These tartlets do the trick. You can serve them right away, but they're better after chilling for about an hour in the refrigerator. A little sprig of mint adds just a touch of color.

special stuffed strawberries

24 large fresh strawberries

½ cup spreadable strawberry
   cream cheese

3 tablespoons sour cream

1 Remove stems from the strawberries. Place point side up on a cutting board. Cut a deep "X" in the top of each berry. Carefully spread berries apart.

2 In a small bowl, beat cream cheese and sour cream until smooth. Pipe or spoon filling into each berry. Refrigerate until serving.

YIELD: 2 DOZEN.

Marcia Orlando, Boyertown, Pennsylvania

These sweet bites can be made ahead of time...and they look really pretty on a tray. I sometimes sprinkle the piped filling with finely chopped pistachio nuts.

cookie brittle

1 cup butter, softened

1 cup sugar

2 cups all-purpose flour

1¼ cups peanut butter chips

½ cup coarsely chopped pecans

1 In a small bowl, cream butter and sugar until light and fluffy. Gradually add flour and mix well. Stir in peanut butter chips.

2 Line a 15-in. x 10-in. x 1-in. baking pan with foil; coat with cooking spray. Gently press dough into the pan; sprinkle with pecans and press into dough.

3 Bake at 350° for 20-25 minutes or until golden brown. Cool on a wire rack. Invert pan and remove foil. Break brittle into pieces; store in an airtight container.

YIELD: ABOUT 4 DOZEN.

Betty Byrnes Consbruck, Gainesville, Florida

This recipe originally called for chocolate chips, but my family and friends like it better when I use peanut butter chips.

caramel apple pizza

Tari Ambler, Shorewood, Illinois

Here's a new take on a classic treat. Folks love the flavor and never guess it's light!

¼ cup butter, softened

¼ cup sugar

¼ cup packed brown sugar

1 egg

2 tablespoons canola oil

1 tablespoon light corn syrup

1 teaspoon vanilla extract

1 cup whole wheat pastry flour

¾ cup all-purpose flour

½ teaspoon baking powder

¼ teaspoon salt

¼ teaspoon ground cinnamon

TOPPING:

1 package (8 ounces) fat-free cream cheese

¼ cup packed brown sugar

½ teaspoon ground cinnamon

½ teaspoon vanilla extract

3 medium Granny Smith apples, thinly sliced

¼ cup fat-free caramel ice cream topping

¼ cup chopped unsalted dry roasted peanuts

1 In a large bowl, cream butter and sugars until light and fluffy. Beat in the egg, oil, corn syrup and vanilla. Combine the flours, baking powder, salt and cinnamon; gradually add to creamed mixture and mix well.

2 Press dough onto a 14-in. pizza pan coated with cooking spray. Bake at 350° for 12-15 minutes or until lightly browned. Cool on a wire rack.

3 In a small bowl, beat the cream cheese, brown sugar, cinnamon and vanilla until smooth. Spread over crust. Arrange apples over the top. Drizzle with caramel topping; sprinkle with peanuts. Serve immediately.

YIELD: 12 SLICES.

fruit-and-cheese bars

½ cup butter, softened

½ cup packed brown sugar

1 cup all-purpose flour

1 package (8 ounces) cream cheese, softened

¼ cup sugar

1 egg

1 tablespoon lemon juice

½ cup chopped mixed candied fruit

1 In a small bowl, cream butter and brown sugar until light and fluffy. Add flour; beat until crumbly. Set aside ½ cup for topping.

2 Press remaining crumb mixture into a greased 8-in. square baking dish. Bake at 350° for 10-12 minutes or until lightly browned.

3 Meanwhile, in a large bowl, beat cream cheese and sugar until smooth. Beat in the egg and lemon juice. Stir in candied fruit. Spread over crust; sprinkle with reserved crumb mixture.

4 Bake 18-20 minutes longer or until firm. Cool on a wire rack. Store in the refrigerator.

YIELD: ABOUT 2½ DOZEN.

Tina Hagen, Emo, Ontario

A pan of these rich bars goes a long way. Colorful candied fruit makes it especially festive.

maple ginger fudge

2 teaspoons plus 2 tablespoons butter, *divided*

2 cups sugar

²/₃ cup heavy whipping cream

2 tablespoons light corn syrup

¼ teaspoon ground ginger

½ teaspoon maple flavoring

½ cup chopped walnuts

1 Line a 9-in. x 5-in. loaf pan with foil and grease the foil with 1 teaspoon butter; set aside. Butter the sides of a small heavy saucepan with 1 teaspoon butter; add the sugar, cream, corn syrup and ginger. Bring to a boil over medium heat, stirring constantly. Reduce heat; cook until a candy thermometer reads 238° (soft-ball stage), stirring occasionally.

2 Remove from the heat. Add maple flavoring and remaining butter (do not stir). Cool to 110° without stirring, about 1 hour. With a portable mixer, beat on low speed for 1-2 minutes or until fudge begins to thicken. With a clean dry wooden spoon, stir in walnuts until fudge begins to lose its gloss, about 5 minutes.

3 Spread into prepared pan. Refrigerate until firm, about 30 minutes. Using foil, lift fudge out of pan. Discard foil; cut fudge into 1-in. squares. Store in an airtight container in the refrigerator.

YIELD: 1¼ POUNDS.

EDITOR'S NOTE: We recommend that you test your candy thermometer before each use by bringing water to a boil; the thermometer should read 212°. Adjust your recipe temperature up or down based on your test.

Steve Westphal, Milwaukee, Wisconsin
I combine two fall favorites—maple and ginger—in this sweet, smooth fudge. One piece just isn't enough!

miniature napoleons

6 tablespoons sugar

2 tablespoons cornstarch

¼ teaspoon salt

1 cup 2% milk

1 egg yolk, lightly beaten

2 tablespoons butter, *divided*

½ teaspoon vanilla extract

1 sheet frozen puff pastry, thawed

½ cup heavy whipping cream

2 ounces semisweet chocolate, chopped

1 In a small saucepan, combine the sugar, cornstarch and salt. Add milk; stir until smooth. Cook and stir over medium heat until mixture comes to a boil. Stir a small amount into egg yolk; return all to the pan. Bring to a gentle boil, stirring constantly; cook 2 minutes longer.

2 Remove from the heat; stir in 1 tablespoon butter and vanilla. Pour into a small bowl; cool to room temperature. Cover surface of custard with waxed paper. Refrigerate, without stirring, for 2-3 hours or until chilled.

3 Unfold puff pastry; place on an ungreased baking sheet. Prick dough thoroughly with a fork. Bake according to package directions. Remove to a wire rack to cool.

4 In a small bowl, beat cream until stiff peaks form. Fold into custard. Use a fork to split pastry in half horizontally. Spread filling over the bottom half; replace top. Cover and freeze for 4 hours or until firm.

5 Cut into 1½-in. x 1-in. rectangles. In a microwave, melt chocolate and remaining butter; stir until smooth. Drizzle over pastries. Freeze until serving.

YIELD: 4½ DOZEN.

Taste of Home Test Kitchen

It can be a challenge to come up with an elegant sweet that works well for a cocktail party. These impressive, bite-size desserts are easy to enjoy while mingling.

peanut butter cheese ball

1 package (8 ounces) cream cheese, softened

1½ cups peanut butter

½ cup confectioners' sugar

1 teaspoon vanilla extract

¾ cup chopped peanuts

Apple slices

1 In a small bowl, beat cream cheese until fluffy. Add the peanut butter, confectioners' sugar and vanilla; beat until smooth.

2 Shape into a ball; roll in peanuts. Wrap in plastic wrap. Refrigerate until serving. Serve with apples.

YIELD: 2½ CUPS.

Tessie Hughes, Marion, Virginia

I've made this change-of-pace cheese ball for many occasions, and it's always well received by old and young alike.

almond bars

1 cup butter, softened

1 cup almond paste

2¼ cups sugar, *divided*

2 eggs

1 teaspoon almond extract

2 cups all-purpose flour

½ cup slivered almonds

1 In a large bowl, cream the butter, almond paste and 2 cups sugar until light and fluffy. Beat in eggs and extract. Gradually add flour just until moistened.

2 Spread into a greased 13-in. x 9-in. baking dish. Sprinkle with remaining sugar; top with almonds.

3 Bake at 350° for 30-35 minutes or until a toothpick inserted near the center comes out clean. Cool on a wire rack. Cut into squares. Store in the refrigerator.

YIELD: 4½ DOZEN.

Cheryl Newendorp, Pella, Iowa

These no-fuss squares make a delicious addition to dessert trays.

stuffed chocolate cherries

Judy Bond, Duncan, British Columbia

A summertime favorite, these cherry delights freeze nicely and make a wonderful treat for unexpected guests.

1½ **pounds fresh dark sweet cherries with stems**

1 **package (8 ounces) cream cheese, softened**

2 **tablespoons ground hazelnuts**

2 **tablespoons maple syrup**

2 **cups white baking chips**

12 **teaspoons shortening, *divided***

1½ **cups milk chocolate chips**

1½ **cups semisweet chocolate chips**

1 Pit cherries through the sides, leaving stems intact. In a small bowl, beat cream cheese until smooth. Stir in hazelnuts and syrup. Pipe into cherries.

2 In a small microwave-safe bowl, melt baking chips and 5 teaspoons shortening at 70% power. Microwave at additional 10- to 20-second intervals, stirring until smooth. In another bowl, repeat with milk chocolate chips and 3½ teaspoons shortening. Repeat with semisweet chips and remaining shortening.

3 Holding stems, dip a third of the stuffed cherries into melted white chocolate; allow excess to drip off. Place on waxed paper; let stand until set. Repeat with remaining cherries and milk chocolate and semisweet chocolate. Dip the white-coated cherries a second time to completely cover; let stand until set.

4 Reheat remaining melted chocolate if necessary. Drizzle white chocolate over cherries dipped in milk or semisweet chocolate. Drizzle milk or semisweet chocolate over white chocolate-dipped cherries. Store in an airtight container in the refrigerator.

YIELD: 5 DOZEN.

coconut peaks

¼ cup butter

3 cups flaked coconut

2 cups confectioners' sugar

¼ cup half-and-half cream

1 cup (6 ounces) semisweet chocolate chips

2 teaspoons shortening

1 Line a baking sheet with waxed paper; set aside. In a large saucepan, cook butter over medium-low heat until golden brown, about 5 minutes. Remove from the heat; stir in the coconut, confectioners' sugar and cream.

2 Drop by rounded teaspoonfuls onto prepared baking sheet. Refrigerate until easy to handle, about 25 minutes.

3 Roll mixture into balls, then shape each into a cone. Return to baking sheet; refrigerate for 15 minutes.

4 Meanwhile, in a microwave, melt chocolate chips and shortening; stir until smooth. Dip bottoms of cones into chocolate; allow excess to drip off. Return to waxed paper to harden. Store in an airtight container in the refrigerator.

YIELD: ABOUT 3 DOZEN.

Patricia Shinn, Fruitland Park, Florida

I found this gem on a slip of paper in a cookbook I got at a yard sale. The unique treats get fabulous flavor from the browned butter.

banana-chip mini cupcakes

1 package (14 ounces) banana quick bread and muffin mix

¾ cup water

⅓ cup sour cream

1 egg

1 cup miniature semisweet chocolate chips, *divided*

1 tablespoon shortening

1 In a large bowl, combine the muffin mix, water, sour cream and egg; stir just until moistened. Fold in ½ cup chocolate chips.

2 Fill greased or paper-lined miniature muffin cups two-thirds full. Bake at 375° for 12-15 minutes or until a toothpick inserted near the center comes out clean. Cool for 5 minutes before removing from pans to wire racks to cool completely.

3 For frosting, in a small microwave-safe bowl, melt shortening and remaining chocolate chips; stir until smooth. Frost cupcakes.

YIELD: 3½ DOZEN.

Beverly Coyde, Gasport, New York

These cute little mini-muffins are packed with banana flavor and chocolate chips then topped off with creamy frosting. They make a great, fast snack when the kids come home from school or a nice dessert addition to appetizer buffets.

best beverages

296

302

Whether hosting a poolside party for kids or celebrating the holidays with co-workers, you'll find the ideal way to whet your whistle with this chapter. Consider Berry Yogurt Shakes (p. 297) when enjoying fun in the sun or chase fall's chills with Apple Cherry Punch (p. 296). If it's your turn to play bartender, mix up a Cherry Brandy Old-Fashioned (p. 302) that's sure to impresss.

And if you really want to surprise guests, look at the photos throughout this chapter for simple garnish ideas that promise to make your party a standout.

apple cherry punch

4 cups water

4 cups unsweetened apple juice

1 cup sugar

1 envelope unsweetened cherry soft drink mix

¼ teaspoon ground cinnamon

⅛ teaspoon ground nutmeg

⅛ teaspoon ground cloves

In a large saucepan, combine all ingredients. Bring to a boil over medium heat. Reduce heat; simmer, uncovered, for 15 minutes.

YIELD: about 7 cups.

Joslyn Stock, Hampton, Iowa

Try this cheery red punch in fall or for a festive, fruity touch that brightens the holidays and fills the house with a lovely aroma. It's quick, easy, economical and a hit with all ages!

berry yogurt shakes

2 cups (16 ounces) lemon yogurt

1½ cups fat-free milk

1 cup unsweetened raspberries

Sugar substitute equivalent to
  2 tablespoons sugar

Place all ingredients in a blender; cover and process until smooth. Pour into chilled glasses; serve immediately.

YIELD: 4 SERVINGS.

Jacquie Adams, Colquitlam, British Columbia
We have a few raspberry bushes in our backyard. If my grandchildren don't get the berries first, I use them in recipes like this one. Of course, the kids love the mellow flavor of these shakes. So either way, they win!

golden fruit punch

Cindy Steffen, Cedarburg, Wisconsin

This is a refreshing punch that isn't as sweet as most. My friends and family love the tart flavor.

4 maraschino cherries

1 medium navel orange, thinly sliced

1 small lemon, thinly sliced

1 small lime, thinly sliced

1 can (12 ounces) frozen lemonade concentrate, thawed

1 can (12 ounces) frozen limeade concentrate, thawed

1 can (12 ounces) frozen pineapple-orange juice concentrate, thawed

2 liters diet ginger ale, chilled

1 Arrange fruit in a 5-cup ring mold; add ¾ cup water. Freeze until solid. Add enough water to fill mold; freeze until solid.

2 Just before serving, in a punch bowl, combine juice concentrates with 2 cups water. Stir in ginger ale. Unmold ice ring by wrapping the bottom of the mold in a hot, damp dishcloth. Invert onto a baking sheet; place fruit side up in punch bowl.

YIELD: 21 SERVINGS (4 QUARTS).

iced cranberry-mint tea

4 cups water

2/3 cup loosely packed fresh mint leaves

2 tablespoons sugar

8 lemon herbal tea bags

3 1/2 cups reduced-calorie reduced-sugar cranberry juice

1 tablespoon lemon juice

Ice cubes

Lemon slices, optional

1 In a large saucepan, bring the water, mint and sugar to a boil. Remove from the heat; add tea bags. Cover and steep for 15 minutes.

2 Discard tea bags. Cover and let stand 45 minutes longer. Strain and discard mint leaves. Stir the cranberry and lemon juices into tea. Serve over ice with lemon slices if desired.

YIELD: 8 SERVINGS (2 QUARTS).

Taste of Home Test Kitchen

Raise a toast to friends, family, sunshine and warm weather with this cranberry cooler. Fresh mint and a hint of lemon add refreshing fruity flavor.

frozen lemon-berry margaritas

4 lime wedges

2 tablespoons coarse sugar

2/3 cup thawed lemonade concentrate

1 cup frozen unsweetened raspberries

2 cups ice cubes

1 package (16 ounces) frozen sweetened sliced strawberries, partially thawed

1/2 cup frozen blueberries

1 tablespoon sugar

1/2 cup tequila, optional

1 Using lime wedges, moisten the rims of four margarita or cocktail glasses. Set aside limes for garnish. Sprinkle coarse sugar on a plate; hold each glass upside down and dip rim into sugar. Set aside. Discard remaining sugar on plate.

2 In a blender, combine the lemonade concentrate and raspberries; cover and process until blended. Press mixture through a fine sieve; discard seeds. Return raspberry mixture to blender; add the ice, strawberries, blueberries, sugar and tequila if desired. Cover and process until smooth.

3 Pour into prepared glasses. Garnish with reserved limes.

YIELD: 4 SERVINGS.

Julie Hieggelke, Grayslake, Illinois
Cool down summer months with this absolutely fantastic margarita. It's slightly icy, thick and perfect for those warm-weather parties.

cherry brandy old-fashioned

1 maraschino cherry

1 teaspoon bitters

½ teaspoon chopped crystallized ginger

⅓ cup ice cubes

⅓ cup ginger ale, chilled

1½ ounces brandy

½ to 1 ounce maraschino cherry juice

Maraschino cherry with a stem, optional

In a rocks glass, muddle the cherry, bitters and ginger. Add ice. Pour in the ginger ale, brandy and cherry juice. Garnish with a cherry if desired.

YIELD: 1 SERVING.

Taste of Home Test Kitchen
This old-fashioned recipe features brandy instead of whiskey. The addition of maraschino cherry juice makes it a little sweeter.

sparkling peach bellinis

3 medium peaches, halved

1 tablespoon honey

1 can (11.3 ounces) peach nectar, chilled

2 bottles (750 milliliters *each*) Champagne *or* sparkling grape juice, chilled

1 Line a baking sheet with a large piece of heavy-duty foil (about 18 in. x 12 in.). Place peach halves, cut sides up, on foil; drizzle with honey. Fold foil over peaches and seal.

2 Bake at 375° for 25-30 minutes or until tender. Cool completely; remove and discard peels. In a food processor, process peaches until smooth.

3 Transfer peach puree to a pitcher. Add the nectar and 1 bottle of Champagne or juice; stir until combined. Pour into 12 champagne flutes or wine glasses; top with remaining Champagne or juice. Serve immediately.

YIELD: 12 SERVINGS.

Taste of Home Test Kitchen

We developed this elegant brunch beverage so folks can savor a subtle peach flavor at spring and summer events.

creamy lime coolers

1 cup unsweetened pineapple juice, chilled

1 tablespoon lime juice

2 tablespoons confectioners' sugar

¼ teaspoon grated lime peel

1 cup vanilla ice cream, softened

In a blender, combine the pineapple juice, lime juice, confectioners' sugar and lime peel; cover and process until blended. Add ice cream; cover and process until smooth. Pour into chilled glasses.

YIELD: 2 SERVINGS.

Arlyne Murphy, Somers, New York

My rich, frothy beverage is refreshing any time of year, but its fresh, tropical taste really beats the heat on warm summer days.

frosty mocha drink

1 cup milk

3 tablespoons instant chocolate drink mix

2 tablespoons instant coffee granules

2 tablespoons honey

1 teaspoon vanilla extract

14 to 16 ice cubes

In a blender, combine all ingredients; cover and process until smooth. Pour into chilled glasses; serve immediately.

YIELD: 4 SERVINGS.

Lauren Nance, San Diego, California

I like to make this chilly, chocolate-flavored coffee drink when friends stop by for a visit. I always double the recipe, however, because I know they'll come back for seconds. For a richer and creamier version, replace the milk with half-and-half cream.

basil tomato juice

8 pounds ripe tomatoes, quartered

2 celery ribs, chopped

1 medium onion, chopped

¼ cup finely chopped fresh basil

¼ cup lemon juice

2 tablespoons sugar

1 tablespoon Worcestershire sauce

1 teaspoon salt

¾ teaspoon hot pepper sauce

1 In a stock pot, combine the tomatoes, celery and onion. Bring to a boil. Reduce heat; simmer, uncovered, for 45 minutes or until tender, stirring occasionally.

2 Cool slightly; put tomato mixture through a sieve or food mill. Return to the pan. Stir in the remaining ingredients. Bring to a boil. Remove from the heat and cool. Transfer to a pitcher; cover and refrigerate until chilled.

YIELD: ABOUT 2½ QUARTS.

Bonnie Hawkins, Elkhorn, Wisconsin

Put some zing in your next brunch buffet with this homemade tomato juice. Fresh basil and hot pepper sauce accent the garden-fresh tomato flavor. You can put it in containers and freeze it, if you wish.

blended fruit chiller

Kirsten Gunderson, Ottawa, Ontario

This smoothie is great any time of the day. I especially like to serve it when my kids are in a finicky mood. It's a fun, nutritious treat.

3 cups (24 ounces) fat-free plain yogurt

1 cup unsweetened pineapple juice, chilled

1 cup fresh *or* frozen unsweetened strawberries

1 medium ripe banana, sliced

1/2 cup fresh *or* canned unsweetened pineapple chunks

3 tablespoons honey

1 teaspoon vanilla extract

Place half of each ingredient in a blender; cover and process until blended. Repeat. Pour into chilled glasses; serve immediately.

YIELD: 6 SERVINGS.

cinnamon mocha coffee

⅓ cup ground coffee (not instant coffee granules)

¾ teaspoon ground cinnamon

1 cup 2% milk

2 to 3 tablespoons sugar

2 tablespoons baking cocoa

1 teaspoon vanilla extract

4 cinnamon sticks, optional

Whipped cream, optional

1 In a coffeemaker basket, combine the coffee and ground cinnamon. Prepare 4 cups brewed coffee according to manufacturer's directions.

2 Meanwhile, combine the milk, sugar, cocoa and vanilla in a saucepan. Cook over medium-low heat for 5-7 minutes or until small bubbles appear on the sides of the pan, stirring occasionally (do not boil). Pour hot milk mixture into four coffee cups, then add cinnamon-flavored coffee. Garnish with cinnamon sticks and whipped cream if desired.

YIELD: 4 SERVINGS.

Taste of Home Test Kitchen

The aroma of cinnamon and cocoa makes this coffee hard to resist. Serve at winter get-togethers, brunches or for an after-dinner treat.

champagne punch

4 cups orange juice

1 cup ruby red grapefruit juice

½ cup lemon juice

½ cup lime juice

2 bottles (750 milliliters *each*) Champagne, chilled

In a 3-qt. pitcher, combine the juices. Refrigerate until chilled. Just before serving, stir in Champagne. Serve in Champagne glasses.

YIELD: 16 SERVINGS (3 QUARTS).

Amy Short, Lesage, West Virginia

A blend of four fruit juices pairs well with bubbly Champagne in this party-pleasing punch.

frosty chocolate malted shakes

6 cups low-fat vanilla frozen yogurt

3½ cups fat-free milk

¼ cup sugar-free instant chocolate drink mix

¼ cup malted milk powder

1½ teaspoons vanilla extract

In batches, process all ingredients in a blender until smooth. Pour into tall glasses.

YIELD: 10 SERVINGS.

Dora Dean, Hollywood, Florida

I played around with our favorite milk shake recipe to come up with this lighter version. I serve it all the time, and no one misses the extra fat or calories.

mexican hot chocolate

4 cups fat-free milk

3 cinnamon sticks (3 inches)

5 ounces 53% cacao dark baking chocolate, coarsely chopped

1 teaspoon vanilla extract

Additional cinnamon sticks, optional

1 In a large saucepan, heat milk and cinnamon sticks over medium heat until bubbles form around sides of pan. Discard cinnamon. Whisk in chocolate until smooth.

2 Remove from the heat; stir in vanilla. Serve in mugs with additional cinnamon sticks if desired.

YIELD: 6 SERVINGS.

Patricia Nieh, Portola Valley, California

The entire family will enjoy this festive drink. Cinnamon sticks give it a great flavor that kids will love.

herb garden tea

¼ cup finely chopped lemon balm

¼ cup finely chopped fresh mint

¼ cup lemon juice

¼ cup orange juice

¼ cup honey

2 liters ginger ale

1 In a small bowl, combine the first five ingredients; let stand for 1 hour. Strain; discard herbs.

2 Pour into a 2½-qt. pitcher. Stir in the ginger ale just before serving. Serve in chilled glasses.

YIELD: 9 SERVINGS.

Mary Harrison, Hamilton, Ohio

This aromatic tea is the perfect drink for a summer luncheon. A touch of mint makes it so refreshing.

bottoms-up cherry limeade

¾ cup lime juice

Sugar substitute equivalent to 1 cup sugar

2 liters lime carbonated water, chilled

½ cup maraschino cherry juice

8 maraschino cherries with stems

8 lime slices

1 In a large bowl, combine lime juice and sugar substitute. Cover and refrigerate. Just before serving, stir carbonated water into lime juice mixture.

2 For each serving, place 1 tablespoon cherry juice in a glass. Add crushed ice and about 1 cup of lime juice mixture. Garnish with a maraschino cherry and a lime slice.

YIELD: 8 SERVINGS.

EDITOR'S NOTE: This recipe was tested with Splenda no-calorie sweetener.

Awynne Thurstenson, Siloam Springs, Arkansas
My guests enjoy this refreshing cherry-topped drink. It's just right on a hot southern evening. And it's pretty, too.

cranberry herbal tea cooler

3½ cups water

½ cup orange juice

2 tablespoons sugar

8 orange spice herbal tea bags

4 cups reduced-calorie reduced-sugar cranberry juice

Orange slices

1 In a saucepan, bring the water, orange juice and sugar to a boil. Reduce heat; cover and simmer for 10 minutes. Remove from the heat; add tea bags. Let stand for 4 minutes.

2 Remove and discard tea bags. Transfer to a pitcher; stir in cranberry juice. Refrigerate until chilled. Garnish with orange slices.

YIELD: 8 SERVINGS.

Taste of Home Test Kitchen

You only need to stir together a few ingredients for this delightful take on traditional iced tea. After just one sip, it's sure to be a summertime favorite for years to come.

coffee & cream martini

Clara Coulston Minney, Washington Court House, Ohio

With Kahlua, Irish cream liquor and chocolate syrup, this martini is almost like a dessert. It's an after-dinner drink that's easy to fix and so impressive.

- 2 tablespoons coarse sugar
- 1 teaspoon finely ground coffee

Ice cubes

- 1½ ounces vodka
- 1½ ounces Kahlua
- 1½ ounces Irish cream liqueur

Chocolate syrup, optional

1 Sprinkle sugar and coffee on a plate. Moisten the rim of a martini glass with water; hold glass upside down and dip rim into sugar mixture.

2 Fill a mixing glass or tumbler three-fourths full with ice. Add the vodka, Kahlua and Irish liqueur; stir until condensation forms on outside of glass.

3 Drizzle chocolate syrup on the inside of prepared martini glass if desired. Strain vodka mixture into glass; serve immediately.

YIELD: 1 SERVING.

fruit slush

1 can (46 ounces) pineapple juice

8 cups water

1 can (12 ounces) frozen lemonade concentrate, thawed

1 can (12 ounces) frozen orange juice concentrate, thawed

4 cups sugar

2 cups fresh *or* frozen unsweetened raspberries

2 envelopes unsweetened cherry soft drink mix *or* other red flavor of your choice

ADDITIONAL INGREDIENT:
Grapefruit *or* citrus soda

1 In a 6-qt. container, combine the first seven ingredients. Cover and freeze for 12 hours, stirring every 2 hours. May be frozen for up to 3 months.

2 For each serving, place $\frac{1}{2}$ cup of the fruit slush in a glass. Add $\frac{1}{2}$ cup of soda.

YIELD: ABOUT 5 QUARTS.

Darlene White, Hobson, Montana

I like to mix up this sweet slush using juices, berries and soft drink mix. Then I store it in the freezer for unexpected company. Simply pour a little citrus soda over scoops of the colorful mixture for frosty and refreshing beverages.

grape juice sparkler

1 can (11½ ounces) frozen cranberry-raspberry juice concentrate, thawed

1 bottle (1 liter) club soda, chilled

1 bottle (750 ml) sparkling white grape juice, chilled

20 to 30 fresh raspberries

Just before serving, combine juice concentrate with club soda in a large pitcher. Stir in sparkling grape juice. Place two to three raspberries in the bottom of each glass; add juice.

YIELD: 10 SERVINGS (2 QUARTS).

Taste of Home Test Kitchen

For a nice alternative to wine, give this fruity beverage a try. The kid-friendly drink will appeal to people of all ages.

dill bloody marys

1½ cups Clamato juice, chilled

2 tablespoons dill pickle juice

1 tablespoon Worcestershire sauce

¼ teaspoon celery salt

⅛ to ¼ teaspoon pepper

⅛ teaspoon hot pepper sauce

¼ cup vodka, optional

Ice cubes

2 celery ribs

2 pepperoni-flavored meat snack sticks

2 dill pickle spears

2 pitted ripe olives

In a small pitcher, combine the first six ingredients. Stir in vodka if desired. Pour into two glasses filled with ice; garnish with celery, snack sticks, pickles and olives.

YIELD: 2 SERVINGS.

Jay Ferkovich, Green Bay, Wisconsin

With a nice level of pepper, and just enough dill from the pickle, these Bloody Marys are sure to be crowd pleasing. To make "Contrary Marys," simply leave out the vodka.

creamy hot white chocolate

6 cups half-and-half cream, *divided*

1⅓ cups white baking chips

2 cinnamon sticks (3 inches)

¼ teaspoon ground cinnamon

Dash ground nutmeg

3 teaspoons vanilla extract

In a large saucepan, combine ½ cup cream, chips, cinnamon sticks, cinnamon and nutmeg. Cook and stir over low heat until chips are melted. Stir in remaining cream; heat through. Discard cinnamon sticks. Stir in vanilla.

YIELD: 8 SERVINGS.

Karen Riordan, Fern Creek, Kentucky

We enjoy this hot beverage all year long but especially around the holidays. It's a tasty change of pace from traditional hot chocolate.

bubbly cranberry punch

2 cans (16 ounces *each*) jellied cranberry sauce

1½ cups orange juice

½ cup lemon juice

2 bottles (1 liter *each*) ginger ale, chilled

Ice cubes

In a large pitcher or punch bowl, whisk cranberry sauce until smooth. Whisk in orange and lemon juices. Just before serving, slowly stir in ginger ale. Add ice cubes.

YIELD: 3½ QUARTS.

Rebecca Cook Jones, Henderson, Nevada

Tart and refreshing, this sparkling non-alcoholic punch adds pizzazz to Christmas parties, bridal showers and other festive occasions.

mulled merlot

4 cinnamon sticks (3 inches)

4 whole cloves

2 bottles (750 milliliters *each*) merlot

½ cup sugar

½ cup orange juice

½ cup brandy

1 medium orange, thinly sliced

1 Place cinnamon sticks and cloves on a double thickness of cheesecloth; bring up corners of cloth and tie with string to form a bag.

2 In a 3-qt. slow cooker, combine the wine, sugar, orange juice, brandy and orange slices. Add spice bag. Cover and cook on high for 1 hour or until heated through. Discard spice bag and orange slices. Serve warm in mugs.

YIELD: 9 SERVINGS.

Taste of Home Test Kitchen

Here's a recipe that's sure to warm up your holiday guests!

sweet citrus iced tea

14½ cups water, *divided*

10 individual tea bags

1½ cups sugar

⅔ cup lemon juice

¼ cup thawed orange juice concentrate

Ice cubes

1 In a large saucepan, bring 4 cups of water just to a boil. Remove from the heat. Add the tea bags; let stand for 10 minutes. Discard tea bags.

2 Pour tea into a large container. Stir in the sugar, lemon juice, orange juice concentrate and remaining water. Refrigerate until chilled. Serve over ice.

YIELD: 1 GALLON.

Diane Kirkpatrick, Terre Hill, Pennsylvania

My family has been making iced tea this way ever since I was a child. When I recently prepared some for a church gathering, many people asked for the recipe.

vanilla-almond coffee

1 pound ground coffee

2 tablespoons almond extract

2 tablespoons vanilla extract

Place coffee in a large jar with tight-fitting lid. Add extracts. Cover and shake well. Store in the refrigerator. Prepare coffee as usual.

YIELD: 1 POUND.

Tina Christensen, Addison, Illinois

Instead of buying flavored coffees, I make my own using extracts for baking. You can prepare this with decaffeinated coffee, too.

lemon quencher

Clara Coulston, Washington Court House, Ohio

Tart and refreshing, this citrus beverage is sweetened with just a touch of honey. It makes a lovely summer cooler any time of day.

5 cups water, *divided*

10 fresh mint leaves

1 cup lemon juice

2/3 cup honey

2 teaspoons grated lemon peel

Ice cubes

Mint sprigs and lemon peel strips, optional

1 In a blender, combine 1 cup water and mint leaves; cover and process for 1 minute. Strain mixture into a pitcher, discarding mint. Add the lemon juice, honey, lemon peel and remaining water; stir until blended. Cover and refrigerate for at least 2 hours.

2 Serve in chilled glasses over ice. Garnish with mint sprigs and lemon peel if desired.

YIELD: 8 SERVINGS.

sangria

1 bottle (750 milliliters) red
  Zinfandel *or* other dry red wine

2 cups diet lemon-lime soda

½ cup orange juice

4½ teaspoons sugar

1 cup *each* frozen unsweetened
  blueberries, raspberries and
  sliced peaches

Ice cubes, optional

In a pitcher, stir the wine, soda, orange juice and sugar until sugar is dissolved. Add the frozen fruit. Serve over ice if desired.

YIELD: 9 SERVINGS.

Taste of Home Test Kitchen

Filled with frozen fruit, this fresh blend is a snap to put together and keep cold. And what a thirst-quenching, elegant beverage for summer parties! Serve over ice if desired.

tropical pineapple smoothies

1 cup fat-free milk

1 can (8 ounces) unsweetened crushed pineapple

½ cup unsweetened pineapple juice

3 tablespoons sugar

½ teaspoon vanilla extract

¼ teaspoon coconut extract

6 ice cubes

In a blender, place the first six ingredients; cover and process until smooth. Add ice cubes; cover and process until smooth. Pour into chilled glasses; serve immediately.

YIELD: 3 SERVINGS.

Polly Coumos, Mogadore, Ohio

Around our house, we often make these yummy shakes. To make them healthier, we substitute fat-free milk and ice cubes for the ice cream. They are fast and nutritious!

holiday buffets

357

369

There's no better time to gather with friends than when celebrating a holiday. Welcome guests this spring with the adorable Easter Bunny Bread (p. 340). When Thanksgiving rolls around, surprise everyone with a Turkey Cheese Ball (p. 357), and deck the halls with our savory Herbed Cheesecake (p. 369).

The holidays are a great time to get creative and have fun in the kitchen. Feel free to elaborate on the ideas in this chapter. For instance, shape the cheese ball on page 365 into an egg and serve it at Easter.

valentine cookie bouquet

Marlene Gates, Sun City, Arizona

This cookie bouquet was a blue-ribbon winner at a local fair. It not only makes a great Valentine centerpiece at a party, but it's a tasty gift for a loved one.

1 cup butter, softened

1 cup sugar

¼ cup milk

1 egg

1 teaspoon vanilla extract

2¾ cups all-purpose flour

½ cup baking cocoa

¾ teaspoon baking powder

¼ teaspoon baking soda

24 long wooden skewers

FROSTING:

½ cup butter, softened

2 cups confectioners' sugar

2 to 3 tablespoons maraschino cherry juice

1 In a large bowl, cream butter and sugar until light and fluffy. Beat in the milk, egg and vanilla. Combine the flour, cocoa, baking powder and baking soda; add to creamed mixture and mix well. Cover and refrigerate for 1 hour or until easy to handle.

2 On a lightly floured surface, roll out half of the dough to ⅛-in. thickness. Cut out with a floured 3-in. heart-shaped cookie cutter. Place 1 in. apart on ungreased baking sheets.

3 Place skewers on top of each cookie with one end of each skewer about 1 in. from top of each heart. Gently press into the dough. Place a little extra dough over each skewer; press into cookie to secure.

4 Bake at 350° for 8-10 minutes or until firm. Let stand for 2 minutes before removing to wire racks to cool.

5 Roll out remaining dough on a lightly floured surface. Cut out with a floured 3-in. heart-shaped cookie cutter. Cut out centers with a 1-in. heart-shaped cookie cutter.

6 Bake at 350° for 8-10 minutes or until firm. Let stand for 2 minutes before removing to wire racks to cool.

7 In a small bowl, combine the butter, confectioners' sugar and enough cherry juice to achieve spreading consistency. Gently spread frosting over cookies with skewers; top with cookies with cutout centers.

YIELD: 2 DOZEN.

be-my-valentine pizza

1 tube (13.8 ounces) refrigerated pizza crust

¼ cup shredded Italian cheese blend

¼ cup shredded part-skim mozzarella cheese

2 slices provolone cheese, cut in half

¼ cup pizza sauce

18 slices pepperoni

¼ cup chopped onion

¼ cup sliced ripe olives

1 Unroll pizza dough onto a greased baking sheet; flatten dough. With kitchen scissors, cut into a 10-in. heart. (Use dough trimmings to make breadsticks if desired.) Bake at 425° for 8 minutes.

2 Combine the Italian and mozzarella cheeses; set aside. Arrange provolone cheese over crust to within ½ in. of edges.

3 Spread with pizza sauce. Layer with the pepperoni, onion, olives and cheese mixture. Bake 8-10 minutes longer or until crust is golden brown and cheese is melted.

YIELD: 2 SERVINGS.

Taste of Home Test Kitchen

Refrigerated dough makes short work of this cute and crusty, heart-shaped surprise. Topped with pepperoni, three kinds of cheese, olives, onions and sauce, this yummy appetizer will steal the show at any Valentines party.

st. patty's hot chocolate

3½ cups 2% milk

8 ounces white baking chocolate, chopped

¼ to ½ teaspoon peppermint extract

⅔ cup heavy whipping cream

8 spearmint *or* peppermint candies, crushed

Additional crushed peppermint candies, optional

1 In a large saucepan, heat milk over medium heat until steaming. Add chocolate; whisk until smooth. Stir in peppermint extract.

2 In a large bowl, beat cream until stiff peaks form. Fold in the crushed candies. Ladle hot chocolate into mugs; dollop with whipped cream. Sprinkle with additional candies if desired.

YIELD: 6 SERVINGS.

Taste of Home Test Kitchen

More than a hint of cool mint makes this delicious sipper a special switch from traditional hot chocolate. A dollop of whipped cream with crushed candy lusciously tops each mug.

hot pastrami spread

2 packages (8 ounces *each*) cream cheese, softened

½ cup sour cream

2 packages (2½ ounces *each*) thinly sliced pastrami, chopped

½ cup finely chopped green pepper

⅓ cup chopped pecans *or* walnuts, optional

Thinly sliced pumpernickel bread and light rye bread

1 In a small bowl, beat cream cheese and sour cream until smooth. Stir in pastrami and green pepper.

2 Transfer to a greased 1-qt. baking dish. Sprinkle with pecans if desired. Bake, uncovered, at 350° for 25-30 minutes or until heated though and edges are bubbly.

3 Cut out bread with a shamrock-shaped cookie cutter if desired. Serve with spread.

YIELD: ABOUT 3½ CUPS.

Arlene Wilson, Center Barnstead, New Hampshire
I first tasted this at a church party a few years ago. Everyone raves about it and the dish is always scraped clean. Beside the shamrock-shaped toasts, you can also serve the spread with crackers or bite-sized bagel pieces.

st. patrick's day popcorn

4 quarts popped popcorn

1 cup sugar

½ cup packed brown sugar

½ cup water

½ cup light corn syrup

1 teaspoon white vinegar

¼ teaspoon salt

½ cup butter

8 to 10 drops green food coloring

1 Place popcorn in a large roasting pan; keep warm in a 250° oven. Meanwhile, in a large heavy saucepan, combine the sugars, water, corn syrup, vinegar and salt. Cook and stir over medium heat until mixture comes to a boil. Cook, stirring occasionally, until a candy thermometer reads 250° (hard-ball stage).

2 Remove from the heat; stir in butter until melted. Stir in food coloring. Drizzle over warm popcorn and toss to coat. Cool. Break into pieces. Store in an airtight container.

YIELD: 6 QUARTS.

Karen Weber, Salem, Missouri

Everyone's eyes will be smilin' when they see this candy corn with an Irish twist.

egg salad wonton cups

36 wonton wrappers

3 cups prepared egg salad

⅓ cup chopped green onions

⅓ cup shredded carrot

10 bacon strips, cooked and crumbled

9 cherry tomatoes, quartered

Parsley sprigs

1 Coat one side of each wonton wrapper with cooking spray; gently press into miniature muffin cups, greased side down. Bake at 350° for 10-12 minutes or until golden brown. Remove to wire racks to cool.

2 In a large bowl, combine the egg salad, onions and carrot. Stir in the bacon. Spoon about 1 tablespoon into each wonton cup. Garnish with tomatoes and parsley.

YIELD: 3 DOZEN.

Taste of Home Test Kitchen

Crispy wonton wrappers are a nice contrast to the creamy egg salad in this appetizer. It's a great alternative to deviled eggs.

easter bunny treats

2/3 cup vanilla frosting

30 large marshmallows

Pink gel *or* paste food coloring

Red and pink heart-shaped
decorating sprinkles

60 miniature marshmallows

1 Frost the tops of 12 large marshmallows; stack a large marshmallow on top of each. Quarter the remaining large marshmallows; set aside for ears. Tint 1/4 cup frosting pink. Cut a small hole in the corner of a pastry or plastic bag; place pink frosting in bag.

2 Pipe a ribbon between the stacked marshmallows for bow tie. With white frosting, attach red hearts for eyes and a pink heart for nose. Pipe pink whiskers and smile.

3 For ears, pipe the center of quartered marshmallows pink; attach to head with white frosting. With the remaining white frosting, attach the miniature marshmallows for legs and tail. Let stand until dry.

YIELD: 1 DOZEN.

Holly Jost, Manitowoc, Wisconsin

These cute treats were easy for our kids to assemble, and the
whole family had fun making them.

fruit skewers with ginger dip

2/3 cup reduced-fat spreadable strawberry cream cheese

2/3 cup reduced-fat sour cream

1/4 cup lime juice

3 tablespoons honey

1/2 teaspoon ground ginger

2 cups green grapes

2 cups fresh *or* canned unsweetened pineapple chunks

2 large red apples, cut into 1-inch pieces

1 For dip, in a small bowl, beat cream cheese and sour cream until smooth. Beat in the lime juice, honey and ginger until smooth. Cover and refrigerate for at least 1 hour.

2 On eight 12-in. skewers, alternately thread the grapes, pineapple and apples. Serve immediately with dip.

YIELD: 8 SKEWERS (1 1/2 CUPS DIP).

Cindy Winter-Hartley, Apex, North Carolina

A friend shared this refreshing recipe with us and my husband and I thought it was simply delicious. Laced with lime, ginger and honey, the creamy dip is a party pleaser all year-round.

springtime lime slushy

2 packages (3 ounces *each*) lime gelatin

2 cups boiling water

2 cups cold water

2 quarts lime sherbet

3 cups ginger ale, chilled

1 In a freezer container, dissolve gelatin in boiling water. Stir in the cold water and sherbet until combined. Freeze for 4 hours or until set.

2 Remove from the freezer 45 minutes before serving. For each serving, place 1 cup of slush mixture in a glass; add about 1/3 cup ginger ale.

YIELD: 8 SERVINGS.

Joyce Minge-Johns, Jacksonville, Florida

I rely on a handful of ingredients to fix this lively lime beverage.

bunny pineapple smoothies

2 cups orange juice

2 pints pineapple sherbet

4 cups (32 ounces) pina colada yogurt

4 medium bananas, quartered

1 cup milk

1 teaspoon vanilla extract

2 cups whipped topping, *divided*

1 drop red food coloring

1 In a blender, combine half of the orange juice, sherbet, yogurt, bananas, milk and vanilla; cover and process until smooth. Pour into chilled glasses. Repeat.

2 Place 1½ cups of the whipped topping in a pastry or plastic bag; cut a medium hole in a corner of the bag. Pipe a bunny face on each smoothie.

3 Tint remaining whipped topping with food coloring; place in another bag. Cut a small hole in a corner of the bag. Pipe eyes, nose and inside of ears on each bunny face. Beginning from the nose, gently pull a toothpick through the whipped topping toward the edge of the glass to form whiskers. Serve immediately.

YIELD: 10 SERVINGS.

Taste of Home Test Kitchen

After trying these bunny-topped smoothies, you'll want to hop back to the buffet for extra servings. Flavored with orange juice, pineapple sherbet and pina colada yogurt, they add a tropical taste to Easter gatherings.

horseradish ham cubes

1 package (8 ounces) cream cheese, softened

2 tablespoons prepared horseradish

1 teaspoon Worcestershire sauce

½ teaspoon seasoned salt

⅛ teaspoon pepper

10 square slices deli ham

1 In a small bowl, beat the cream cheese, horseradish, Worcestershire sauce, seasoned salt and pepper.

2 Spread about 2 tablespoons over each ham slice. Make two stacks, using five ham slices for each. Wrap each stack in plastic wrap; chill for 4 hours. Cut each stack into 1-in. cubes.

YIELD: ABOUT 5 DOZEN.

Connie Tolley, Oak Hill, West Virginia

Horseradish and ham have always been perfect partners. Here they combine in a zesty variation of ham roll-ups.

asparagus tart

Mary Relyea, Canastota, New York

The golden crust of this tart is filled with a delightfully light egg bake that includes asparagus spears and Gruyere cheese. Thin wedges are wonderful on a spring appetizer buffet or even when served as a unique side dish.

1 pound fresh asparagus, trimmed

3 cups water

Pastry for single-crust pie (9 inches)

⅔ cup shredded Gruyere *or* Swiss cheese, *divided*

½ cup minced fresh flat-leaf parsley

4 eggs, lightly beaten

¾ cup half-and-half cream

½ teaspoon salt

⅛ teaspoon cayenne pepper

⅛ teaspoon ground nutmeg

1 Cut 2 in. from the top of each asparagus spear; set tops aside. Cut stem ends into ¾-in. pieces. In a small saucepan, bring water to a boil. Add the ¾-in. asparagus pieces; cover and boil for 3-4 minutes. Drain and immediately place asparagus in ice water. Drain and pat dry.

2 On a lightly floured surface, roll out pastry into a 13-in. circle. Press onto the bottom and up the sides of an ungreased 11-in. fluted tart pan with removable bottom; trim edges. Place the blanched asparagus, 1/3 cup cheese and parsley in crust.

3 In a small bowl, combine the eggs, cream, salt, cayenne and nutmeg; pour into crust. Arrange asparagus tops over egg mixture. Sprinkle with remaining cheese.

4 Place pan on a baking sheet. Bake at 400° for 25-30 minutes or until a knife inserted near the center comes out clean. Let stand for 10 minutes before cutting.

YIELD: 16 SERVINGS.

easter bunny bread

2 loaves (1 pound *each*) frozen
bread dough, thawed

2 raisins

2 sliced almonds

1 egg, lightly beaten

Lettuce leaves

Dip of your choice

1 Cut a fourth off of one loaf of dough; shape into a pear to form head. For body, flatten remaining portion into a 7-in. x 6-in. oval; place on a greased baking sheet. Place head above body. Make narrow cuts, about 3/4 in. deep, on each side of head for whiskers.

2 Cut second loaf into four equal portions. For ears, shape two portions into 16-in. ropes; fold ropes in half. Arrange ears with open ends touching head. Cut a third portion of dough in half; shape each into a 3 1/2-in. oval for back paws. Cut two 1-in. slits on top edge for toes. Position on each side of body.

3 Divide the fourth portion of dough into three pieces. Shape two pieces into 2 1/2-in. balls for front paws; shape the remaining piece into two 1-in. balls for cheeks and one 1/2-in. ball for nose. Place paws on each side of body; cut two 1-in. slits for toes. Place cheeks and nose on face. Add raisins for eyes and almonds for teeth.

4 Brush dough with egg. Cover and let rise in a warm place until doubled, about 30-45 minutes. Bake at 350° for 25-30 minutes or until golden brown. Remove to a wire rack to cool.

5 Place bread on a lettuce-lined 16-in. x 13-in. serving tray. Cut a 5-in. x 4-in. oval in center of body. Hollow out bread, leaving a 1/2-in. shell (discard removed bread or save for another use). Line with lettuce and fill with dip.

YIELD: 1 LOAF.

Taste of Home Test Kitchen

With its toothy grin, lovely golden crust and tummy that's perfect for serving dip, this charming rabbit is sure to bring a smile to guests young and old.

asparagus ham roll-ups

16 fresh asparagus spears, trimmed

1 medium sweet red pepper, cut into 16 strips

8 ounces Havarti cheese, cut into 16 strips

8 thin slices deli ham *or* prosciutto, cut in half lengthwise

16 whole chives

1 In a large skillet, bring 1 in. of water to a boil. Add asparagus; cover and cook for 3 minutes. Drain and immediately place asparagus in ice water. Drain and pat dry.

2 Place an asparagus spear, red pepper strip and cheese strip on each slice of ham. Roll up tightly; tie with a chive. Chill until serving.

YIELD: 16 SERVINGS.

Rhonda Struthers, Ottawa, Ontario

Havarti cheese, asparagus and red peppers make these tasty roll-ups ideal for a spring celebration. Fresh chive ties give them a fussed-over look, but they're a cinch to make.

fudgy patriotic brownies

1 cup butter, cubed

4 ounces unsweetened chocolate, chopped

2 cups sugar

1 teaspoon vanilla extract

4 eggs

1¼ cups all-purpose flour

½ teaspoon salt

1 cup chopped pecans

FROSTING:

¼ cup butter, cubed

2 ounces unsweetened chocolate, chopped

3 cups confectioners' sugar

5 to 6 tablespoons milk

1 teaspoon vanilla extract

Red, white and blue decorating icing

1 In a microwave-safe bowl, melt butter and chocolate; stir until smooth. Stir in sugar and vanilla. Add eggs, one at a time, stirring well after each addition. Combine flour and salt; stir into chocolate mixture until combined. Stir in pecans.

2 Spread into a greased 13-in. x 9-in. baking dish. Bake at 325° for 35-40 minutes or until a toothpick inserted near the center comes out clean. Cool on a wire rack.

3 For frosting, in a small heavy saucepan, melt butter and chocolate over low heat; stir until smooth. Remove from the heat. Stir in the confectioners' sugar, milk and vanilla until blended.

4 Frost brownies; score into 24 bars. Using a small star-shaped cookie cutter, lightly press a star outline in the center of each brownie. Outline stars with red, white and blue icing.

YIELD: 2 DOZEN.

Julie Moyer, Union Grove, Wisconsin
A rich chocolate frosting makes these brownies really tasty.
I always come home with an empty pan
when I take them to potlucks.

firecracker shrimp

½ cup apricot preserves

1 teaspoon canola oil

1 teaspoon soy sauce

½ teaspoon crushed red pepper flakes

1 pound uncooked large shrimp, peeled and deveined

1 In a small bowl, combine the apricot preserves, oil, soy sauce and pepper flakes. Thread shrimp onto metal or soaked wooden skewers.

2 Grill, uncovered, over medium heat or broil 4 in. from the heat for 2-3 minutes on each side or until shrimp turn pink, basting frequently with apricot mixture.

YIELD: 10-12 SERVINGS.

Mary Tallman, Arbor Vitae, Wisconsin
These delightful grilled shrimp are coated in a sweet and spicy glaze. The marinade comes together in moments.

watermelon salsa

2 cups chopped seedless watermelon

1 can (8 ounces) unsweetened crushed pineapple, drained

¼ cup chopped sweet onion

¼ cup minced fresh cilantro

3 tablespoons orange juice

⅛ teaspoon hot pepper sauce

Tortilla chips

In a large bowl, combine the first six ingredients. Cover and refrigerate for at least 1 hour. Serve with tortilla chips.

YIELD: 3 CUPS.

Betsy Hanson, Tiverton, Rhode Island
On hot days, this refreshing salsa with watermelon, pineapple and cilantro is sure to satisfy.

cascading fruit centerpiece

Ellen Brown, Aledo, Texas

It's exciting and fun to build this pretty centerpiece, which I've made for holidays, weddings and bridal showers.

PINEAPPLE GINGER DIP:
- 2 packages (8 ounces *each*) cream cheese, softened
- 5 tablespoons unsweetened pineapple juice
- 2 tablespoons confectioners' sugar
- 1 tablespoon grated orange peel
- 1 tablespoon lemon juice
- 1½ to 2 teaspoons ground ginger
- ¼ cup flaked coconut, toasted

CENTERPIECE:
- 1 fresh pineapple
- 1 large grapefruit
- 1 large navel orange
- 1 medium lemon
- 8 Styrofoam rounds (four 10 in. x 1 in., four 6 in. x 1 in.)
- 2 wooden dowels (one 8 in. x ¼ in., one 4½ in. x ¼ in.)

Floral metal greening pins
- 3 to 5 pounds green grapes
- 3 to 5 pounds red grapes
- 1 pound fresh strawberries

Silk flowers with leaves
- 3 cups yogurt of your choice

1 In a small bowl, combine the first six ingredients. Stir in coconut. Chill until serving.

2 Cut off pineapple top with a fourth of the pineapple attached; set aside. For dip bowl, cut a third from bottom of pineapple; remove fruit, leaving a ½-in. shell. Remove peel from center section of pineapple; core and cut pineapple into chunks.

3 Cut the grapefruit, orange and lemon in half widthwise. Remove pulp from one half of each; set aside. Stack two 10-in. Styrofoam rounds and two 6-in. rounds; cover each stack with heavy-duty foil. Repeat with remaining rounds. On a 19-in. x 15-in. platter, pile the stacks on top of each other, staggering them and anchoring with dowels.

4 Place pineapple top on the top circle; position lemon, orange and grapefruit cups on other circles. Place pineapple bowl on platter.

5 With pins, attach clusters of grapes onto circles. Add strawberries, pineapple chunks and more grapes to cover foil and platter. Decorate with flowers.

6 Just before serving, fill pineapple bowl with dip. Fill lemon, orange and grapefruit cups with yogurt.

YIELD: 1 FRUIT CENTERPIECE.

watermelon cookies

¾ cup butter, cubed, softened

¾ cup sugar

1 egg

½ teaspoon almond extract

2¼ cups all-purpose flour

¼ teaspoon salt

¼ teaspoon baking powder

Red and green food coloring

Dried currants

Sesame seeds

1 In a large bowl, cream butter and sugar until light and fluffy. Beat in egg. Beat in extract. Combine the flour, salt and baking powder; gradually add to creamed mixture and mix well; set aside.

2 Add enough red food coloring to tint remaining dough deep red. Roll into a 3½-in.-long log; wrap in plastic wrap and refrigerate until firm, about 2 hours.

3 Divide 1 cup of reserved dough into two pieces. To one piece, add enough green food coloring to tint dough deep green. Leave remaining dough plain. Wrap each piece separately in plastic wrap; chill until firm, about 1 hour.

4 On a floured sheet of waxed paper, roll white dough into a 8½-in. x 3½-in. rectangle. Place red dough along short end of rectangle. Roll up and encircle red dough with white dough; set aside.

5 On floured waxed paper, roll the green dough into a 10-in. x 3½-in. rectangle. Place log of red/white dough along the short end of green dough. Roll up and encircle log with green dough. Cover tightly with plastic wrap; refrigerate at least 8 hours or overnight.

6 Unwrap dough and cut into ⅛-in. slices. Place 1 in. apart on ungreased baking sheets. Lightly press dried currants and sesame seeds into each slice to resemble watermelon seeds.

7 Bake at 375° for 6-8 minutes or until cookies are firm but not brown. While still warm, cut each cookie in half or into pie-shaped wedges. Remove to wire racks to cool.

YIELD: 3 DOZEN.

Ruth Witmer, Stevens, Pennsylvania

Turn any summer celebration into a memorable event with these cute-as-can-be cookies.

antipasto-stuffed baguettes

1 can (2¼ ounces) sliced ripe olives, drained

2 tablespoons olive oil

1 teaspoon lemon juice

1 garlic clove, minced

⅛ teaspoon *each* dried basil, thyme, marjoram and rosemary, crushed

2 French bread baguettes (8 ounces *each*)

1 package (4 ounces) crumbled feta cheese

¼ pound thinly sliced Genoa salami

1 cup fresh baby spinach

1 jar (7¼ ounces) roasted red peppers, drained and chopped

1 can (14 ounces) water-packed artichoke hearts, rinsed, drained and quartered

1 In a blender, combine the olives, oil, lemon juice, garlic and herbs; cover and process until olives are chopped. Set aside ⅓ cup olive mixture (refrigerate remaining mixture for another use).

2 Cut the top third off each baguette; carefully hollow out bottoms, leaving a ¼-in. shell (discard removed bread or save for another use).

3 Spread olive mixture in the bottom of each loaf. Sprinkle with feta cheese. Fold salami slices in half and place over cheese. Top with the spinach, red peppers and artichokes, pressing down as necessary. Replace the bread tops. Wrap the loaves tightly in foil. Refrigerate for at least 3 hours or overnight.

4 Serve cold, or place foil-wrapped loaves on a baking sheet and bake at 350° for 20-25 minutes or until heated through. Cut into slices; secure with a toothpick.

YIELD: 3 DOZEN.

Dianne Holmgren, Prescott, Arizona

These Italian-style sandwiches can be served as an appetizer or even as a light lunch. A homemade olive paste makes every bite delicious.

red-white-and-blue berry delight

½ cup sugar

2 envelopes unflavored gelatin

4 cups white cranberry-peach juice drink, *divided*

1 tablespoon lemon juice

2 cups fresh strawberries, halved

2 cups fresh blueberries

CREAM:

½ cup heavy whipping cream

1 tablespoon sugar

¼ teaspoon vanilla extract

1 In a large saucepan, combine sugar and gelatin. Add 1 cup cranberry-peach juice; cook and stir over low heat until gelatin is completely dissolved, about 5 minutes. Remove from the heat; stir in lemon juice and remaining cranberry-peach juice.

2 Place strawberries in an 8-cup ring mold coated with cooking spray; add 2 cups gelatin mixture. Refrigerate until set but not firm, about 30 minutes. Set aside remaining gelatin mixture.

3 Stir blueberries into the remaining gelatin mixture; spoon over the strawberry layer. Refrigerate overnight. Unmold onto a serving platter.

4 In a small bowl, beat cream until it begins to thicken. Add sugar and vanilla; beat until stiff peaks form. Serve with gelatin.

YIELD: 8 SERVINGS.

Constance Fennell, Grand Junction, Michigan

Loaded with fresh strawberries and blueberries, this luscious treat is perfect for any Fourth of July celebration!

bloodshot eyeballs

2 cups confectioners' sugar, *divided*

½ cup creamy peanut butter

3 tablespoons butter, softened

½ pound white candy coating, coarsely chopped

24 brown Reese's pieces *or* milk chocolate M&M's

1 tablespoon water

¼ to ½ teaspoon red food coloring

1 In a small bowl, combine 1 cup confectioners' sugar, peanut butter and butter. Shape into 1-in. balls; place on a waxed paper-lined pan. Chill for 30 minutes or until firm.

2 In a microwave, melt white candy coating; stir until smooth. Dip balls in coating; allow excess to drip off. Place on waxed paper. Immediately press a Reese's candy onto the top of each eyeball for pupil. Let stand for 30 minutes or until set.

3 In a small bowl, combine the water, food coloring and remaining confectioners' sugar. Transfer to a heavy-duty resealable plastic bag; cut a small hole in a corner of bag. Pipe wavy lines downward from pupil, creating the look of bloodshot eyes. Store in an airtight container.

YIELD: 2 DOZEN.

Taste of Home Test Kitchen

Little ghouls will find these peanut butter "eyeballs" a scary sensation to nibble!

cheesenstein

Nila Grahl, Gurnee, Illinois

This creamy, fun dip will be the hit of every Halloween party! I've done several variations of this cheese ball. My daughters really love it.

2 packages (8 ounces *each*) cream cheese, softened

¼ cup mayonnaise

1 tablespoon Worcestershire sauce

1 teaspoon hot pepper sauce

2 cups (8 ounces) shredded cheddar cheese

6 bacon strips, cooked and crumbled

3 green onions, thinly sliced

2 cartons (4 ounces *each*) whipped cream cheese

Moss-green paste food coloring

1 can (4¼ ounces) chopped ripe olives, drained

2 pepperoncinis

3 colossal ripe olives

2 slices peeled parsnip

Black decorating gel

1 pretzel rod

1 small cucumber

Assorted fresh vegetables

1 In a large bowl, beat the cream cheese, mayonnaise, Worcestershire sauce and pepper sauce until smooth. Stir in the cheddar cheese, bacon and onions. Shape into a 5-in. x 4-in. x 3-in. rectangle; wrap in plastic wrap. Refrigerate until chilled.

2 Unwrap rectangle; place on a serving platter with a 3-in. side on top. Tint whipped cream cheese green; spread over top and sides of rectangle.

3 Add chopped ripe olives for hair and pepperoncinis for ears. Cut one colossal olive in half; add parsnip slices and olive halves for eyes. With black decorating gel, pipe the brow, mouth and stitches.

4 Break pretzel rod in half; add a colossal olive to each end. Press into sides of head for bolts. Cut a small piece from end of cucumber for a nose (save remaining cucumber for another use). Serve with vegetables.

YIELD: 3 CUPS.

EDITOR'S NOTE: Look for pepperoncinis (pickled peppers) in the pickle and olive section of your grocery store.

crunchy monster claws

1 small sweet yellow pepper

2 tablespoons all-purpose flour

2 teaspoons plus 1 tablespoon Cajun seasoning, *divided*

3 eggs, lightly beaten

1½ cups cornflake crumbs

2 tablespoons chopped green onion

1 pound boneless skinless chicken breasts, cut lengthwise into ¾-inch strips

Barbecue sauce

1 Cut yellow pepper into 15 triangles; set aside. In a large resealable plastic bag, combine flour and 2 teaspoons Cajun seasoning. Place eggs in a shallow bowl. In another shallow bowl, combine the cornflake crumbs, green onion and remaining Cajun seasoning.

2 Place a few pieces of chicken in bag; seal and shake to coat. Dip in eggs, then in crumb mixture. Place on a greased baking sheet. Repeat. Bake at 350° for 15-20 minutes or until juices run clear.

3 Cut a small slit into one end of each chicken strip; insert a pepper triangle into each. Serve with barbecue sauce.

YIELD: 15 APPETIZERS.

Mary Ann Dell, Phoenixville, Pennsylvania

Cajun seasoning adds flavor, and a crunchy coating helps keep these chicken fingers moist. They're perfect for any Halloween party.

pumpkin pie dip

1 package (8 ounces) cream cheese, softened

2 cups confectioners' sugar

1 can (15 ounces) solid-pack pumpkin

5 teaspoons ground cinnamon, *divided*

½ teaspoon ground ginger

4 sheets refrigerated pie pastry

4 teaspoons sugar

1 In a large bowl, beat cream cheese until fluffy. Add the confectioners' sugar, pumpkin, 1 teaspoon cinnamon and ginger; beat until smooth. Cover and refrigerate until serving.

2 Roll out pie pastry on a lightly floured surface to ¼-in. thickness. Cut with a floured 2½-in. autumn-shaped cookie cutter. Place on an ungreased baking sheet. Reroll scraps if desired. Combine sugar and remaining cinnamon; sprinkle over cutouts.

3 Bake at 425° for 6-8 minutes or until firm. Remove to wire racks. Serve with pumpkin dip.

YIELD: 3½ CUPS (ABOUT 4½ DOZEN CUTOUTS).

Kari Egger, Portland, Oregon

This dip is yummy with cinnamon-sugar cutouts I make from extra pie crust dough. It's good with gingersnaps and sugar cookies, too.

chutney stuffed eggs

12 hard-cooked eggs

6 bacon strips, cooked and finely crumbled

¼ cup chutney, chopped

3 tablespoons mayonnaise

Cut eggs in half lengthwise; remove yolks and set whites aside. In a large bowl, mash yolks. Add the bacon, chutney and mayonnaise; mix well. Pipe or spoon into egg whites. Refrigerate until serving.

YIELD: 1 DOZEN.

Mrs. Patrick Dare, Fergus, Ontario

My aunt shared this recipe with me many years ago. The chutney is a very tasty addition to the time-honored appetizers.

yummy mummy with veggie dip

1 loaf (1 pound) frozen bread dough, thawed

3 pieces string cheese

2 cups (16 ounces) sour cream

1 envelope fiesta ranch dip mix

1 pitted ripe olive

Assorted crackers and fresh vegetables

1 Let dough rise according to package directions. Place dough on a greased baking sheet. For mummy, roll out dough into a 12-in. oval that is narrower at the bottom. For the head, make an indentation about 1 in. from the top. Let rise in a warm place for 20 minutes.

2 Bake at 350° for 20-25 minutes or until golden brown. Arrange strips of string cheese over bread; bake 1-2 minutes longer or until cheese is melted. Remove from pan to a wire rack to cool.

3 Meanwhile, in a small bowl, combine sour cream and dip mix. Chill until serving.

4 Cut mummy in half horizontally. Hollow out bottom half, leaving a ¾-in. shell. Cut removed bread into cubes; set aside. Place bread bottom on a serving plate. Spoon dip into shell. Replace top. For eyes, cut olive and position on head. Serve with crackers, vegetables and reserved bread.

YIELD: 16 SERVINGS (2 CUPS DIP).

Heather Snow, Salt Lake City, Utah

I came up with this idea for dressing up a veggie tray for our annual Halloween party, and everyone got really "wrapped up" in it.

witch's caviar

2 cans (4¼ ounces *each*) chopped ripe olives, undrained

2 cans (4 ounces *each*) chopped green chilies, undrained

2 medium tomatoes, seeded and chopped

3 green onions, chopped

2 garlic cloves, minced

1 tablespoon red wine vinegar

1 tablespoon olive oil

½ teaspoon pepper

Dash seasoned salt

Tortilla chips

In a large bowl, combine the first nine ingredients. Cover and refrigerate overnight. Serve with tortilla chips.

YIELD: 4 CUPS.

Darlene Brenden, Salem, Oregon

I like to serve this dip with triangle-shaped tortillas because they look like pointy witch hats.

autumn tea

5 individual tea bags

5 cups boiling water

5 cups unsweetened apple juice

2 cups cranberry juice

½ cup sugar

⅓ cup lemon juice

¼ teaspoon pumpkin pie spice

Place the tea bags in a large heat-proof bowl; add boiling water. Cover and steep for 8 minutes. Discard tea bags. Add the remaining ingredients to tea; stir until sugar is dissolved. Serve warm or over ice.

YIELD: 3 QUARTS.

Sandra McKenzie, Braham, Minnesota

I've been creating beverages made with various types of tea at gatherings, and people are always surprised by the results. This blend features flavors we associate with fall— apple, cranberry and pumpkin pie spice.

turkey cheese ball

2 packages (8 ounces *each*)
  reduced-fat cream cheese

6 ounces deli smoked turkey,
  finely chopped

1 cup (4 ounces) shredded
  cheddar cheese

1 tablespoon finely chopped onion

1 tablespoon Worcestershire sauce

½ teaspoon garlic powder

DECORATIONS:

3 packages (3 ounces *each*)
  cream cheese, softened

2 tablespoons milk

Brown, orange and yellow paste
  food coloring

6 large oval crackers

1 large sweet red pepper

1 small yellow summer squash

1 cup pecan halves

Assorted crackers

1 In a small bowl, beat the first six ingredients until combined. Shape into a ball; wrap in plastic wrap. Refrigerate for 1 hour or until firm.

2 In another small bowl, beat cream cheese and milk until smooth. Divide among four small bowls. With food coloring, tint one bowl brown, one dark orange and one light orange (using yellow and orange); leave one bowl plain.

3 Transfer each mixture to a heavy-duty resealable plastic bag; cut a small hole in a corner of each bag.

4 For turkey tail feathers, decorate the top halves of large oval crackers with tinted cream cheese.

5 Using the red pepper, form the turkey head, neck and wattle. For beak, cut a small triangle from summer squash; attach with cream cheese. Add eyes, using brown and plain cream cheese. Insert pecan halves and decorated crackers into cheese ball. Serve with assorted crackers.

YIELD: 1 CHEESE BALL (3 CUPS).

EDITOR'S NOTE: This recipe was tested with Townhouse Oval Bistro crackers.

Taste of Home Test Kitchen
While the real bird is roasting, you can present your guests
with this tasty Thanksgiving turkey cheese spread.

cranberry turkey crostini

1 package (12 ounces) fresh *or* frozen cranberries

1 medium tangerine, peeled and seeded

1/2 cup red wine vinegar

1/4 cup chopped shallots

1/2 cup sugar

1/4 cup chopped seeded jalapeno peppers

1/4 teaspoon pepper

30 slices French bread (1/4 inch thick)

Cooking spray

1 package (8 ounces) reduced-fat cream cheese

1/2 pound shaved deli smoked turkey

1 Place cranberries and tangerine in a food processor; cover and process until coarsely chopped. Set aside.

2 In a small saucepan, bring vinegar and shallots to a boil. Reduce heat; simmer, uncovered, for 5 minutes or until mixture is reduced to 1/3 cup, stirring occasionally. Stir in the sugar, jalapenos, pepper and reserved cranberry mixture. Cook for 5 minutes over medium heat, stirring frequently. Transfer to a small bowl; refrigerate until chilled.

3 Place bread on ungreased baking sheets; lightly spray bread on both sides with cooking spray. Broil 3-4 in. from the heat for 1-2 minutes on each side or until lightly browned. Spread each slice with 1 1/2 teaspoons cream cheese; top with turkey and 1 tablespoon cranberry mixture.

YIELD: 2 1/2 DOZEN.

EDITOR'S NOTE: When cutting hot peppers, disposable gloves are recommended. Avoid touching your face.

Bridgetta Ealy, Pontiac, Michigan
I wasn't quite sure what to expect when I made these, but they're fantastic. The jalapenos balance out the other ingredients perfectly.

nutty caramel apple dip

1 package (8 ounces) cream cheese, softened

½ cup apple butter

¼ cup packed brown sugar

½ teaspoon vanilla extract

½ cup chopped salted peanuts

3 medium apples, sliced

In a small bowl, beat the cream cheese, apple butter, brown sugar and vanilla until combined. Stir in the peanuts. Serve with apple slices. Refrigerate leftovers.

YIELD: 2 CUPS.

EDITOR'S NOTE: This recipe was tested with commercially prepared apple butter.

Darlene Brenden, Salem, Oregon
Looking for a standout appetizer that could double as a dessert? Try this fast, no-fuss favorite that whips up easily.

squash appetizer cups

1½ cups shredded zucchini

1½ cups shredded yellow summer squash

½ cup diced onion

¼ cup shredded Parmesan cheese

¼ cup shredded Colby cheese

2 tablespoons minced fresh parsley

1½ teaspoons minced fresh marjoram *or* ½ teaspoon dried marjoram

1 garlic clove, minced

1 cup biscuit/baking mix

½ teaspoon seasoned salt

Dash pepper

4 eggs, lightly beaten

½ cup canola oil

1 In a large skillet, saute the zucchini and yellow squash over medium heat until reduced to about 1½ cups, about 10 minutes. Transfer to a small bowl. Add the onion, cheeses, parsley, marjoram and garlic.

2 In a large bowl, combine the biscuit mix, seasoned salt and pepper. Stir in eggs and oil just until combined. Fold in squash mixture.

3 Fill greased miniature muffin cups three-fourths full. Bake at 350° for 20-25 minutes or until golden brown and a toothpick inserted near the center comes out clean. Cool for 5 minutes before removing from pans to wire racks. Serve warm. Refrigerate leftovers.

YIELD: ABOUT 3 DOZEN.

Lori Bowes, Waterford, Michigan

These cheesy, moist bites always go fast! If I'm in a hurry, I bake the mixture in a greased 9 x 13-in. pan and cut into squares.

creamy guacamole spread

2 large ripe avocados,
   peeled and cubed

½ cup mayonnaise

¼ cup chopped onion

2 teaspoons lemon juice

2 teaspoons Worcestershire sauce

1 teaspoon salt

1 teaspoon hot pepper sauce

Assorted crackers or fresh
  vegetables

In a blender, combine the first seven ingredients. Cover and process until blended. Serve with crackers or vegetables.

YIELD: 2 CUPS.

Lynn Thomas, Lakewood, New York

All my brothers and sisters like to bring appetizers to our holiday gatherings. This delectable dip came from my brother and is always a favorite.

zippy cranberry appetizer

Marie Hattrup, The Dalles, Oregon

Tart cranberry flavor blends nicely with mustard and horseradish in this out-of-the-ordinary spread.

½ cup sugar

½ cup packed brown sugar

1 cup water

1 package (12 ounces) fresh *or* frozen cranberries

1 to 3 tablespoons prepared horseradish

1 tablespoon Dijon mustard

1 package (8 ounces) cream cheese, softened

Assorted crackers

1 In a large saucepan, bring sugars and water to a boil over medium heat. Stir in the cranberries; return to a boil. Cook for 10 minutes or until thickened, stirring occasionally. Cool.

2 Stir in horseradish and mustard. Transfer to a large bowl; refrigerate until chilled. Just before serving, spread cream cheese over crackers; top with cranberry mixture.

YIELD: 2½ CUPS.

appetizer wreath

2 tubes (8 ounces *each*) refrigerated crescent rolls

1 package (8 ounces) cream cheese, softened

½ cup sour cream

1 teaspoon dill weed

⅛ teaspoon garlic powder

1½ cups chopped fresh broccoli florets

1 cup finely chopped celery

½ cup finely chopped sweet red pepper

Celery leaves

1 Remove crescent dough from packaging (do not unroll). Cut each tube into eight slices. Arrange in an 11-in. circle on an ungreased 14-in. pizza pan.

2 Bake at 375° for 15-20 minutes or until golden brown. Cool for 5 minutes before carefully removing to a serving platter; cool completely.

3 In a small bowl, beat the cream cheese, sour cream, dill and garlic powder until smooth. Spread over wreath; top with broccoli, celery and red pepper. Form a bow garnish with celery leaves.

YIELD: 16 SERVINGS.

Shirley Privratsky, Dickinson, North Dakota
I have lots of fun with this festive wreath. I often place a bowl of stuffed olives in the center.

christmas cheese balls

4 packages (8 ounces *each*) cream cheese, softened

4 cups (1 pound) shredded cheddar cheese

1 cup chopped pecans

¼ cup evaporated milk

1 can (4¼ ounces) chopped ripe olives, drained

2 garlic cloves, minced

½ teaspoon salt

Minced fresh parsley, chopped pecans and paprika

Assorted crackers

1 In a small bowl, beat the cream cheese and cheddar cheese. Stir in the pecans, milk, olives, garlic and salt. Divide into thirds; roll each into a ball.

2 Roll one ball in parsley and one in nuts. Sprinkle one with paprika. Cover and refrigerate. Remove from the refrigerator 15 minutes before serving. Serve with crackers.

YIELD: 3 CHEESE BALLS.

Margie Cadwell, Eastman, Georgia

Christmas at our house just wouldn't be complete without these rich cheese balls. Friends and family ask for them every year.

holiday wassail

4 cups hot brewed tea

1 cup sugar

1 bottle (32 ounces) cranberry juice

1 bottle (32 ounces) apple juice

2 cups orange juice

¾ cup lemon juice

2 cinnamon sticks (3 inches *each*)

24 whole cloves, *divided*

1 orange, sliced

In a large kettle, combine tea and sugar. Add the juices, cinnamon sticks and 12 of the cloves. Bring to a boil and boil for 2 minutes. Remove from the heat. Serve warm or cool. Garnish punch bowl with orange slices studded with remaining cloves.

YIELD: 12-16 SERVINGS.

Lucy Meyring, Walden, Colorado

With cranberry juice, cinnamon sticks and cloves, this richly colored beverage tastes like Christmastime.

santa's snack mix

2 cups Honey-Nut Cheerios

2 cups chow mein noodles

1 cup honey-roasted peanuts

½ cup raisins

½ cup holiday milk chocolate M&M's

½ cup peanut butter chips

½ cup vanilla *or* white chips

In two wide-mouth quart jars, layer all of the ingredients. Cover the jars. Decorate the tops of jars with fabric and ribbon if desired. To serve, pour into a bowl and stir to combine.

YIELD: 7 CUPS.

Lori Daniels, Beverly, West Virginia

For the holidays, I love to make homemade gifts such as this tasty treat.

santa claus cookies

12 ounces white baking chocolate, chopped

1 package (1 pound) Nutter Butter sandwich cookies

Red colored sugar

32 vanilla *or* white chips

64 miniature semisweet chocolate chips

32 red-hot candies

1 In a microwave, melt white chocolate at 70% power for 1 minute; stir. Microwave at additional 10- to 20-second intervals, stirring until smooth.

2 Dip one end of each cookie into melted chocolate, allowing excess to drip off. Place on wire racks. For Santa's hat, sprinkle red sugar on top part of chocolate. Press one vanilla chip off-center on hat for pom-pom; let stand until set.

3 Dip other end of each cookie into melted chocolate for beard, leaving center of cookie uncovered. Place on wire racks. With a dab of melted chocolate, attach semisweet chips for eyes and a red-hot for the nose. Place on waxed paper until set.

YIELD: 32 COOKIES.

Mary Kaufenberg, Shakopee, Minnesota

I use just six ingredients to create these cute Kris Kringle confections. Store-bought peanut butter sandwich cookies turn jolly with white chocolate, colored sugar, mini chips and red-hots.

herbed cheesecake

3 packages (8 ounces *each*) cream cheese, softened

2 cups (16 ounces) sour cream, *divided*

1 can (10¾ ounces) condensed cream of celery soup, undiluted

3 eggs

½ cup grated Romano cheese

3 garlic cloves, minced

1 tablespoon cornstarch

2 tablespoons minced fresh basil *or* 2 teaspoons dried basil

1 tablespoon minced fresh thyme *or* 1 teaspoon dried thyme

½ teaspoon Italian seasoning

½ easpoon coarsely ground pepper

Assorted crackers

1 In a large bowl, beat the cream cheese, 1 cup sour cream and soup until smooth. Add the eggs, Romano cheese, garlic, cornstarch, basil, thyme, Italian seasoning and pepper; beat until blended.

2 Pour into a greased 9-in. springform pan. Place pan on a baking sheet. Bake at 350° for 55-60 minutes or until center is almost set. Cool on a wire rack for 10 minutes. Carefully run a knife around edge of pan to loosen; cool 1 hour longer.

3 Refrigerate for at least 4 hours or overnight. Remove sides of pan. Spread remaining sour cream over top. Serve with crackers. Refrigerate leftovers.

YIELD: 24 SERVINGS.

Julie Tomlin, Watkinsville, Georgia

Cheesecake isn't just for dessert! This savory version is a favorite that keeps dozens of people happily munching.

feta cheesecake

7 crisp sesame breadsticks,
crushed (about 2/3 cup)

3 tablespoons butter, melted

1 cup ricotta cheese

8 ounces crumbled feta cheese

1/2 cup heavy whipping cream

1 tablespoon cornstarch

1 teaspoon prepared horseradish

2 eggs, lightly beaten

1 carton (12 ounces)
cranberry-orange sauce

1/2 cup chopped pecans, toasted

1 teaspoon minced fresh thyme

1/2 teaspoon minced fresh
rosemary

Assorted crackers

1 In a small bowl, combine breadstick crumbs and butter. Press onto the bottom and 1 in. up the sides of a greased 9-in. springform pan. Place on a baking sheet. Bake at 350° for 5 minutes. Cool on a wire rack.

2 In a large bowl, beat the ricotta, feta and cream until smooth. Add the cornstarch and horseradish; mix well. Add eggs; beat on low speed just until combined. Fold in the cranberry-orange sauce, pecans, thyme and rosemary. Spoon into crust. Place pan on a baking sheet.

3 Bake at 350° for 30-35 minutes or until center is almost set. Cool on a wire rack for 10 minutes. Carefully run a knife around edge of pan to loosen; cool 1 hour longer.

4 Cover and refrigerate overnight. Let cheesecake stand at room temperature 30 minutes before serving. Serve with crackers.

YIELD: 24-30 SERVINGS.

Josephine Piro, Easton, Pennsylvania

I modified a cheese spread into a cheesecake by lightening the filling with part skim ricotta, crushed cranberry and orange and other ingredients.

puff pastry holly leaves

1 package (17.3 ounces) frozen
 puff pastry, thawed

1 egg

1 tablespoon water

4 ounces cream cheese, softened

1 cup (4 ounces) crumbled
 feta cheese

1/2 cup minced fresh parsley

1/2 cup prepared pesto

24 pimiento pieces

1 Unfold pastry sheets onto a lightly floured surface. From each sheet, cut out 12 leaves with a floured 3 1/2-in. leaf-shaped cookie cutter. Place on ungreased baking sheets. With a toothpick, score veins in the leaves. In a small bowl, beat the egg and water; brush over the pastry.

2 Bake at 400° for 12-14 minutes or until golden brown. Remove to wire racks to cool.

3 In a large bowl, combine the cheeses, parsley and pesto. Split pastry leaves in half. Spread 1 tablespoon cheese mixture over bottom halves; replace tops. Add a pimiento piece on each for a holly berry. Refrigerate leftovers.

YIELD: 2 DOZEN.

Angela King, Walnut Cove, North Carolina
These elegant appetizers look like you've slaved in the kitchen, but they can be assembled in a jiffy. They always earn raves at my office holiday party.

Alphabetical Index

General Index

cooking terms

HERE'S a quick reference for some of the cooking terms used in *Taste of Home Appetizers*:

baste
To moisten food with melted butter, pan drippings marinades or other liquid to add more flavor and juiciness.

beat
A rapid movement to combine ingredients using a fork, spoon, wire whisk or electric mixer.

blend
To combine ingredients until just mixed.

boil
To heat liquids until bubbles form that cannot be "stirred down." In the case of water, the temperature will reach 212°.

bone
To remove all meat from the bone before cooking.

cream
To beat ingredients together to a smooth consistency usually in the case of butter and sugar for baking.

dash
A small amount of seasoning, less than 1/8 teaspoon. If using a shakera dash would comprise a quick flip of the container.

dredge
To coat foods with flour or other dry ingredients. Most often done with pot roasts and stew meat before browning.

fold
To incorporate several ingredients by careful and gentle turning with a spatula. Used generally with beaten egg whites or whipped cream when mixing into the rest of the ingredients to keep the batter light.

julienne
To cut foods into long thin strips much like matchsticks.

mince
To cut into very fine pieces. Used often for garlic or fresh herbs.

parboil
To cook partially, usually used in the case of chicken, sausages and vegetables.

partially set
Describes the consistency of gelatin after it has been chilled for a small amount of time. Mixture should resemble the consistency of egg whites.

puree
To process foods to a smooth mixture. Can be prepared in an electric blender, food processor food mill or sieve.

saute
To fry quickly in a small amount of fat, stirring almost constantly. Most often done with onions mushrooms and other chopped vegetables.

score
To cut slits partway through the outer surface of foods.

stir-fry
To cook meats and/or vegetables with a constant stirring motion in a small amount of oil in a wok or skillet over high heat.